A REGIONAL

THE RAILWAYS OF

General Editor: DAVID ST⎯⎯⎯THOMAS

VOLUME III

GREATER LONDON

£4.50

London at the dawn of the railway age was small and compact. The great changes about to take place, largely due to the new means of transport, can be appreciated by comparing this 1838 view of the London & Croydon Railway with the present scene from the Vesta Road (S.E.4) overbridge, three miles out from London Bridge. New Cross station is in the middle distance with the London & Greenwich viaduct beyond.

A REGIONAL HISTORY OF
THE RAILWAYS OF GREAT BRITAIN

Volume III

GREATER LONDON

by
H. P. White

WITH FRONTISPIECE AND 43 PLATES
18 ILLUSTRATIONS IN TEXT
INCLUDING REGIONAL MAPS,
AND LARGE FOLDING MAP

DAVID & CHARLES: NEWTON ABBOT

ISBN 0 7153 5337 3

First published 1963
New edition 1971

Set in eleven on twelve point Baskerville
and printed in Great Britain
by J. M. Dent & Sons Limited
for David & Charles (Publishers) Limited
South Devon House   Newton Abbot   Devon

Contents

List of Illustrations

ix

facing page

IN TEXT

LIST OF TABLES

Sources of the Photographs

The author is indebted to Mr B. N. Nunns for help in obtaining illustrations, especially for the frontispiece, photographed from part of 'View of the London and Croydon Railway from the deep cutting made through the hill at New Cross' by E. Duncan, by permission of the Librarian, Guildhall Library; for plate 35, from the *Great Eastern Magazine*, by courtesy of the Eastern Region; and for plate 36, from the *Railway Gazette*, by courtesy of the editor.

Thanks are also due to the Curator of Historical Relics, British Railways Board, for plates 1, 3, 4, 15, 20, 21, 22, 23, 25, 26, 27, 34, 41, 43; Locomotive & General Railway Photographs for plates 2, 7, 9, 10, 11, 12, 13, 14, 24, 29, 30, 31, 32, 33, 42; the London Transport Board, for plates 16, 17, 18, 19, 28; Hunting Surveys Ltd for plate 6; the Public Relations department, Southern Region, for plate 5; the Librarian and Curator, Walthamstow Museum, for plate 39. Plates 8, 37, 38, 40 are by the author.

CHAPTER I

London and its Parts

London, thou art of townes *A per se,*
Soveraign of cities, seemliest in sight,

. . . . .

Of merchaunts full of substaunce and of myght:
London, thou art the flour of cities all.

WILLIAM DUNBAR (1465–1520?)

ONE Briton in four now lives in Greater London and its adjoining counties. But the dominance of London is far from being new. Ever since Roman times it has been the largest city in Britain; for the greater part of the period it has been the commercial heart of England; for at least half the time it has been the political capital; and today it is the largest single industrial centre.

In the early seventeenth century it was considered to be such a phenomenal size as to be socially and economically undesirable. James I, himself an immigrant, attempted Canute-like to stem the flood-tide of growth by decree. But a century later Defoe was asking 'Whither will this monstrous city then extend?' In the 1820's, when the city numbered over 1·25 million, William Cobbett was castigating its growth as draining provincial England of wealth, culture and talent: 'The increase of London, the swellings of the immortal Wen.'

Yet his Great Wen was on the threshold of unparalleled expansion. In 1831 the compact urban area of some 18 square miles housed 1·65 million. A century and a quarter later, in 1961, the population of the sprawling mass, covering over 700 square miles with continuous building, numbered 8,171,902. The period of expansion is by no means over, though with the

1

more rigid application of the 'Green Belt' this is taking place discontinuously in the surrounding towns and villages.

The causes of this explosive expansion are numerous, but one of the most important was the transport revolution brought by the steam railway. This led to increased trade and industry, new opportunities for employment, the ease of maintaining a food

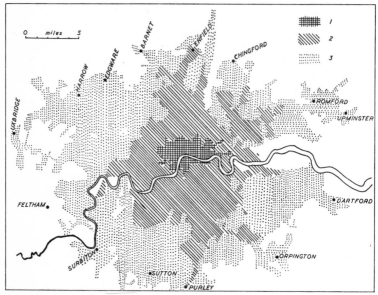

FIG. 1. The suburban sprawl—London's growth in terms of area: 1, The built-up area in 1801. 2, The built-up area in 1914. 3, The built-up area in 1951.

supply, and above all the possibility of separation of home and work. The expansion of the built-up area, which since 1920 has been even more marked than that of population, was made possible chiefly by the electric railway. It is the main purpose of this book to examine the effects of railway development upon London's growth, and conversely the consequences of that growth upon the evolution of the existing railway system and its traffic.

Just as an artist, to understand the face he is painting, must study the bone structure beneath, to understand London we must in imagination first strip away the surface layer of buildings and streets and consider the terrain beneath. For us the story began at least sixty million years ago when the London Basin, that great downfold in the sheet of chalk covering southern England, began to be filled up with clays, gravels and sands. This took millions of years and was followed by a long period during which the erosive forces of nature moulded the present landscape. Then, but a geological yesterday, the ice-sheets swept across England to the line of the Thames's ancestor. When they finally retreated they had deposited further layers of sands, gravels and boulder clays. Subsequently the Thames has left a number of gravel terraces as it cut down through the soft rocks of the London Basin.

Until the latter part of the nineteenth century main drainage, both of rain-water and sewage, was almost unknown. G. A. Sekon, the transport historian, tells us the house he lived in at Hammersmith in 1870 depended on cesspit and well. Thus subsoil dictated settlement. The most favoured sites were on free draining sand or gravel, while the impervious clays were avoided as long as possible. Even today the more exclusive as well as the older suburbs are associated with a gravel subsoil.

The result of all this geological activity has been that the outer rim of the London Basin is formed by two divergent ranges of chalk hills reaching eastward from Salisbury Plain. The more southerly is the North Downs, which stretch unbroken to the white cliffs of Dover. The more northerly, the Chilterns, runs in a north-easterly direction until petering out in the heart of East Anglia far beyond London's sphere of influence. Each range is in fact a plateau with a steep outward-facing slope. The reverse slopes dip away, imperceptibly for the most part, towards London. They are seamed with deep valleys, many of which lead back to gaps through the summits.

These have enabled the railways from London to cross the chalk barriers by more moderate gradients. From Paddington the West of England line follows the Thames through the Goring Gap; the West Coast line from Euston climbs up the Gade-Bulbourn valley to the Tring Gap; and the Brighton line uses the dry valleys south of Croydon to reach the Merstham Gap.

Between the North Downs and the rather narrow terraces

south of the Thames and east of Croydon is a wide area of gravel-capped hills interspersed by tracts of clay. Those nearest the river extend from Blackheath through Denmark Hill and Herne Hill. The heights continue southward through Chislehurst, Hayes and Croydon. Westward they are less extensive, but form the high ground of Wimbledon Common and Richmond Park.

The northern part of the Thames Basin is more complex. The Chiltern plateau, descending gradually southward, is clearly bounded by a low-lying vale on the slopes of which lie Uxbridge, Watford, St Albans and Hertford. Within this arc most of southern Hertfordshire is occupied by a clay plateau about 400 feet high and from it long fingers of high ground, usually capped by sand and gravel, reach out south-westward. The longest, most southerly and best known is the Hampstead Ridge from Finchley through Highgate and Hampstead out as far as Ealing. This plateau descends steeply on to the flat clay plain of Middlesex bounded approximately by the main lines from Paddington and from Euston.

East of the River Lea the rolling clay country of Epping Forest, Chigwell and Ongar has a similar abrupt southern slope and similar southward extensions of sand and gravel-capped hills in the regions of Brentwood, Ockendon and Laindon. But there is no equivalent of the clay plain here.

The gravel terraces north of the Thames are several miles wide. On them both City and West End grew up. Westward they extend continuously to the great loop of the river in which are London Airport and the Staines reservoirs. Eastward they extend through Stratford, Ilford and Romford to the low south Essex hills.

This then is the landscape in which London has grown up, a city which has been described with some truth as a collection of villages. London was never a legal or political entity until the creation of the Greater London Council in 1965 to administer almost the whole conurbation.

But the 'collection of villages' goes deeper. A variety of communities are found in close proximity. This is nowhere better seen than at Aldgate Pump on Sunday morning. Westward the sabbath calm of the City is unbroken, but eastward

Aldgate High Street and Middlesex Street (Petticoat Lane) teem with life. A few minutes' walk takes one from the *bourgeois* exclusiveness of Bayswater to the proletarian racial *mélange* of Notting Hill, while Camden Town and Holloway pass with dramatic suddenness into Hampstead and Highgate.

Lest it be assumed that these frontiers belong to the older parts only and that the suburban sprawl produces and is the product of a monotonous uniformity, it must be added that even here the distinctions are clear enough. First, the outward spread swamped established communities which still survive. This is particularly to be noticed in the Thames-side towns, Richmond, Kew and Twickenham, but also in Harrow, Romford and Bromley (Kent). Secondly, housing densities, house sizes and the presence or absence of industry near by result in adjoining neighbourhoods being socially distinct – Woodford from Walthamstow, Sudbury from Alperton, Chislehurst from Sidcup.

But whatever else it may be, London is the main centre of population. It also has the greatest concentration of industry in this highly industrialized country. In 1960 19·7 per cent of all persons engaged in manufacturing industry worked within Greater London, which housed 15·9 per cent of the population. In spite of its being a centre of administration and service industries, 34·7 per cent of those employed in Greater London were in manufacturing. This industrial development is based on the large labour force and on the vast market it forms. Another basis is the electric power from the generating stations which line the Thames, largely fed with Northumberland and Durham coal brought by ship, and with oil from Thames-side refineries.

In 1955 there were 13,300 factories and workshops employing a million and a half workers. These establishments vary from the clothing workshops of the East End, each employing a dozen or so, to the engineering works of Thames-side, each of which employs thousands. There is a notable concentration on engineering and electrical industries, chemicals, clothing, leather, furniture and printing. But almost every conceivable kind of industrial activity is represented.

London is the largest port in Britain. In 1967, 16 million tons of dry cargo and 19·1 million of petroleum were imported and exported, while 2·4 million and 8·5 million tons respectively went coastwise. The net registered tonnage of shipping entering and leaving the port was nearly 80 million tons. Almost the whole range of goods manufactured in the country is repre-

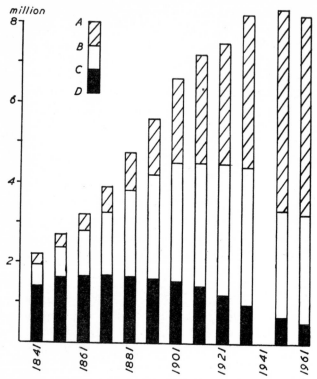

Fig. 2. The population explosion—London's growth in terms of population: In each column A–D represents the total population of the area now covered by Greater London, C–D that of the Central Area and surrounding boroughs, B–D that of the area now covered by the County of London. Broadly, B–C can be equated with the Inner Suburban Zone and A–B with the Middle.

sented among the exports. British Railways maintained a special export service from eighty-one manufacturing centres to the port by which over 100,000 loaded wagons a year were passed in 1963, in addition to the very large quantitities of goods arriving by road or coastwise.

Finally, it must be noted that not only is London the administrative capital, it is also the commercial capital, one of the major
commodity and money markets of the world. It is also the main
social centre of the country.

To assist then in appreciating the complexities of Greater
London a regional division has been attempted of this seemingly
amorphous sprawl, some twenty-five miles from Croydon to
Enfield and from Southall to Dagenham.

In many ways Greater London still bears traces of its dual
origin in the twin cities of London and Westminster. London,
the present *City*, grew up on a part of the terrace gravels which
overlooked the river on the inside of a bend where the water
was deep. Here on the site of the Roman town grew up the
medieval City within walls which can be traced in street
patterns and names. Today merchants and bankers are in sole
possession in the giant cubic office blocks soaring phoenix-like
from the ashes of the second world war, with shops at ground
level to cater for the needs of City workers.

Half a million people work in the City during the day, but
the resident population numbered only 4,771 in 1961. J.
Westergaard of the Centre for Urban Studies has pointed out
that in 1951 the City's 'job ratio' (the number employed per
100 of the resident working population) reached the fantastic
figure of 9,430.

Westminster grew up on Thorney Island in the marshy estuary
of the Tyburn. Here the court was established and with it grew
up the machinery of government, which still remains centred on
the Palace of Westminster (popularly the Houses of Parliament).
In 1961, 85,223 people lived in the City of Westminster (which
includes some of the West End). These are many more than in
the City, but the difference between the daytime and resident
population still remains striking, and Westminster had a job
ratio of 758 in 1951.

Just as finance is localized within the City, so administration
is localized here. Not only are there the main government
departments in the Whitehall area, but Scotland Yard and,
just across the river, though not within Westminster, the
Greater London Council. Another example of localization

common in London is the concentration of consulting engineers at the Abbey end of Victoria Street.

Later in time and clearly distinguishable from Westminster (though not so clearly in the popular mind) is the *West End*, which grew up during the eighteenth century as a residential area and which expanded during the nineteenth into Belgravia and Marylebone. Streets and squares were regularly laid out and still retain notable examples of Georgian architecture. Yet behind the mansions squalid slums were apt to lurk.

But the character of the West End is much changed. It has become one of the main social centres of the country, its shops, theatres and cinemas catering for the whole of the Home Counties. Since the first world war, too, commerce has been spilling over from the City. The few large houses not taken over as offices are now subdivided into flats, the West End mansion now being as much of an anachronism as the slums of Central London. In January 1956 employment in the West End (including Westminster) was 750,000 and has grown since.

These three entities, City, Westminster and West End, with the former slum areas separating them, we may collectively call *Central London*. For the 1960 Royal Commission on Local Government it included the City, Westminster, Holborn, Finsbury and Marylebone, while for London Transport its limits are at Hyde Park Corner, Euston Road and City Road. But all would agree it is characterized by its large day and small night population.

In its 1960 census London Transport recorded 1,270,000 people arriving daily in Central London between 7.0 and 10.0 a.m. Of these, 927,000, or 73 per cent, travelled by train – 489,000 (38·5 per cent) by Underground and 438,000 (34·5 per cent) by British Railways; 222,000 (17·4 per cent) came by bus and the remaining 121,000 (9·6 per cent) arrived, in spite of the fearful congestion they created, in cars, on motor-cycles and on push-bikes.

This immense daily tide, flowing between 7.0 and 10.0 a.m. and ebbing between 4.0 and 7.0 p.m., is the main theme of our story. For it is no new phenomenon. The 1905 Royal Commission on Locomotion in London stated 'one of the most important . . . problems of London locomotion is the movement

TABLE I

PASSENGERS AT LONDON TERMINI – 1960
WEEKDAY AVERAGES*

(Figures in thousands)

Station	Arrivals			Departures			Total 24 hrs	Two peak hours as percentage of total
	24 hrs	7–10 a.m.	Peak hour	24 hrs	4–8 p.m.	Peak hour		
S. Region								
Cannon St	37	35	23	38	36	25	75	64%
Charing Cross	61	44	26	64	45	25	125	41%
Holborn (1)	37	33	19	30	26	17	67	54%
London Bridge	104	74	42	95	67	38	199	40%
Victoria (2)	81	55	33	82	59	33	163	40%
Waterloo (3)	99	72	45	97	70	38	196	42%
TOTAL	419	313	188	406	303	176	825	44%
W. Region								
Paddington	32	7	6	32	NA	6	64	19%
L.M. Region								
Broad St	NA	6	4	NA	4	3	NA	—
Euston (4)	NA	5	4	NA	4	3	NA	—
St Pancras	16	6	4	17	6	3	33	21%
Marylebone	6	5	4	6	5	3	12	58%
E. Region								
Fenchurch St	21	18	12	21	18	13	42	60%
King's Cross	15	6	3	15	6	3	30	20%
Liverpool St	90	61	44	91	67	42	181	48%
London Transport								
Baker St	NA	15	8	NA	15	9	NA	—
Moorgate	NA	19	12	NA	15	11	NA	—

* Based on censuses carried out on selected days at each station.
(1) Including Blackfriars and Elephant and Castle.
(2) Excluding continental passengers.
(3) South Western Division station only.
(4) Suburban passengers only.
NA Not available.
Peak hour – the heaviest sixty minutes.

of population from the Suburbs towards the Centre every morning and back again in the afternoon and evening'. It has tremendous social implications and is vital in the economy and operation of the transport system.

Next may be distinguished *Industrial London*. This is not a single region, but a number of zones into which industry is concentrated. The chief one extends along the river below Tower Bridge, to Thames Haven on the north bank and beyond the Medway on the south. In the dock areas many industries work on imported raw materials—flour milling, sugar refining, paint manufacture and so on. Below the docks are engineering works and chemical plants, while here is concentrated the major proportion of the country's cement and paper production.

To the east of the City is a crescentic concentration of the clothing industry carried on in hundreds of small workshops, and a great diversity of other industries, chiefly furniture, engineering and metal goods. Such is the congestion here that many firms in the last forty years have migrated to the Lea Valley between Stratford and Cheshunt, where numerous metal, light engineering, furniture and food processing factories have been set up.

The remaining large area of industry is new and rapidly expanding, spreading discontinuously through the outer suburbs of West London. Many of the factories are aligned along arterial roads and main-line railways, others are grouped on estates and yet others intermingled with smaller and cheaper houses.

The main concentrations are: Cricklewood–Colindale around the North Circular Road; Willesden–Wembley, where the Wembley Park Estate was one of the earliest industrial estates in the country; the Park Royal Estate off the Oxford Road; and along the Western Region main line and almost parallel Great West Road. Products are too diverse to allow generalizations. In 1960 a trip along the Great West Road from Brentford to London Airport passed factories producing soft drinks, windscreen wipers, razor blades, tyres, cosmetics and a variety of other contributions to the contemporary way of life.

Encircling Central London from Camden Town eastward and then southward as far as Lambeth is the *Inner Arc*, a zone of suburban development which preceded the railways.

Some parts, such as Islington, date from the late eighteenth or early nineteenth century, but others, Spitalfields among them, had grown up as early as the sixteenth. Nowadays all these areas have common characteristics. Whatever social class first colonized them, the whole arc is now uncompromisingly working class. Industry is inextricably mixed up with housing, and the entire zone is one of rapid depopulation. It thus shares with Central London the further characteristic of having a larger daytime than resident population. Shoreditch's job ratio is 200 and Stepney's 180.

Once the home of a teeming, overcrowded population, the zone included many of the horrifying slums portrayed by Dickens and Mayhew. In 1901 nearly 250,000 people lived in Stepney. A full half of the area was occupied by factories and roads, so the real population density was 300 per acre – and an acre is the size of a football pitch. But rising living standards and clearances, accelerated but not initiated by bombing, have meant that, while the zone is by no means salubrious, there are few slums in the sense there were even thirty years ago.

Population declined steadily after 1900, and rapidly between 1940 and 1950. Thus in 1961 Stepney had shrunk to 91,940. Similarly Bethnal Green, stationary at 129,000 in 1891 and 1901, had fallen to 47,018 in 1961, and Bermondsey, which numbered 119,452 in 1921, housed but 51,815.

The suburban ring which grew up for the most part between 1870 and 1914 may be termed the *Inner Suburban Zone*. It varies so greatly in social structure, appearance and housing densities that it is difficult to generalize. Places like Blackheath, Dulwich, Putney and Swiss Cottage were characterized by large villas generally in their own grounds. Lewisham, Battersea, Hornsey and Leyton consisted largely of small semi-detached or terrace houses occupied by clerks, small tradesmen and skilled artisans. In places like West Ham, Tottenham and the mushrooming old towns of Deptford and Woolwich working-class housing was frequently sub-standard and jerry-built, and was interspersed with factories far too closely for modern standards. But the gross overcrowding and appalling slums of the Inner Arc were absent save in a few areas, the North Woolwich and Poplar docklands among them.

Great changes have occurred over the years. Mr Pooter, hero of George and Weedon Grossmith's *Diary of a Nobody*, a respectable managing clerk, who today would live in Finchley or Barnet, in 1888 had quite a large house in Holloway and kept a maid. Considerable social contrasts still remain within Lewisham, Wandsworth and other large boroughs.

The inner suburbs have a similar pattern of population development, a spectacular increase between 1891 and 1911, followed by a period of stagnation or slight growth until 1939. Now they are declining, but slowly and with few signs of increasing rates of decline. Tottenham may be taken as typical. Between 1881 and 1901 its population grew from 46,560 to 136,774. By 1931 it was 157,667, but in 1951 it had fallen to 126,929 and to 113,126 ten years later. Hammersmith grew from 71,939 in 1881 to 121,521 in 1911. Twenty years later it was 135,532 and, in 1951, 119,387 (110,147 in 1961). Between 1938 and 1948 the population of Lewisham fell by 4 per cent, and by 2·6 per cent between 1951 and 1961. This compares with rates of decline in Southwark of 35 and of 11·4 per cent.

This zone, diverse though it is, has sufficiently coherent characteristics to be recognizable as a unit. Outside is another, the *Middle Suburban Zone*, one of rapid expansion during the inter-war period, especially in the 1929–39 decade. Again, house types and general appearance show wide variety and consequently so does the social composition. But times had changed sufficiently for the very large villas of pre-1914 to be no longer wanted. The medium-sized detached houses and general 'desirability' of such places as Chislehurst, Sanderstead, Pinner and Stanmore contrasted with the small semi-detached villas which proliferated elsewhere, though we must not forget there is a hierarchy even among the semi-detached. There were also the estates, large towns in themselves, built by the L.C.C. at Grove Park, St Helier, Becontree and elsewhere.

These new suburbs had housing densities lower than those in the Inner Suburban Zone and much lower than in the Inner Crescent. In 1951 Chislehurst and Sidcup housed 18 persons to the acre, Croydon 26·3, Barking 20·9 and Finchley 20·1. This compares with 76·8 persons per acre in Bethnal Green and 86 in Islington. But lest it be thought these are special cases of overcrowding, it should be noted that Chelsea had a density of 77 per acre and Kensington 71·9. The mean for the whole of Greater London was 18·1.

South of the Thames the new suburbs grew up around and transformed pre-existing settlements, whether erstwhile villages such as Bexley, Orpington or Sutton, or Victorian outer suburbs created by the steam railway such as Sidcup, Bickley or Surbiton.

There are plenty of examples of this process in the northern suburbs, where Harrow, Edgware, Finchley and Romford grew to their present sizes. But everywhere the real nucleating force was the railway station rather than the old settlements. South of London the country had by 1900 been covered with a close network of lines and stations. On the other hand, particularly in the north and north-west, a number of branches were pushed out at dates subsequent to 1920 into open country in anticipation of housing development. Around the stations on these lines large communities sprang up where previously there had been no more than a farm or two. Examples are Oakwood and Cockfosters on the Piccadilly extension, Queensbury and Kingsbury on the Stanmore line, and Rayners Lane and East-cote on the Uxbridge line. In the south this happened only along the 1939 line to Chessington and around a few newly opened stations such as Petts Wood.

Whatever their origin, the growth of these suburbs between 1921 – or more particularly 1931 – and 1939 was enormous. A few examples only must suffice here. Hornchurch, Essex, more than doubled its population from 17,489 in 1931 to 39,389 in 1951. Near by, Romford expanded from 19,442 in 1921 to 88,002 in 1951. Enfield, which had grown only from 60,738 in 1921 to 67,752 in 1931, grew to 110,465 in the next twenty years. In the north-west growth was even more spectacular. Edgware grew from 1,516 in 1921 to 17,513 in 1951, and Ruislip from 9,112 to 16,035 between 1921 and 1931 and to 68,288 by 1951.

During the 1951–61 decade in most cases growth declined sharply or ceased. Ruislip–Northwood increased by only 6·2 per cent, while Hendon and Enfield declined by 2·8 and 0·9 per cent. On the other hand Romford increased by 30·2 per cent. Examples from southern suburbs are described in Chapter III.

With the more rigid interpretation of the Green Belt since the war, the edge of the continuously built-up area, the 'conurbation', was, with few exceptions, much the same in 1961 as in 1939. But with the great increase in car ownership it is no longer sufficient to take the conurbation as co-extensive with the London Region. It is more realistic to adopt the newly developed concept of 'City Region'.

Following this we can define an *Outer Suburban Zone*, which reaches out as far as Clacton, Thanet and West Sussex and up the Thames valley at least to Henley. Northward, however, the edge of the Chilterns appears to be the frontier and Luton is more of the midlands than of London. In this discontinuous zone dormitory functions are normally subordinate to agriculture, industry or catering for holiday makers. But almost every station within the zone has its quota of commuters to Central London, sometimes two or three thousand, sometimes no more than a dozen.

This is the zone of present population growth, where New Towns such as Basildon, Harlow and Crawley have sprung up and where speculative building has been resumed on the scale experienced in the Middle Zone in the 1930's. The 1951–61 population increase in Dartford Rural District (Kent) was 41·9 per cent, in Burgess Hill (East Sussex) 64·1 per cent and in Rayleigh (Essex) 103·9 per cent.

However, as is to be expected, the termini of the intensive suburban services lie closely round the edge of the conurbation. Because of this coincidence this is the area selected for consideration in this book. 'Intensive' has been taken for this purpose to imply a regular-interval service from Central London in the off-peak hours of at least three stopping trains per hour by one or more routes (1961 timetables).

These termini include Dartford (9 trains per hour), Orpington (4), Coulsdon (6 to the adjacent stations of Smitham, Coulsdon North and South), Surbiton (6) and Twickenham (10) on the Southern Region. North of the Thames the termini are Uxbridge, LT (4–5), West Ruislip, LT and WR (6), Stanmore (6), Edgware (5–10), High Barnet (5) and Cockfosters (6–8),

LT, Enfield (4), Chingford (4) and Broxbourne (3), ER, and Upminster, LT and ER (4–7).

There are certain exceptions to this. Where intensive services extend beyond the Middle Zone their termini have been taken as regional boundaries. They are Dorking North, SR (3), Rickmansworth, LT (3), Watford Junction, LT and LMR (8) and Shenfield, ER (3). Again, although the services are not 'intensive', there is a clear frontier at Gordon Hill on the ER's Hertford North line.

This leaves a number of main lines even yet without 'intensive' suburban services, and here convenient points were selected arbitrarily, at West Drayton on that of the WR, at Elstree on the St Pancras line and at Potters Bar on the East Coast line. Next there are several dead-end branches extending into open country which must be included for the sake of convenience. Among them are the Ongar line into the heart of rural Essex and the SR's Thames Valley branch to Shepperton. Finally the activities of two companies, the Metropolitan and the London, Tilbury & Southend, must be considered as a whole, being both as essentially of London as the North London and the District.

Greater London owes its present social and economic structure largely to railway developments. But each region stands in a different relationship to the railways serving it. Central London had taken shape before the Railway Age, but its present functions and social structure were the result of the dispersal of its resident population, made possible only by railway development. Rapid transit within Central London, too, is possible only by diverting a considerable portion of the traffic to the railways below the streets.

Industrial London is the creation almost equally of river, road and rail, each predominating locally according to the position or product of a particular plant.

The Inner Arc, mostly antedating the railways but partly created by them, has now almost abandoned the rail. Here is a story of closed stations and abandoned services equal to that of remoter rural England.

The Inner Suburban Zone was the creation of the steam suburban railway. Where services were adequate and fares reasonable, as on the southern lines or the Great Eastern, the suburbs spread rapidly outwards. Where suburban traffic was neglected, notably by the GWR and LNWR, open country could soon be reached. After 1900 competition from trams and buses became acute, especially for short journeys. But distances to Central London are longer than in the Inner Arc, and where electrified the rail has maintained a competitive position, which has improved since fares have been equalized.

The Middle Suburban Zone was similarly the creation of the electric railway, and in this rail has still the monopoly of traffic to and from Central London because of the wide time differential. In 1951 the average speed of buses was 11·4 m.p.h. and of suburban trains 20·4. Average journeys by bus were 2·2 miles, 5·6 by tube, and 10 by British Railways.

This zone is the principal source of the peak traffics, for between 20 and 30 per cent of the employed population resident in areas such as Orpington, Sutton, Harrow and Romford work in Central London. Nor is short-distance traffic entirely lacking, especially since fares have been equalized. The private car and television have already begun to affect off-peak traffic, though not to the extent that they have cut into bus revenues.

In the Outer Suburban Zone commuter traffic is generally small in volume, though Tonbridge and Tunbridge Wells have 3,000 season ticket holders and there are places in Surrey and the Chilterns of nearly equal importance. Occasional visits for business or pleasure to Central London also keep traffic at a reasonable level. There is little competition from buses and the Shenfield electrification quickly reduced the large volume of traffic on parallel Green Line routes. Nor are receipts yet affected much by private cars since the time factor is important, season tickets and day returns are highly competitive, and the parking problem looms large.

In this brief assessment, routes radiating from Central London have been stressed, for analysis of the 1951 census figures has shown there are few traffic currents apart from those to and from Central London and local journeys crossing no more than one local government boundary. These latter are more economically handled by bus, and almost all the peripheral and cross-country routes have suffered decay.

While commuting traffic must naturally remain the principal theme, it is possible to distinguish other traffic currents in the bewildering complexity of London's rail system.

Passenger
   1. Long-distance traffic to and from London.
   2. Through traffic involving exchange between termini. Long-distance services over the country as a whole are chiefly concentrated on London and this class of traffic is large. In the past it was specifically catered for. Today, save for the suitcases with which it encumbers peak-hour tube trains, it is almost indistinguishable from the urban.
   3. Urban traffic. That is, movement within Central London.
   4. Suburban traffic. That is, movement chiefly to and from Central London, but also between suburbs.

Freight
   1. Long-distance traffic consigned to or dispatched from the marketing, distributing and manufacturing centre which is London.
   2. 'The water outlet.' Port traffic has always been a prize. But owing to the organization of the port of London, where a large proportion of the cargo is loaded from or discharged into a fleet of over 8,000 lighters, wharves anywhere along the Thames served railway companies equally as well as direct connections with the docks and were as much sought after.
   3. Interchange traffic between the northern and southern lines.
   4. Local traffic. But it is important to note that even prior to the motor age this was comparatively unimportant.

The proportion of long-distance to suburban traffic and of passenger to freight naturally varied widely. But only the District and the Tubes handled no freight at all. In other respects, at least in their early days, both the Metropolitan and the District were orthodox steam railways, which until the beginning of the present century handled the bulk of the traffic.

After 1900 many steam services were electrified, but for suburban traffic only, except for the SR's extensions of the

1930's. All main-line companies continued to intermingle electric suburban trains with steam-hauled expresses and goods trains. But electrification has been continuously extended and, between 1958 and 1962 all remaining suburban services converted to diesel traction. With electrification to Bournemouth in 1967 the last main line steam workings into London ceased.

After their electrification the development of the Metropolitan and the District diverged from that of other companies. They assumed the functions of what was called in the U.S.A. 'rapid transit', specializing in the mass movement of urban and suburban traffic by very intensive services of multiple-unit electric trains.

The tubes have a somewhat different history. Built to deal with urban traffic, they originally extended only to the inmost suburbs and from the very first were exclusively 'rapid transit' lines. But with the projection of Bakerloo trains over the LNWR to Watford in 1917 they entered a new phase of extension into the Middle Zone, though still retaining their extreme specialization. These extensions were sometimes over new branches, but often they were along existing routes (generally on new lines parallel to the steam-operated ones).

It is notable that but one tube line ever penetrated far south of the river, the early and universal electrification of the Southern's suburban system having forestalled others. The southern lines offer a number of other contrasts with those north of the river and are logically dealt with as a unit.

Before going further it must be explained that the structure of local government was reorganized with the creation of the Greater London Council in 1965 to administer virtually the whole of the area covered by this book. Within this area, London Boroughs were created with entirely new boundaries rather than simple amalgamations of pre-existing Boroughs and Urban Districts. For the sake of historical and statistical continuity, however, the divisions as they existed in 1964 have been retained in this edition.

CHAPTER II

The Southern Termini and their Approaches

When I think of . . . the Cannon Street and Charing Cross railway stations, I am not sure the prospect is not even fairer than in Fleet Street. See how they belch forth puffing trains . . . gorging and disgorging incessantly those human atoms whose movement is the life of the City.

SAMUEL BUTLER.

LONDON IN 1836

LONDON's first railway was opened between Spa Road and Deptford on 8 February 1836. At that time the population numbered some 1·75 million, crowded into an area about that of present-day Brighton and Hove. Orchards and market gardens spread over the gravel terraces westward from Chelsea, around Barking and up the Lea Valley. On the tracts of clay were large fields of wheat, hay for London's horses and pasture for cattle. Parks of country houses crowned the gravel-capped hills.

The outward spread of the suburbs, which the new railways were to facilitate, had already begun. Since 1800 St John's Wood, Camden Town and Islington had grown up with good-class housing. Southward pleasant squares, interspersed with sordid slums, which the railways were to empty impartially, extended to the City and Westminster. To the east houses were rapidly replacing the fields of Bethnal Green and Stepney. Between Commercial Road and the river building extended to Limehouse church, and master mariners lived in the neat villas of Wapping and Shadwell.

On the south bank continuous building connected Rother-hithe with Lambeth. For the most part it was an area of overcrowded and noisome slums. But away from the river middle-class housing had filled in the area up to the New Kent Road and was reaching out into Walworth and Kenning-ton and even out to Camberwell.

To the west Pimlico and Belgravia had recently linked Chelsea village with Westminster, though along the river the latter still petered out in the Millbank slums. Park Lane and Edgware Road still clearly defined the city's north-western limits.

Along the Bath Road, Kensington, Hammersmith and Turnham Green villages were linked with London by ribbon development, but along the Uxbridge Road open country was soon reached. Only the small villages of Kilburn and Edgware interrupted the solitudes along the Edgware Road. A ribbon of building extended through Tottenham to Upper Edmonton, while beyond, unusually for Middlesex and south Essex, the villages along the Enfield Road were large and closely spaced. Along the Colchester Road desultory building reached out to Bow and a wide ribbon had grown up along the East India Dock Road. Along the roads leading southward, ribbon development reached Brixton Hill and Upper Tooting. The environs of London were sparsely peopled, villages were small and scattered and towns few.

In 1831 the City still housed a tenth of Greater London's population. Counsel for the defence in an 1840 murder trial lived at 17 Old Jewry, but the wealthier merchants and pro-fessional men had already moved out to the West End or the rural seclusion of Sydenham, Clapham or Stoke Newington. Cobbett sneered that 'between Sutton and the Wen there is, in fact, little besides houses, gardens, grass plots and other matters to accommodate the Jews and Jobbers and their mistresses. . . .' Their chief clerks were seeking houses in Penton-ville, Islington or Newington. Lowten, Mr Perker's clerk (*Pickwick Papers*), lived in Camden Town and walked to Gray's Inn. But thousands of poorer folk lived in Holborn, Smithfield and Moorgate. The industrial suburbs of Spitalfields and Shoreditch were become increasingly overcrowded. But the

SOUTHERN TERMINI I

(1) *London Bridge at the turn of the century. On the extreme left is the entrance to the High Level through platforms. Next to it is Beazley's* SER *station (the Low Level), and beyond the* LBSCR *station and hotel.*

(2) *The Brighton side at London Bridge is now covered by a great three-arched roof. In 1880 the intensive local services were handled by trains of uncomfortable four-wheelers hauled by small and well-kept tank engines.*

(3) *In 1900 Charing Cross was still a gateway to the Continent, and here boat trains for both Dover and Folkestone are loading at adjacent platforms. The photograph was taken before the collapse of the arched roof.*

SOUTHERN TERMINI II

(4) 'Brighton Baroque' at Victoria—the rebuilt LBSCR station just after the first world war. The much smaller SE & CR station can just be seen on the left.

(5) The foot of the incline from Grosvenor Bridge. The great length of the platforms on the Brighton side of Victoria can be appreciated. The arched roof of the Chatham side is in the background.

(6) Waterloo. The lower roofs cover the older 'Windsor' station. Note the SER viaduct and the bridge across Waterloo Road which carried the connecting spur.

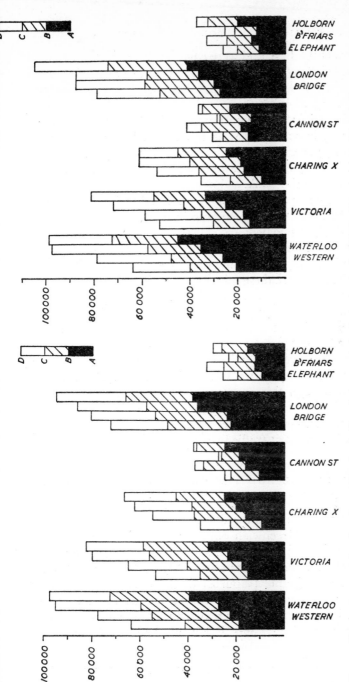

Fig. 3. Passengers at the Southern Region's London termini: *Left*, Arrivals. *Right*, Departures. These diagrams, based on annual censuses, show the average number of passengers on an ordinary weekday during the census period, usually over two weeks in February. For each station the columns represent (*left to right*) the figures for 1930, 1939, 1948, and 1960. In each column A–D represents twenty-four hours, A–C 7 a.m. to 10 a.m. for incoming passengers and 4 p.m. to 8 p.m. for departing passengers, while A–B represents the busiest hour (morning for incoming, evening for departing).

evil slums of the East End were never as bad as those of Central London. In 1849 Calmel Buildings in Orchard Street (the south end of Baker Street) housed 944 human beings in twenty-six three-storey houses.

Thus even in 1836 separation of work and home had begun, though people could still walk to and fro. Distances were still reasonable, generally a mile, rarely more than two. Islington, Bethnal Green, Limehouse and Walworth are all just under two miles from the Bank.

The 1846 Royal Commission on London Traffic found a greater number of people coming in to work from the Surrey side. In 1836, 75,000 pedestrians crossed Blackfriars Bridge daily and 100,000 London Bridge. The bridges converged on the southern suburbs, making the City and most of the West End accessible. Nor were these suburbs as yet extensive and property values were lower on the south bank. Thus the southern lines had a large traffic potential, they could reach convenient bridgeheads without undue cost and their stations were among the best placed.

There were eventually four southern companies and each sought both a City and a West End terminus. Three threads thus run through this chapter: a dogged and costly progress towards the heart of both City and West End; inter-company rivalry: and successive enlargements of stations and approaches to deal with constant traffic increases.

LONDON BRIDGE AND THE CHARING CROSS EXTENSION

London Bridge is the oldest London terminus, and is now the busiest. Its nucleus was the simple two-platformed structure of the London & Greenwich officially opened on 14 December 1836. Col. George Landmann, its engineer, suggested a viaduct to cross the numerous lanes of the Bermondsey slums, 'One of the most abominable [suburbs] in the environs of London', says an 1858 Guide, and of the numerous market gardens beyond. Even the promotors realized that revenue from suburban traffic on this 3·75-mile line would be inadequate, so they envisaged letting off arches as dwellings, shops and warehouses reached by toll paths alongside. The arches understandably proved unpopular for houses, but are still widely used as business premises.

Because of the continued addiction to walking, receipts were disappointing until tolls could be levied on 'foreign' users. Eventually there were three such, the Croydon, the Brighton and the SER. The London & Croydon was formally opened on 1 June 1839 from Corbett's Lane Junction to the present West Croydon, 10·25 miles from London Bridge. Two of the stations were named after inns in default of nearby villages. Anerley, another, was named after the villa of a Scots merchant and means 'lonely'. The Company's policy was to encourage tourist traffic amidst this long-vanished Arcady.

In 1853 Measom's *Guide* describes Anerley as a 'holiday resort', but by then the area around the new Crystal Palace was becoming fashionable for suburban villas. A Guide of 1858 states that the area round Sydenham was rapidly being built over and at Penge half-finished streets were enveloping Beulah Spa.

The original London Bridge would have been quite inadequate, and before it was opened the Croydon obtained powers for a separate station on the *north* side. Then, on 7 August 1840, the Greenwich were authorized to widen their viaduct on the *south* side for the use of their tenants; this came into use on 10 May 1842. Consequently the terminal stations were exchanged and the former Greenwich station was administered by a Joint Committee of the Brighton, Croydon and SER.

The Greenwich tolls were high and the Company was apt to be intransigent. The SER therefore hatched a scheme to break the stranglehold. On 4 July 1843 it obtained powers for a mile branch from Bricklayers' Arms Junction on the Croydon to a 'Grand West End Terminus'.

Sir William Cubitt, engineer to the SER, selected a site on the Old Kent Road as being clear of building and 'near the Bricklayers' Arms, a travellers' resting place'. Westminster Bridge is in fact more conveniently reached from here than from London Bridge. BRICKLAYERS' ARMS was opened on 1 May 1844, but was never a success for passengers, though later connected with the North Kent (p. 45) at North Kent East

TABLE 2

THE USER OF TRACKS ON THE EASTWARD APPROACH TO LONDON BRIDGE

	From 17 June 1928	1901	13 August 1866	24 February 1850	10 May 1842	14 December 1836
			North Side of Viaduct	*North Side of Viaduct*		
1.	Down No. 1 Eastern	Down No. 1 SECR				
2.	Down No. 2 Eastern	Down No. 2 SECR				
3.	Down No. 3 Eastern	Down No. 3 SECR	Up Greenwich			
4.	Up No. 2 Eastern	Up No. 2 SECR	Down Greenwich & SER	Up Greenwich		
5.	Up No. 1 Eastern	Up No. 1 SECR	Up SER	Down Greenwich & North Kent	Down Greenwich	Down Greenwich
6.	Down Local Central	Down LBSCR	Down LBSCR & SER	Up North Kent	Up Greenwich	Up Greenwich
7.	Down Through Central	Up LBSCR	Up LBSCR & SER	Down SER & LBSCR	Down SER, L&C, L&B †	
8.	Up Through Central	Up LBSCR	Up LBSCR & SER	Up SER & LBSCR	Up SER, L&C, L&B	
			South Side of Viaduct			
9.	Up Local Central	Down South London	Down South London	Up Croydon Local		
10.	Down South London	Up South London *	Up South London			
11.	Up South London	Up South London	Up South London			

* Reversible from 1909 to 1928.

† L & C, London & Croydon; L & B, London & Brighton.

Junction. From February 1852 regular services ceased and the terminus became a goods depot. The locomotive shed closed in 1961, and in 1969 a centralized parcel depot opened.

But the SER had achieved its purpose, for the Greenwich reduced the tolls from 3d. to 1¼d. per passenger and in 1845 leased the line to the larger company, giving it control of the London Bridge approach. On this traffic was rapidly growing and in 1847 powers were obtained for two more lines, on the north side. It will be seen in Table 2 that down Greenwich and North Kent trains shared a single down line. This was the origin of right-hand running on the Greenwich, then with a self-contained 15-minute shuttle service. After 1850, especially with the opening of the Crystal Palace, traffic continued to grow.

In 1846, 625,000 passengers used the station, in 1850, 5·6 million, and in 1854, 10·8 million. By 1858 about 7·5 million were using the SER side and 6 million the Brighton. To accommodate this traffic, most of which was to and from the West End, a new station was designed by Samuel Beazley. But as the result of a quarrel the Brighton left the joint station and built its own to the south, just in time to deal with the Crystal Palace traffic.

The *Illustrated London News* of 24 July 1858 described the new stations and their traffic:

> The Greenwich traffic, which seldom includes any luggage, is connected by two lines of rail. . . . Next to the right are the North Kent rails [both these sections were obliterated when the High Level was built]. . . . Its neighbour group [the present Low Level] belongs to the Dover line, three rails, two platforms and a carriage road. The Brighton, Croydon and Crystal Palace series of lines comes last, chumming together under one span of roof [up to the present platform 17], but sociably contriving matters so that special pairs of rails are appropriated for the arrival and departures of the long and short trains [i.e. long distance and local].
>
> Of ordinary trains during the month of July there start to Greenwich 49 *per diem*, on the North Kent line 29, to Dover and Margate 15, to Brighton and the South Coast 14, to Croydon and Epsom 24, to Beckenham and other short stations 11 and to the Crystal Palace etc. 25, total 167. This

catalogue does not include the excursion trains nor the 'special trains' which convey grand ambassadors on their missions or bring up Royal visitors *en route* to Buckingham Palace.

On 30 June 1862 the LBSCR obtained its South London Act for a line from London Bridge to Victoria. In connection with this three more tracks, Brighton property, were brought into use on the south side of the viaduct on 13 August 1866, together with the present platforms 19–23. On 1 January 1880 the roads were continued on to Bricklayers' Arms Junction on a separate viaduct, the South Bermondsey Spur (see Figure 4).

The six through platforms of the High Level station date from the Charing Cross extension, when the Dover station (now the Low Level) became the continental freight depot. In 1901 Southwark Depot was opened for continental freight (since 1960 used for parcels traffic after the new Hither Green depot opened), and from 2 June 1902 the Low Level was used again for passengers, this time with four platforms. By 1902, 23·7 million passengers were using the Brighton side and 6 million the South Eastern; ninety-six trains arrived before 10.30 a.m.

The frontage of London Bridge, though still sadly war-shattered, is little altered. In contrast with the opulent glories of other termini it is severely plain, but is pleasant if freshly stuccoed. Behind the Brighton side is a vast glass roof with three arched bays, but the Low Level and the long tunnels up to the High Level are dark and dismal. In July 1961 plans were released for a new station, but by 1970 were not implemented.

London Bridge is essentially the station of the Common Man and it is hard to imagine 'grand ambassadors' ever using it. Nor is it a gateway for holiday crowds any more. Excursionists and hop-pickers no longer come from the once overcrowded neighbourhood.

On an average 1961 weekday 104,000 passengers arrived, an 18·6 per cent increase over 1939. Seventy-one per cent came between 7.0 and 10.0 a.m. Crowds poured across the bridge into the City or streamed through the 'hole in the wall' from the Brighton side up to the High Level to insert themselves some-how into overcrowded Charing Cross trains. Thirty-eight thousand of them would return during the evening peak hour.

But outside the two daily business periods there is only a trickle of short-distance travellers. At night the whole station is busy with mail, newspapers and parcels. Among the departures in 1961 were eight parcels trains, some carrying passengers almost as an afterthought, and the 11.50 p.m. including the South Eastern Travelling Post Office. Some 500 up trains pass through the High Level on weekdays and there are over 400 arrivals at the terminal platforms.

Schemes for a 'Grand Terminal Station' on the noisome alleys of the Hungerford Market were mooted in 1845. But not until 8 August 1859 was the Charing Cross Railway incorporated, the SER being spurred on by proposals for Victoria (p. 32). The 1·9 miles over the crowded roof-tops cost £4 million and the new terminus was opened on 11 January 1864 for local traffic (using a Villiers Street entrance) and on 1 May for all traffic. An intermediate station at Blackfriars Road was closed when Waterloo Junction (Waterloo from 7 July 1935) was opened on 1 January 1869. Today about 22,000 passengers a day use the latter's four platforms, half of them at peak hours. For the rest of the day most of them are going to and from the main station.

A city terminus on Cannon Street was authorized on 28 June 1861 and opened on 1 September 1866. It had a triangular approach from the double-tracked Charing Cross line, but later a third track was laid for a shuttle service at 5-minute intervals between Charing Cross and Cannon Street, a reflection of the chronic congestion existing even then in the Strand and Fleet Street. The service disappeared as other trains became more numerous.

Until the end of 1916 the majority of trains were reversed in Cannon Street before continuing to Charing Cross, and by 1900 the situation on the triangle was chaotic. Its sides were too short for increased train lengths and according to an SE & CR report it would sometimes be completely blocked by trains fouling each other. It was the main cause of the line's bad record of timekeeping. In 1904 between 5.0 and 6.0 p.m. on weekdays twenty-five down trains and almost as many up passed through London Bridge and all but two or three had to be reversed in Cannon Street. By 1902 a widening programme

TABLE 3

THE EVENING RUSH HOUR THROUGH LONDON BRIDGE
HIGH LEVEL – OCTOBER 1906

Charing Cross	Cannon Street	London Bridge	
p.m.	p.m.	p.m.	
5.2	5.11	5.14	Dartford via Greenwich
5.8	5.17	5.20	Redhill and Reading
	5.18	5.21	Mid-Kent
5.11	5.20	5.23	Erith via Bexleyheath
		5.27*	Dartford Loop
	5.25	5.28	Dartford via Blackheath and North Kent
5.17	5.25	5.29	Caterham
	5.30	5.32	Bromley North
5.21	5.31	5.34	Erith via Greenwich
	5.34	5.37	Mid-Kent
5.27	5.37	5.40	Maidstone via Dartford Loop
5.30	5.38	5.42	Bexhill via Orpington
5.33	5.42	5.45	Plumstead via Blackheath
	5.42	5.45	Gillingham via Dartford Loop
5.37	5.46	5.49	Wadhurst via Orpington
		5.51	Mid-Kent
	5.50	5.53	Dartford via Blackheath and North Kent
	5.50	5.53	Orpington
5.42	5.52	5.55	Plumstead via Greenwich
5.46	5.56	5.59	Mid-Kent
5.50	5.58	6.1	Redhill and Gomshall
5.53	—	6.1	Plumstead via Blackheath
	6.0	6.2	Bromley North
	6.3	6.6	Dartford via Bexleyheath
5.59	6.8	6.11	Dartford via Greenwich
	6.10	6.13	Mid-Kent
6.7	—	6.14	Blackheath
15	23	27	trains

* From Low Level.

Summary of Destinations

	1906	1962
Main Line	3	14
Bromley North	2	4
North Kent via Greenwich	4	5
North Kent via Blackheath	5	4
Bexleyheath	2	7
Dartford Loop	3	8
Mid-Kent	5	9
Croydon Line	3	0
	27	51

had been completed, but it left a legacy of so many flat junctions that operating the present intensive service is a real *tour de force*. The side of the triangle carrying all the Charing Cross trains remains only double; from London Bridge to Spa Road there are only two up roads, while beyond this the three down and three up lines must be sorted by a series of flat junctions into three pairs of up and down (see Figure 4).

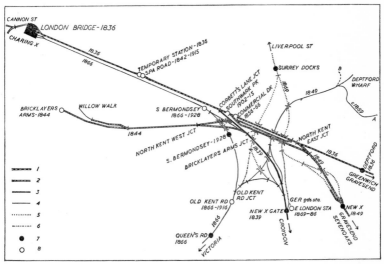

FIG. 4. The approaches to London Bridge. 1, London & Greenwich. 2, South Eastern. 3, London & Croydon. 4, London, Brighton & South Coast. 5, East London. 6, East London (abandoned). 7, Passenger stations. 8, Closed passenger stations. A, Foreign Cattle Market. B, Surrey Commercial Docks.

By 1902, 13·5 million passengers a year were using Cannon Street and 10·2 million Charing Cross. Traffic continued to grow, particularly after 1918, and delays were almost as bad as ever. But no more widening was attempted and it was left to the Southern to deal with the situation by electrification and power signalling.

N. Hawkshaw, engineer to the Charing Cross Railway, designed magnificent single-arched roofs for both stations. At 3.40 p.m. on 5 December 1905 a heavy beam fell from Charing Cross roof. Passengers were hastily cleared from the 3.50 for

Hastings and an incoming continental express was stopped outside. A few minutes later the two outer bays of the roof collapsed, much of the wreckage falling through the roof of the adjacent theatre. About thirty men were working on the roof and a hundred more in the theatre, but casualties were mercifully light. Seven workmen were killed but no railwayman or passenger. The arched roof was replaced by the present flat one.

In 1926 Cannon Street's nine platforms, five short and narrow, were rebuilt to provide eight faces and a large circulating area. In 1956 a start was made on complete rebuilding. The roof was taken down, the platforms extended across the circulating area and a new one provided under the ex-hotel building. Completion was delayed due to a dispute with the Corporation of London over design, but was largely completed in 1965.

With the westward spread of commerce and more frequent journeys from suburbs to West End for shopping or theatre-going, Charing Cross, with six platforms, is now very much busier than Cannon Street with eight, about three times as many passengers now using it as did in 1902.

In 1960, 352 trains arrived daily, 89 before 10.30 a.m. as opposed to 45 in 1902. An average of 125,000 passengers a day passed through the station, an 11 per cent increase on 1939. Ninety thousand arrive and leave during the six busiest hours, but, because of its great convenience for the West End, there is a constant flow of suburban travellers. In season holiday crowds are conspicuous. On summer Saturdays in 1960, 8,000 or more left by Dover line trains between 8.30 a.m. and 3.0 p.m. and about half as many again by those to Hastings. But Charing Cross is essentially a suburban station.

There is less variety in Cannon Street's passenger traffic, the station being used almost exclusively by City-bound commuters. With the rebuilding of the City, peak-hour traffic has more than recovered from the low level to which it had fallen in 1946. Thus, while 4,600 fewer passengers arrived daily in 1960 compared with 1939, peak-hour arrivals were *up* by a similar figure. Of the 36,700 passengers arriving on an average 1960 day all but 2,200 came in between 7.0 and 10.0 a.m. and 23,100 during the single busiest hour. In 1952, 89 trains arrived before 10.30 a.m. compared with 37 in 1902. Outside peak hours only a skeleton service is provided Mondays to Fridays. From 1936 to 1939 and again after 1960 it was used by relief continental services and, unlike Charing Cross, parcels were dealt with on a large scale.

Occasionally town planners develop peculiar ideas about railway stations. Both Charing Cross and Cannon Street are superbly convenient for Central London and nearly 200,000 passengers use them daily. Yet more than once it has been proposed that Hungerford Bridge should become a road and that the railways should be cut back south of the river. The 1931 Commission on Cross-River Traffic roundly condemned these ideas.

VICTORIA

The Brighton also cherished ideas for a West End terminus, but nothing concrete transpired until Paxton's masterpiece was moved from Hyde Park to Sydenham after the 1851 Exhibition. In expectation of consequent excursion traffic the West End of London and Crystal Palace Railway was floated. On 4 August 1853 powers were obtained for a 5·75-mile line from the LSWR to an end-on junction with the LBSCR's spur from Sydenham. Powers were also obtained for short extensions – to the Thames at New Chelsea Bridge and to Norwood Junction. The next year a branch was sanctioned from Bromley Junction, 0·8 mile beyond Crystal Palace, to Farnborough (Kent).

The new company's line traversed open country and local traffic would be sparse. But the Brighton was interested in it as an approach to Waterloo and, when the LSWR proved unco-operative, to Pimlico, as the Thames-side terminus was to be called. Wandsworth Common to Crystal Palace was opened for public traffic on 1 December 1856 and worked by the Brighton. The Norwood extension opened on 1 October 1857 and Pimlico station on 29 March 1858. Pimlico portions were now detached at East Croydon from London Bridge trains.

Although the West End line crossed under the LSWR it was not until 1863, when the district was rapidly being built over, that an exchange station was opened. Although in Battersea, this has always been Clapham Junction. Its seventeen platforms are in a V, enclosing Clapham Yard, the main carriage depot for Waterloo. Over 2,500 trains now pass through in twenty-four hours, making it one of the busiest traffic junctions in the world, though it is little used as an exchange station. Local traffic is heavy; 4·3 million tickets were issued in 1938 and there has been little subsequent change. It also had a large milk depot.

The West End line also attracted the interest of the London, Chatham & Dover, for its Farnborough Extension provided the opportunity for an approach to London independent of the South Eastern (Vol. II, p. 40). The Extension was opened on 3 May 1858 as a double line to Beckenham, where there was a junction with the SER (p. 46), and a single one thence to Bromley (now Shortlands).

Although planned as a route into mid Kent proper, it never got any further. It was continued by the Mid-Kent (Bromley to St Mary Cray) Company, incorporated on 21 July 1856. Its line was opened to Southborough Road (now Bickley) on 5 July 1858 and was linked with the LCDR's line from Rochester on 3 December 1860, when the first through trains reached Victoria. The LBSCR bought the West End line on 1 July 1859 and a year later the Farnborough Extension became part of the LCDR, which enjoyed running powers but no traffic rights over the WE & CPR.

Meanwhile, on 23 July 1858, the Victoria Station and Pimlico Company had been incorporated to build 73 chains from the WE & CPR at what is now Stewarts Lane Junction to a new terminus across the river, on the site of the Grosvenor Canal basin, the cheapest land in this rapidly developing area. Victoria Street had been opened as recently as 1851 and Belgravia newly laid out by Sir Thomas Cubitt. The Brighton, subscribing half the necessary capital, became entitled to half the station. This part was opened on 1 October 1860, Pimlico being closed and subsequently absorbed into Battersea goods depot. The other half was leased to the LCDR and the GWR. It was not ready until 25 August 1862, and until then LCDR trains used a temporary station.

The circuitous and steeply graded approach to Victoria was

unsatisfactory and large sums were spent on improvements. The LBSCR received powers in 1860 for a cut-off from Windmill Bridge Junction (north of Croydon) to Balham Junction, avoiding Crystal Palace. This was first used on 1 December 1862 and was quadrupled under powers of 1896. On 29 July 1862 a high level line was sanctioned from Pouparts Junction (east of Clapham Junction) over, instead of under, the LSWR to the south end of Grosvenor Bridge. This was opened on 1 December 1867.

By one of the most important Acts in its history, the Metropolitan Extensions Act of 6 August 1860, the LCDR obtained an independent and easier access from Penge Junction (west of Beckenham) to Stewarts Lane, again avoiding Crystal Palace. It was opened between Stewarts Lane and Herne Hill on 25 August 1862 and on to Beckenham on 1 July 1863. The Crystal Palace route ceased to be a main line, but housing development soon brought a heavy local traffic which remains.

The LCDR was still unsatisfied and obtained in its New Lines Act of 1864 powers for a three-track high-level line from Factory Junction (Wandsworth Road) to Grosvenor Bridge, avoiding the steep dip to Stewarts Lane. This line came into use on 1 January 1867. The observant traveller can still distinguish the old approach among the maze of lines below him.

The GWR came by way of the West London Extension (p. 126), opened on 2 March 1863. From Latchmere Junction connections led to the Windsor and Brighton sides of Clapham Junction and to the WE & CPR and LCDR at Longhedge Junctions (named after a nearby farm). Mixed gauge was provided and on 1 April 1863 a service of both broad- and narrow-gauge trains from Southall inaugurated. By October 1866 these were solely narrow-gauge and the service ceased from 22 March 1915, though the GWR remained a lessee of Victoria until 1933. The ex-GWR goods depot at South Lambeth remains important.

The complex history of the stations south of Grosvenor Bridge is summarized in Figure 5. The bridge itself originally carried two mixed-gauge tracks, but in 1866 it was widened. On the old section the broad-gauge rails were removed and a third track added. The Brighton now had exclusive use of these, for on the east side a new section was built carrying two standard and two mixed tracks for the other users. By its 1898 and 1899 Acts the Brighton gained powers to rebuild its own side, adding two extra tracks and making nine in all.

Victoria was provided with seven platforms and ten tracks on the Brighton side and eight platforms and six tracks on the

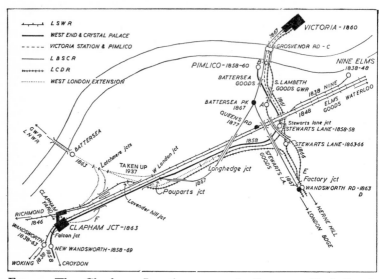

FIG. 5. The Clapham Junction area: A, Battersea Park Road, 1867–1916. B, Battersea Park & Steamboat Pier, 1860–70. C, Opened 1870. LBSCR side closed 1907; LCDR side closed 1911. D, LCDR side closed 1916. E, Wandsworth Road Goods (Midland). F, Falcon Lane Goods (LNWR).

other. The Victoria Street frontage was ramshackle indeed, while the LCDR provided the uninteresting buildings which face Wilton Road.

The 1898–9 Acts authorized the Brighton to rebuild their side. There was no room to provide extra platforms, so the existing ones were lengthened and the tracks arranged to allow trains to arrive at or leave the inner ends while the outer ends were occupied. A much more impressive frontage was provided and the new station formally reopened on 1 July 1998. The next year the SE & CR completed its new Victoria Street frontage.

In 1924 the Southern knocked a wide opening in the party wall and administered the two stations as one. But it still remains a binary station with train services segregated and duplicated booking offices, buffets and so on. The ex-LBSCR frontage, which includes a large hotel, is in flamboyant 'Brighton Baroque'. The former SE & CR side (erected 1907–9) is much plainer but includes the large arch inscribed 'The Gateway to the Continent'.

At holiday times the Chatham side is crowded with cross-Channel travellers of all nationalities, and up to 30 boat trains may leave and as many arrive in a day. There are also the Kent Coast holiday-makers. In 1962, 16 trains left for Margate and Ramsgate between 8.0 a.m. and noon on peak Saturdays with about 10,000 passengers. But at other times this part of the station may be almost deserted, and the basic 1962 service included but two suburban and three main line departures in the hour. Even at rush hours it is under-used.

In contrast, platforms 9–17, the Brighton side, are always busy. Trains, normally too long for the platforms to be used in tandem, arrive and depart every few minutes. In 1962 there were in the average hour 10 suburban departures, 8 main-line and a solitary steam or diesel train for the Oxted line, 19 in all. In summer and at the daily peaks passenger traffic reaches gargantuan proportions.

In 1902, 29·4 million people used Victoria, 18·6 million the Brighton side and 10·8 million the Chatham. Today, in spite of a decline in travel from the inner suburbs, this has grown to over 50 million. On an average 1960 weekday 81,286 passengers (excluding continental) arrived, an increase of 35·5 per cent over 1939; 54,556 came between 7.0 and 10. a.m., an increase of 56·1 per cent over 1939, which is a measure of the growing concentration of commerce in the West End. The proportion of passengers arriving between 7.0 and 10.0 a.m. is 67 per cent of the total, but nevertheless this is the lowest concentration of all Southern termini except Waterloo.

Victoria serves the Continent, the Sussex and Thanet resorts, prosperous inland towns and the middle-class suburbs stretching continuously from Dulwich and Streatham to the North Downs. After 1962 it entered the air age. British United Airways'

terminal was erected over platforms 15–16. In 1967 some
750,000 air passengers used the rail link with Gatwick Airport.
Its links with the West End improved beyond recognition with
the opening of the Victoria Line (p. 109).

THE 'CITY LINE'

The Metropolitan Extensions Act of 1860 also gave the LCDR
access to the City, authorizing a 4.5-mile line from Herne Hill
across the river to join the Metropolitan Railway at Farringdon
Street (p. 85).

The scheme involved the demolition of houses north of
Camberwell accommodating some 3,000 people. Because a
further Act of 25 July 1864 entailed even more demolitions,
Clause 134 required the LCDR to 'run a train every morning of
the week from their Loughborough Park and Peckham
Junction stations to their Ludgate station' and back in the
evening at 'one penny per journey' to convey workmen who,
it was presumed, would be rehoused farther out. In fact, H. J.
Dyos has shown that unskilled workmen were dependent on
casual employment and were unable to live away from the
work they had to compete for daily. Thus railway building
through the inner suburbs for the time being increased the
already bad overcrowding. Only the more highly paid were
able to move out to better housing. The workmen's trains,
started in 1865, left both Ludgate Hill and Victoria for the
other terminus *via* Herne Hill at 4.55 a.m. and returned at
6.15 p.m. (2.30 p.m. Saturdays).

The 'City Line' was far more than the Chatham could cope
with financially. It was soon afloat on and then awash in a sea
of speculation. But the possibilities for through traffic were vast.
To the north the GNR and the Midland could be reached and
to the south were the LBSCR and LSWR at Clapham Junction,
and from there the West London led to the GWR and LNWR.
All these companies were approached to partake financially
and all eventually profited from the scheme, even if the
Chatham did not. Among their gains was the right to work
trains to their own goods and coal depots in South London.

From Herne Hill to the Elephant and Castle the line was

THE CHANGING SCENE AT GROVE PARK

(7 and 8) *The widening of lines in response to increased traffic has brought great changes in the railway scene. In the upper picture a down goods train passes Grove Park station on the* SER *main line from Charing Cross by Sevenoaks and Dover about 1900. In the lower picture a ten-coach electric train leaves for Bromley North in 1958. Both photographs were taken from the signal box in the angle between main and branch lines.*

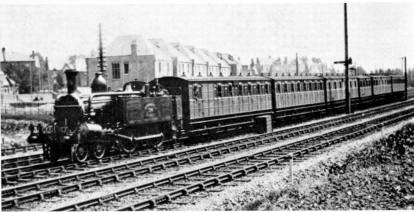

STEAM SUBURBAN I

(9) *A North London train from Broad Street climbs the heavy gradients of the* GNR's *'Northern Heights' line about 1900.*

(10) *A Metropolitan train of the same period near Willesden Green gives an impression of even greater antiquity. But speculative building is going up fast in anticipation of the imminent electrification.*

(11) *A small ex-*GER *2-4-2 tank about 1925 drags its long train of six-wheelers up Brentwood Bank, where the line is now quadrupled and electrified.*

opened on 6 October 1862 and thence to Blackfriars on 1 June 1864. This was a terminus on the south bank of the river and the building (on the up side) became part of Blackfriars goods depot, which had a long disused wharf on the river. Closed in 1965, empty trains from Cannon Street are stabled on the site. The site was so limited that the marshalling of freight trains, hitherto normally done at goods stations, had to be carried out at Herne Hill Sorting Sidings, one of the first of such yards in the country.

The Thames was eventually bridged, and by 21 December 1864 a temporary station at Ludgate Hill was in use, a permanent station being opened on 1 June 1865. Gloomy and inconvenient, it had two island platforms which were replaced in 1910 by a single, broader one.

On 1 January 1866 LCDR passenger trains began running into the Metropolitan's Farringdon Street station and the connection was soon carrying a wide variety of passenger and freight services. Then, by an Act of 13 July 1871, the Chatham became committed to yet another grandiose project. A nominally independent Holborn Viaduct Station Company (for the bankrupt Chatham was not allowed to raise capital) was authorized to build a 292-yard branch from the Ludgate–Farringdon line to a new terminus, complete with hotel, fronting on the new thoroughfare of Holborn Viaduct of 1869. It was opened on 2 March 1874. On 1 August a low-level station, Snow Hill ('Holborn Viaduct Low Level' from 1912), was opened at the foot of the 1 in 39 incline; it was closed on 1 June 1916.

Finally, on 10 May 1886 a parallel bridge across the Thames was opened with at the northern end yet another new station, St Paul's, the original Blackfriars being closed. Just to make the story more complex, on 1 February 1937 St Paul's was renamed Blackfriars. When Ludgate Hill was rebuilt the rear wall of the present Blackfriars was pierced to make two of the five platforms through ones.

The existing layout was completed by the opening by the SER on 1 June 1878 of the Union Street spur up from the Charing Cross line to share in the through traffic. Inevitably there was trouble over bookings on the SER–GNR service, but the spur has remained a useful link.

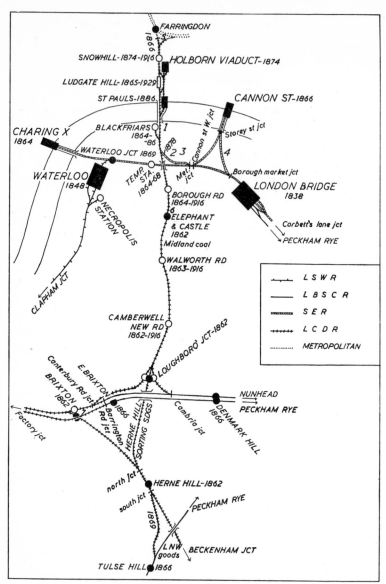

FIG. 6. The LCDR and SER approaches to City and West End: ownership of lines through Brixton and Denmark Hill shown as built. On completion the northern pair were taken over by the LCDR and the southern by the LBSCR. 1, Blackfriars Goods. 2, Southwark continental depot. 3, Ewer Street locomotive depot. 4, Cannon Street locomotive depot. 5, West Street junction. 6, GNR coal depot. 7, Midland coal depot.

Less than 700 yards separate the inner end of Holborn from the country end of Blackfriars. Ludgate Hill thus became increasingly redundant, especially after the through trains ceased in 1916. The Wimbledon trains were the last to call (p. 60), and with their electrification it was closed on 3 March 1929, but the station remains a disused shell.

The difficulties of inter-terminal transfer through the congested streets of mid-Victorian London can scarcely be imagined even by moderns fretting in buses immured in endless traffic jams. Holborn was easily the nearest southern terminus to King's Cross and St Pancras and thus attracted a considerable transfer traffic. All LCDR main-line trains, including continental ones, carried a City portion attached or detached at Herne Hill, which consequently became the Chatham's key point.

But by 1899 E. L. Ahrons, the great railway writer, was saying of Holborn 'no London Station may be said to have had such an ephemeral existence'. Watching the thin trickle of humanity at 5.15 p.m. we cannot but agree, but with the rebuilding of the district traffic is on the increase. In 1963 the bombed frontage was replaced by a large office block.

Outside the small hours there are no services beyond Gillingham in peak periods and Sevenoaks at slack times, when there are but 4 departures an hour. But Holborn dealt with a very heavy parcels traffic, including continental, and three of its six platforms, too short for electric trains, were so used.

Just as the Underground destroyed the through services and consequently the importance of Holborn and Blackfriars, trams and buses ate deeply into the revenue of the Metropolitan Extensions, and of fifteen stations but six remain. The intensive Ludgate–Victoria services perished during the first world war and even since electrification there have been successive reductions in service intervals. Though use at certain stations is greatly increased, these services do not tap the full potentialities of the Middle Zone as do those from Charing Cross and Victoria.

In 1902, 19·2 million passengers used Holborn, Ludgate and St Paul's. Use declined with the loss of Inner Zone traffic until electrification. The growth of L.C.C. estates at Bellingham and St Paul's Cray and of private building at St Mary Cray and

Swanley increased numbers until in 1960 they were back to the 1902 level.

On an average day in 1960, 37,000 passengers arrived at Holborn, Blackfriars and Elephant, but 87.7 per cent came between 7.0 and 10.0 a.m. Total arrivals were 5,000 a day up on 1939, but 6,000 more came during the busiest hour alone.

Cut into the stone entrance arch of Blackfriars the names Baden Baden, Nice and Constantinople evoke the ghosts of a vanished age. They are ghosts more easily conjured on a winter night waiting on the vibrating wooden platform for a near empty train to Ravensbourne or Haydons Road than at Charing Cross or Victoria. Though the 'City Line' was still vital as a north–south freight link with some 90 trains a day in 1962, all regular freight and parcels services were withdrawn in 1969.

WATERLOO

Compared with previous complexities, the story of Waterloo is straightforward. The original proposal came from a company projecting a line to Richmond. The move awoke the South Western to the possibility of developing suburban traffic. Their Nine Elms terminus had been opened on 21 May 1838 on a riverside site in South Lambeth at the edge of the built-up area. Easily reached by steamer, it was however much too remote to encourage short-distance travellers.

So the South Western persuaded the Richmond Company to build their line from what is now Clapham Junction and to leave the rest to them. Parliamentary powers were obtained on 31 July 1845 for the two-mile extension to the south end of Waterloo Bridge. In their new-found enthusiasm the LSWR directors pressed for further extensions. A scheme was presented to the 1846 London Traffic Commission for a joint station in Union Street, Southwark, with the projected London, Chatham & North Kent. This was sanctioned but foundered with the rejection of the other company's Bill. A proposal to share in the SER's 1845 Hungerford Market terminus also died with that scheme's collapse.

The Richmond Company opened its six-mile line on 27 July

1846 and sold out to the LSWR a year later. In 1847 the Windsor, Staines & South-western (Richmond to Windsor) was incorporated to extend the line from Richmond, the first of piecemeal extensions in the Thames valley which ensured that the 'Windsor Line' fed an increasing volume of traffic into Waterloo. From the latter to the site of Clapham Junction four tracks were provided, two for the Main and two for the Windsor Line, so from the first the two streams of traffic have been segregated.

These four lines fed a six-road terminus with four platforms, the buildings being designed by Sir Francis Tite, who had built Nine Elms and Southampton Terminus. Waterloo was opened on 11 July 1848 and Nine Elms given over to goods traffic until closure in 1968 (traffic diverted to South Lambeth). The approach lines were on a viaduct which curved between the grounds of Lambeth Palace and Vauxhall Gardens through what even then was a seedy neighbourhood.

Over the remainder of the century Waterloo grew into a hideous labyrinth of wooden sheds covering odd groups of platforms with a locomotive depot in their midst. A foot or two below its general level the concourse was crossed by the mercifully little-used line to the SER. The station was pilloried in *Three Men in a Boat* and was properly swept into oblivion with the old century.

In 1866 an extension was built on to the north side. With its own booking office and approach road, it dealt with Windsor Line traffic. At that time 48 up Main and 54 up Windsor trains were arriving daily. Many of them were fly-shunted into their platform.

When the Charing Cross Railway was opened in 1864 the siding between platforms 2 and 3 was extended across the concourse to join it. Never of great value, it disappeared with the rebuilding, though traces of a platform can be seen at the bottom of the footway up to the South Eastern station.

In 1879 two more platforms came into full use. Officially the 'South Station', railwaymen knew them as 'Cyprus', it being the year after the island was acquired. In September 1885 another extension, in partial use the previous year, was completed, the existing Windsor Line platforms, numbers 16–21.

Kitchener then being active, it was dubbed 'Khartoum'. Simultaneously two extra lines were provided, the six-road approach being considered sufficient 'for all time'. Some 700 trains a day were now being dealt with.

Then, on 9 August 1899, powers were obtained for what was virtually a new station. The first platforms, on the south side, were ready by 1909 and by 1914 the present numbers 1–11 were in use. Meanwhile, in 1902, 31 million passengers passed amid the turmoil of rebuilding. The new station was formally inaugurated by Queen Mary on 21 March 1922. By that time the station was dealing with 707 electric and 326 steam trains on an average day.

In connection with rebuilding the viaduct was again widened to take five Main and three Windsor tracks as far as Vauxhall and four Main and four Windsor on to Clapham Junction, save for there being a single down Windsor road through Queen's Road (Battersea) station.

Waterloo, pride of the Southern and its administrative head-quarters, is just old enough to be receiving adverse comments from architectural critics now extolling St Pancras. But what-ever its aesthetic shortcomings, as a station it is superb, and handsome is as handsome does. Even its spacious concourse could be none too large for the holiday crowds, but normally there is free and convenient access to all platforms. Because the station is built on transverse arches the parcels office is below and the parcels and mail reach the platforms by lift from a long tunnel. A parallel tunnel allows peak-hour crowds to reach the centre part of the platforms direct from the City Tube and the Underground. Significantly, the new Waterloo had no hotel; by 1900 it was in the wrong part of London.

Platforms 1–6 deal with main-line suburban trains. Formerly, departures were from 7–11 and arrivals at 12–15, but with the passing of steam the distinction became blurred. Between 11 and 12 is a broad taxi-road with parcels bays at the far end. The Windsor Line platforms, 16–21, are separated by an office block known as 'The Village'. Outside the north wall are carriage sidings on the site of a proposed extension rendered unnecessary by reduced platform occupation consequent on electrification. Here also is the hoist used to bring up Waterloo

& City stock for overhaul and down which an M7 0-4-4 tank once plunged.

Traffic at Waterloo is steadily expanding. In 1961 the annual census figures were 2,000 up for arrivals alone on those of the previous year and 11,000 up on 1956. 640 trains brought in 100,514 passengers; 71,687 came during the 7.0–10.0 a.m. peak, representing a concentration into this period of 71·6 per cent. But this is low for a Southern terminus and reflects the amount of long-distance traffic. The 1961 arrivals were 20 per cent up on 1939, but the whole of the increase of 19,500 is accounted for by arrivals in the busiest hour alone. Once again use in slack hours is actually down on that before the war.

In spite of much long-distance traffic the atmosphere of Paddington and King's Cross is lacking, perhaps because Waterloo is parvenu, brash and wholly twentieth century. Suburban traffic is of course much heavier, and makes it a very close second to London Bridge as the busiest London station. But the more spacious inner and middle suburbs of south-west London are served, and there are never the jostling peak-hour mobs of Charing Cross or Liverpool Street, though this may be more a reflection of Waterloo's large concourse than of more gracious living by its commuters.

As a gateway to the Isle of Wight, Bournemouth and the West Country, Waterloo had very large holiday traffic. On a summer Saturday in 1960, 41 crowded trains left for those places between 8.0 a.m. and noon with about 20,000 passengers. The highest number of holiday-makers leaving in one day in recent years is 45,386 by 119 trains. Almost daily mountains of baggage in the taxi-road proclaim the arrival or departure of an ocean liner special, of which there may be 10 in a day. Always there are the uniforms of all three armed forces and six times a year there is the schools traffic. It is difficult to sum up this terminus's character briefly.

After 6 September 1964 its traditional role as a terminus for the West Country was much reduced. On that day all trains ceased to run beyond Exeter St David's, except for the night newspaper train that continued for some time. Though the frequency of the basic service to Exeter at the time of writing has not been reduced, few extra trains are now run.

Waterloo is sufficiently convenient for the West End, especially since it was connected by both the Bakerloo and Northern
Tubes. But it is remote from the City, which goal the LSWR
made two serious attempts to reach. First it subscribed to the
LCDR's 'City Line' and thus gained running powers. Herne
Hill was reached from Wimbledon (p. 60) and, started in
1869, the service still operates.

But much more successful was the floating of the Waterloo
and City Electric Railway to build a 2-mile Tube from Waterloo
to a station near the Bank of England. This was opened on
8 August 1898 and absorbed by the LSWR in 1907. It was
worked as an extension of the South Western suburban system,
through tickets being available. It is the only one of London's
tubes to be owned and worked by British Railways.

Peak-hour traffic is very heavy and the platforms at the Bank
are scarcely cleared in the morning before the arrival of the
next train, though the 'Travolators' installed in 1960 have
done much to increase the capacity of the long slope up to the
surface. In 1960 its users averaged 41,200; 84·7 per cent (34,900)
travelled in the two peak periods and 58·3 per cent in the busiest
morning and evening hour. At other times traffic is very light
and one-car trains suffice.

CHAPTER III

The Southern Suburbs

On the right a delightful cluster of villages appears—Camberwell, Peckham, Dulwich, Norwood.

Illustrated London News, December 1844.

THE SOUTH EASTERN RAILWAY

THE service on the London & Greenwich, leased by the SER in 1845, was suburban and intensive, every 15 minutes for many years. The South Eastern thus had suburban interests almost from its beginning. These were reinforced by the building of its NORTH KENT line, on which grew up a large local traffic between London and the Thames-side towns.

The Admiralty refused to countenance an extension of the Greenwich line on the grounds that the instruments in the Royal Observatory would be upset. So when a line to Gravesend was authorized in 1845 the junction was at North Kent East, and thence through Lewisham, Woolwich and Dartford, 22·5 miles in all. Beazley, architect of London Bridge, designed the stations, and examples of his work survive at Erith, Dartford and Gravesend.

The North Kent, abounding in sharp curves and short but steep grades, was opened by the SER on 30 July 1849. New Cross was on the outer fringe of London, but Woolwich, Dartford and Gravesend were among the largest and most important towns in Kent, hitherto served by steamers. By 1868 there were 46 down weekday trains to Greenwich and 34 on the North Kent. Only 15 of these went beyond Plumstead, described in 1876 as 'a new district of workers' houses and small villas'. By

1906, 49 down trains ran via Greenwich and 40 via Lewisham, 35 continuing beyond Plumstead.

After 1870 Thames-side began to be industrialized. Woolwich, population 25,785 in 1841, had grown to 146,397 by 1961 and Dartford from 5,619 to 45,643. In 1841 Erith's population of 2,082 included 221 harvest labourers; during the present century, with the establishment of large engineering works, it grew to 45,043 in 1961.

The south bank of the lower Thames is largely concerned with engineering, especially electrical. But there is a wide variety of other industries – paint, plaster, glass, chemicals, tanning and milling, to name but a few. Below Dartford extend paper-mills, cement plants and the Grain oil refineries. Erith is important for coal and petrol imports brought coastwise, and two or three trains a day were run to Lower Sydenham gas-works. Freight and passenger traffic are equally important and 28 goods trains a day were run in 1961. Thamesmead housing project on Plumstead marshes, taking shape in 1970, is expected to double peak traffic on the line.

In 1855 the MID-KENT Railway was authorized, and opened on 1 January 1857 as a 4·75-mile line from Lewisham to the Farnborough Extension at Beckenham. In 1862 a 3·5-mile extension was sanctioned from New Beckenham to Croydon (Addiscombe Road) – Addiscombe after 1925 – on the very outskirts of the town. This was opened on 1 April 1864, the year the SER absorbed the Mid-Kent, having always worked it. Later branches were from Elmers End to Hayes and Woodside to Selsdon. The Ladywell Loop which by-passes Lewisham was opened about 1865.

Trains from London were divided at New Beckenham, one portion rounding the curve into Beckenham Junction, the other being for Addiscombe. There were shuttle services on the Hayes and Selsdon Road lines. For some time the district remained rural, but between 1880 and 1910 rows of terrace houses grew up round the stations, except for New Beckenham, which served an area of large houses. Continuous building, however, was not completed until the 1930's.

Consequently traffic did not develop until after 1900 and the present densities were not attained until after electrification.

In 1868, 19 down trains passed Ladywell on weekdays. The June 1904 timetable shows 27 trains splitting at New Beckenham, 3 more for Beckenham Junction only and 1 for Addiscombe Road. There were 10 connections for Selsdon Road and 19 for Hayes.

The MAIN LINE to Tonbridge was opened to all traffic on 1 May 1868 from a junction on the North Kent where St Johns

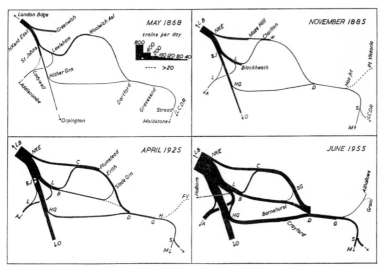

Fig. 7. Suburban services in North Kent: The thickness of the lines represents the number of suburban trains on an ordinary weekday.

now stands (Vol. II, p. 43), though there had been a service to Chislehurst since 1 July 1865. In the early years there was no suburban service. Later some trains ran to Bromley, but otherwise the stations were served by slow trains for Tonbridge and beyond. In the early 1900's a speculative builder laid out Hither Green with small villas, offering free season tickets from the new station. But until 1920 there was scarcely any building beyond, except of large houses around Chislehurst and Elmstead Woods; by 1939, however, the built-up area had spread beyond Orpington. In 1868 Chislehurst was the only station between New Cross and Orpington, where there are now six.

On 30 June 1862 the SER obtained powers for a 10-mile line from a junction with the proposed main line at Hither Green to the North Kent at Dartford Junction. The DARTFORD LOOP was opened on 1 September 1866, cutting the distance to Dartford by three miles and allowing higher speeds. Fast trains with no Woolwich stop were therefore diverted from the North Kent. Through freight traffic increased after Hither Green Yards were laid out in 1899 and the spur thither from Lee Junction laid in. In 1961 21 regular and 5 conditional goods train used the Loop daily.

In spite of public opinion the SER refused to promote any line between the North Kent and the Loop. This task was left to local enterprise in the shape of the BEXLEY HEATH [sic] Company, incorporated on 20 August 1883. The route was eventually from Blackheath on the North Kent to a triangular junction with that line east of Slade Green.

The grudging co-operation of the SER was obtained, but money was short and progress slow, opening being delayed until 1 May 1895. There was no collation, though a temperance band played. England had come far since the roaring forties. The SER, learning of building developments at Bexleyheath, bought the bankrupt company at a large discount.

Both the Loop and the Bexleyheath lines enjoyed a remarkably good service, and consequently by 1904 clusters of prosperous villas had sprung up round the stations, and the new settlements of Bexleyheath, Eltham Park, New Eltham and Sidcup had emerged. But between stations was extensive farming land. There were 27 down weekday trains on the Loop and 32 on the Bexleyheath.

It remains to mention the other SER branches. The 2-mile gap between GREENWICH and CHARLTON was not finally closed until 1878. In 1865 a Bill was deposited, but the Act authorized only the 1·25 miles from Charlton Junction to Maze Hill. There was no incentive to complete this appendix, not opened until 1 January 1873. The remaining 0·75 mile was finally built by 1 February 1878 and from 4 March main-line trains were diverted through Greenwich and the local service extended thence to Plumstead.

From Charlton Junction a mile-long branch runs to the

Thames at ANGERSTEIN WHARF, the SER's 'water outlet'. It was built by a local industrialist, John Angerstein, and opened in August 1852. Line and wharf were leased to the SER, who bought them in 1898. Several factories, a large gasworks and a railway sleeper and engineering depot are served. The line was electrified for goods locomotives in 1960. There are numerous other industrial branches from the North Kent, and mention must be made of the Woolwich Arsenal system which was linked with the Southern at Plumstead.

The WEST WICKHAM & HAYES Company was incorporated in 1880 to build a 3·5-mile branch from the Mid-Kent at Elmers End to Hayes and was purchased by the SER the next year. Opened on 29 May 1882, it was the only successful scheme of a number put forward to develop the thinly peopled country between the Mid-Kent and the Chatham lines. In view of the thousands of houses since built and the 1,414 season-ticket holders at West Wickham alone in 1957, it seems strange that the original justification for the branch was to make more accessible country much favoured by Londoners for day outings.

The WOODSIDE & SOUTH CROYDON, a 2·5-mile link between the Mid-Kent at Woodside and the Oxted line at Selsdon Road (Selsdon from 1935), was opened on 10 August 1885 as part of the Croydon & Oxted joint scheme (Vol. II, p. 94).

THE BROMLEY DIRECT COMPANY promoted a 1·5-mile branch from the Tonbridge line at Grove Park. The line was opened on 1 January 1878, and absorbed by the SER on 21 July 1879. The old market town was described in an 1876 Guide as being 'easy of access and consequently much in favour with City merchants'. The LCDR then had the monopoly and the SER were interested in the potential suburban traffic. In 1958, 404,000 ordinary tickets and 35,000 seasons were issued at Bromley North.

THE LONDON, CHATHAM & DOVER RAILWAY

The LCDR at first concentrated on reaching Victoria and Ludgate Hill and on establishing an intensive service between, for this was then the only section within the built-up area. In 1885 there were over 80 trains each way between the termini.

By its New Lines Act of 1864 the Chatham became involved in the Brighton's South London scheme. Two more tracks were built alongside its existing Victoria line between Wandsworth Road and Barrington Road Junction (Brixton). The Brighton would continue these four lines eastward to a point just beyond

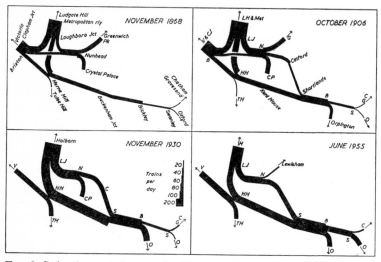

FIG. 8. Suburban services on the Chatham line. Number of passenger trains on an ordinary weekday calling at one or more suburban stations. Note the decay of services in the inner suburbs and the rise of those in the outer.

Peckham Rye. On completion the Chatham took over exclusive use of the northern pair and the Brighton that of the southern. Today the station architecture betrays the original builder, the baroque palace of Denmark Hill of Brighton origin contrasting with the mean Chatham erection at Clapham.

Two curves were built from the northern pair of lines to Loughborough Junction on the 'City Line'. The west-facing one allowed the Ludgate–Victoria service to be diverted from Herne Hill and increased. The eastern one allowed access to the City from stations to the east.

The CRYSTAL PALACE & SOUTH LONDON JUNCTION Company was authorized on 17 July 1862 to build a line from Peckham Rye to a vast covered terminus at Crystal Palace. It was opened on 1 August 1865 together with the line on to Brixton. As was so often the case, the Chatham were too late, for the Crystal Palace excursion traffic was already falling. The district was beginning to develop, however, and intermediate stations were later built. But the houses were villas of the *nouveaux riches* in very large grounds and potential traffic was limited. Services were suspended during both wars, and on 20 September 1954 the branch beyond Nunhead achieved the melancholy distinction of being the only part of the 'Southern Electric' system to be abandoned completely so far in Greater London.

On 28 July 1863 the GREENWICH PARK branch was authorized from the Crystal Palace line where Nunhead was opened on 1 September 1871. It was opened to Blackheath Hill on 18 September 1871, and to Greenwich Park on 1 October 1888. But the route was circuitous and Greenwich had lost its former importance. However, in the time when for the majority a day by the sea was at best an annual event, 'outings' to Greenwich Park were popular and brought some traffic. In 1904 there were 57 down trains, many of them shuttle services from Nunhead. The branch succumbed, along with most of the Chatham's inner suburban services, to tramway competition, being closed on 1 January 1917.

On 12 August 1889 a nominally independent Shortlands & Nunhead Company was incorporated to build a 5-mile line between those places. The CATFORD LOOP was opened on 1 July 1892 and has always been regarded as a relief to the main line, which could not be widened because of Penge Tunnel. But in addition there was an intensive service to Catford, the limit of the built-up area in 1910, and a much less frequent one on to Bickley. The Ravensbourne valley above Catford remained almost completely clear of building and Beckenham Hill was reputedly the quietest suburban station of all until the edge of the Bellingham L.C.C. estate reached it.

It is not generally realized that, save for the inner areas, where road competition is keenest, the ex-LCDR lines even today traverse districts with very low housing densities for the most part. This, added to the comparative inconvenience of Holborn and Victoria, largely explains the limited traffic on this section.

THE SOUTH EASTERN & CHATHAM RAILWAY COMPANIES MANAGING COMMITTEE

Almost all the housing development described took place after 1870 and most of it after 1900. After the 1899 fusion the Managing Committee were thus left to deal with rapidly expanding traffic from the fringes of the Inner Suburban Zone. Accordingly a suburban service was provided on the SER's main line as far as Orpington (which had been quadrupled by 1904). This also became the terminus of Chatham line trains, extended from Bickley and increased in number. Locomotive and carriage workings were altered so that they could be based on suburban depots, and large locomotive sheds and carriage sidings were built at Slades Green (the British Transport Commission dropped the s), Orpington and Purley. But the financial aftermath of the 'feud' (see Vol. II, chap. III) and the first world war prevented them from tackling the problem more seriously. Traffic in 1921 was up by 26 per cent on that of 1914 and shorter hours had intensified the peak. By 1923 the situation had got almost completely out of hand and the new Southern Company were left with the task of bringing some order out of chaos.

THE LONDON, BRIGHTON & SOUTH COAST RAILWAY

In describing the Brighton's approach to London many of its lines have been mentioned. The last major link was the 10·5-mile line from Peckham Rye to SUTTON opened on 1 October 1868. Just north of Tulse Hill the line crossed over the LCDR main line, that company providing a spur between Herne Hill and Tulse Hill (1 January 1869). South of Tulse Hill the West End line crossed overhead and connecting spurs were built to allow through running from Tulse Hill to Crystal Palace (1 November 1870) and to Clapham Junction (1 August 1871). South of that the Brighton main line was crossed and spurs laid in to allow through running from Victoria to Sutton (1 October 1868) and from Peckham to Selhurst (1 January 1886). Finally connections were made by severe curves with the West Croydon and Wimbledon line at Mitcham Junction and with the West Croydon and Epsom line at Sutton.

Study of a map reveals that within the angle of the main lines from London Bridge and Victoria converging on East Croydon there are no dead-end branches. Instead there is a maze of intersecting lines and connecting spurs which allow an almost limitless combination of routes. First may be noted three loops connecting London Bridge and Victoria; the South London line via Denmark Hill; a middle loop via Crystal Palace; and an outer loop via a Norwood–Selhurst spur opened on 1 December 1862. In addition the Peckham–Sutton line intersects the middle and outer loops and is connected to them. So there is yet a fourth route from London Bridge to Victoria via Tulse Hill and Streatham Hill. 'Roundabout' services are also possible from London Bridge and back again either via Crystal Palace or via Selhurst. Finally there are numerous routes to destinations beyond the outer loop, via East and West Croydon and Sutton.

The fullest use of all these routes has always been made, especially in peak hours. A few examples from 1904 must suffice. On weekdays there were 95 departures from London Bridge to Victoria, 59 over the South London line, 23 via Crystal Palace, 2 via Tulse Hill and Streatham Hill, and 11 via Selhurst.

TABLE 4

LBSCR PEAK-HOUR DEPARTURES FROM LONDON BRIDGE –
JUNE 1904

5.30	London Bridge via Norwood, Selhurst and Tulse Hill
5.31	Victoria via South London Line
5.36	Victoria via Sydenham and Crystal Palace
5.43	Stoat's Nest (Coulsdon North) via Norwood
5.46	Sutton via Norwood
5.46	Dorking via Tulse Hill and Mitcham Junction
5.50	West Croydon via Norwood
5.50	Battersea Park via South London Line
5.53	Victoria via Sydenham and Crystal Palace
6.0	Brighton *[Continued overleaf*

6.0	Horsham via Tulse Hill and Mitcham Junction
6.2	Victoria via Tulse Hill and Streatham Hill
6.5	Brighton
6.7	Crystal Palace via Sydenham
6.10	Sutton via Norwood
6.13	Streatham Common via Norwood and Selhurst
6.15	Wimbledon via Tulse Hill and Tooting
6.16	Victoria via Norwood and Selhurst
6.18	Battersea Park via South London Line
6.25	Victoria via Sydenham and Crystal Palace
6.30	Victoria via Tulse Hill and Streatham Hill
6.30	Stoat's Nest via Norwood
22	Departures (43 in 1962)

It is difficult to describe South London concisely owing to the apparently random distribution of neighbourhoods as exclusive as Dulwich, as slum-like as parts of Brixton or of small terrace houses as in Balham and Thornton Heath. But the application of two principles provides some explanation. The higher ground, especially if gravel-capped, was the most sought after. The largest and most expensive houses were on the heights of Forest Hill, Crystal Palace and Tulse Hill. Rows of small houses filled the surrounding low ground in Balham, Tooting and Norbury. Secondly, the wealthier always tended to move outward as the poorer moved in, forced from the inmost suburbs by overcrowding and clearances. Charles Booth said in 1902: 'Southwark is moving to Walworth, Walworth to North Brixton and Stockwell, while the servant keepers of outer South London go to Croydon.'

Between 1841 and 1871 the area within the arc of the South London line had become completely built over and growing suburbs reached out to Balham, Norwood and Streatham, the last described in 1871 as 'a suburb of mansions, villas and genteel residences'. By 1914 the suburbs along and within the South London line had become exclusively working class, and suburban building had filled up the triangle within the London Bridge–Selhurst–Victoria loop.

A good service to both City and West End was provided from all the stations within the built-up area. Sets of austere four-wheelers were used which lasted until electrification, although seven-coach bogie sets were coming in after 1900. Tram, bus and tube competition has been very severe, but early electrification, frequent trains and competitive fares retained much of the traffic and prevented closures. Nowadays, however, at peak hours the 'roundabouts' are much less crowded than outer suburban trains.

Most of the London Bridge–East Croydon–Purley traffic was carried in South Eastern trains, though the Brighton started a suburban service to Coulsdon North on 5 November 1899 and built there a large station and depot. They also ran by various routes to Sutton and beyond, but the outer suburban services did not really develop until after 1923.

There remain some other lines to mention. The SOUTH LONDON was opened between London Bridge and Loughborough Park (now East Brixton) on 13 August 1866 and the remainder on 1 May 1867. At first traffic disappointed, but with the introduction of the famous 'Terrier' 0-6-0 tanks, hauling close-coupled four-wheelers at 15-minute intervals, traffic soon improved to such an extent that eleven or twelve coaches were needed.

The DEPTFORD WHARF branch was opened from New Cross Gate on 2 July 1849 and has been used only for goods traffic ever since. Deptford and Battersea Wharves were the Brighton's 'water outlet' and at the former the Brighton built up a considerable coal traffic, distributing imports as far as Brighton. Coal was landed for railing to power-stations and gas-works at Croydon until the branch was closed on 1 January 1964.

The country west of Croydon was very thinly peopled in the mid nineteenth century, but there was a demand for a line to Wimbledon along part of the defunct Surrey Iron Railway's route. The WIMBLEDON & CROYDON Company was incorporated in 1853, promoted by local enterprise personified in G. P. Bidder, a well-known railway contractor. The line was opened on 22 October 1855 and worked by Bidder until leased to the Brighton the next year.

It still wears a curiously rural air. Though electrified, it is largely single track, and at Waddon Marsh and Beddington Lane the signalman issues tickets from his box. Yet there have been extensive industrial developments at Waddon and growth of housing everywhere, which bring a heavy freight, now including block oil trains, and steady passenger traffic.

The line from West Croydon to EPSOM was opened on 10 May 1847, and the EPSOM DOWNS branch from Sutton on 22 May 1865. The CATERHAM RAILWAY from Purley, which figured so largely in the quarrels between the Brighton and South Eastern, was opened on 5 August 1856, and the CHIPSTEAD VALLEY line from Purley to Tattenham Corner in stages between 2 November 1897 and 4 June 1901. Both these last were SER lines in the heart of Brighton territory. The history of all four has been dealt with in Volume II.

These lines were pushed out into the rather poor farming country of the North Downs with only a few small villages. Some commuters moved out over the years, but building did not really get under way until the 1920's and is still in progress. Services were therefore sparse until after electrification and for long a rail motor dealt with normal traffic on the Epsom Downs branch.

THE LONDON & SOUTH WESTERN RAILWAY

The suburban services of the South Western have always fallen into two sections, those down the Main and those down the Windsor Line. From the former the two most important branches are probably the New Guildford, dealt with later, and that to Epsom, which in the early days the LSWR were most anxious to reach, for once the Brighton got there Surbiton would no longer be the railhead for the racing. They were thwarted several times, until the WIMBLEDON & DORKING Company was incorporated on 27 July 1857 with powers to build a 5·75-mile branch from Epsom Junction (the site of Raynes Park station). Opened on 4 April 1859, it was worked by the LSWR, which absorbed it in 1862. There was no place of any importance between Wimbledon and the market town and former spa of Epsom and traffic was small save on race days.

Turning to the Windsor Line, it will be recalled that Richmond was reached on 27 July 1846 and Datchet on 22 August 1848 (*see* Vol. II, p. 132). The 1847 Act of incorporation empowered the Windsor, Staines & South-western (Richmond to

Windsor) also to build a 7·25-mile line from Barnes to a triangular junction with the Windsor Line beyond Whitton. The HOUNSLOW LOOP, called after what was then the only important place on the line other than Brentford, was opened to Isleworth on 22 August 1849 and to Feltham Junction on 1 February 1850, the curve to Whitton Junction being opened for passengers on 1 January 1883. Passenger traffic has always been purely local, and since 1900 has suffered severely from trams, buses and extensions of the District. But it is an essential link for through freight traffic (p. 128), formerly all marshalled at Feltham Yard (1919); after 1965 block trains predominated. Feltham would be the junction for a branch to London Airport.

Farther up the river, Kingston-on-Thames, where Saxon kings were crowned, was the second largest Surrey town in 1841, with 8,147 inhabitants. Opposition, particularly by coaching interests, had kept early main lines away and the consequences were becoming serious. Not only was coaching dead, the maltings were suffering from grain being railed direct to London instead of reaching Kingston by water, and retail trade was hit. Instead, Kingston-on-Railway (Surbiton) was growing fast and Richmond was benefiting from its Windsor Line station.

There was local satisfaction when in 1859 a branch from Twickenham on the Windsor Line was authorized. It was opened on 1 July 1863, but did little to assuage Kingston's ambitions, for the route to London was circuitous and slow. In 1865 powers were obtained for an extension to Wimbledon via Malden (now New Malden), opened on 1 January 1869. To cross the High Street involved the building of a new high-level through station, completely rebuilt in 1934-5. From Twickenham to Malden has always been the KINGSTON LOOP.

Measom's *Guide* of 1856 mentions housing developments in the Battersea area, but the site of Clapham Junction was well on the outskirts of London and open country lay between it and the town of Wandsworth and village of Wimbledon. Far into the country were the market towns of Hounslow, Richmond, Teddington and Kingston, the objectives of the railway developments just outlined. They prospered amidst fertile market gardens, and Measom comments on the 'fine market gardens' of Isleworth, justly famed for raspberries and strawberries.

But London was now in easy reach and this salubrious region was sought after by business men following in the footsteps of fashionable and leisured eighteenth-century Londoners. The towns grew apace. 'Barnes has nearly doubled in size in the last ten or twelve years', says a Guide of 1876. By 1914 con-tinuous building had spread along the Windsor and Main Lines as far as Richmond and Wimbledon respectively.

The rapidly developing Surrey countryside, still a South Western monopoly, attracted the District's envious eyes. With its backing the Kingston & London Company obtained powers in 1881 for a line from the Putney Bridge terminus of the District to Kingston and thence to Guildford via Cobham. The LSWR, forgetful of its fighting youth, or reserving its enmity for the arch-enemy at Paddington, met these proposals with a sweet reason which paid off in the Transfer Act of 1882.

The LSWR agreed to build the line between Guildford and Surbiton (the NEW GUILDFORD line opened 2 February 1885), but linked it with their own main line at Hampton Court Junction. A line from Kingston to Putney Bridge was to be built jointly by the LSWR and the District. But ultimately this was diverted from the South Western's Kingston stronghold to Wimbledon and was built solely as a South Western concern. The 3·5-mile WIMBLEDON & PUTNEY line was opened on 3 June 1889 and on 1 July a flying junction went into service from the Windsor Line at Point Pleasant to East Putney. What was virtually a separate terminus was provided at Wimbledon and into it ran District trains from Putney Bridge and LSWR ones from Waterloo, but the latter ceased in 1941. The Southern Region still however finds it very useful as a relief line and to reach Longhedge Junction. Although their trains never call, the intermediate stations are manned and maintained by the Southern. Wimbledon station was completely rebuilt in 1929 and the ten platforms deal with about 50,000 passengers a day. The goods department handled some 93,000 wagons a year in 1961.

The pattern of the LSWR's suburban services differed from those of other southern companies. The residential areas served beyond Wandsworth and Earlsfield had the reputation of being more exclusive; certainly housing densities were generally lower. Commuters, too, tended to travel in from farther afield. Thus there never were intensive inner suburban services, nor were there any equivalents of the Crystal Palace, Bickley or Dartford services apart from the 'roundabouts' on the Kingston and Hounslow Loops and the Hampton Court trains. Otherwise suburban stations were served by stopping trains bound for such distant terminals as Windsor, Reading, Guildford and Dorking.

These ran through heaths, past golf courses, villas in large grounds, and pleasant Thames backwaters. Except perhaps at Beckenham, Chislehurst, Sevenoaks and Reigate there was nothing like it on other lines. There was therefore an attention to passenger comfort that must have driven South Eastern or Great Eastern users apoplectic with envy.

The 1904 timetables show 31 down trains over the Hounslow Loop and as many on the Kingston Loop via Twickenham. There were 22 down trains to Wimbledon via East Putney, 29 to Hampton Court and 22 to Epsom.

A few other branches remain for mention. That to HAMP-TON COURT was the earliest: 1·75 miles long, it was opened from Hampton Court Junction, west of Surbiton, on 1 February 1849. W. J. Chaplin, the LSWR's Chairman, was unenthusiastic, but considered it a public necessity. In true Victorian tradition, virtue was rewarded and the South Western always did handsomely from visitors and residents. In 1865, 13 of the 47 Main Line departures from Waterloo were for Hampton Court. In 1955, 300,000 tickets were collected and 10,000 seasons issued.

From the Kingston Loop a branch was promoted by the THAMES VALLEY Company incorporated in 1862. Opened on 1 November 1864, it ran from Strawberry Hill through the market gardens for 6·5 miles to Shepperton. Even today the district beyond Hampton is not fully built up and race meetings at Kempton Park provide the heaviest traffic. In later years a triangular junction was completed to allow through running from Kingston.

The TOOTING, MERTON & WIMBLEDON was authorized in 1864 to build a connecting line from Streatham Junction on the Peckham–Sutton line. The next year it passed to the LSWR and LBSCR jointly and was opened on 1 October

1868. At Tooting the line forked, one branch reaching Wimbledon via Haydons Road, the other via Merton Park on the Wimbledon and Croydon, the last 0·75 mile of which became joint property as well. On 1 January 1869 the LSWR started its Wimbledon and Ludgate Hill service and there were also LBSCR trains. The southern loop was closed to passengers between Tooting and Merton Park on 3 March 1929, but it remained open for goods until 5 August 1968.

'SOUTHERN ELECTRIC': BEGINNINGS*

By 1900 complete separation of work and residence had become general for the middle class. But though this was becoming common for many workmen, the 1905 Royal Commission were convinced that lower fares were necessary to encourage migration of the working class and so reduce overcrowding. In the end this did not come about until the 1930–50 period and mainly because fares rose more slowly than the real value of wages. But even so the journey to work was steadily lengthening and journeys per head by local railway, which numbered 10 a year in 1867, had increased to 30 in 1895 and 42 in 1902.

On the other hand the tram had come as a rival mass transporter, at least for short journeys. Journeys by this means had increased from 12 per head a year in 1880 to 52 in 1902. In the 1890's the London County Council had begun to acquire tramways, and in 1901 became an operator. As social policy very low fares were charged to reduce housing congestion by migration. Electrification began in 1901 and was accompanied by route extensions far into the suburbs. By 1911 journeys per head had leapt to 113.

But during the same decade the rail figure had remained stationary. On some lines there had been a serious decline in patronage and an even more alarming contraction in the revenue. Falling receipts on a line such as the South London or that of the North London Railway could not be offset by reducing service frequency. Facilities became even less attractive and yet more custom was lost. The alternative to closure was electrification. Operating costs would be reduced and

* See Volume II, Chapter 9.

would allow an increased service and competitive fares. Conversely, on lines with increasing traffic the greater acceleration from the frequent stops would allow increased track occupation and save the expense of widening. These considerations underlie all suburban electrification projects.

C. E. Lee has pointed out, however, that the electrification policy was originally adopted by the LBSCR to counter the projects for an electric railway to Brighton. Powers to electrify were obtained in 1903, and next year it was decided to convert a test section between Peckham Rye and Battersea Park on the South London. But it was not until 1906 that tramways competitive with the South London were electrified.

Whatever the ultimate cause, electrification was timely. The LBSCR told the 1905 Royal Commission they had lost $1\frac{1}{4}$ million passengers in the previous six months to and from 'the Croydon direction', and between 1903 and 1908 passenger journeys over the South London fell from 8 to $3\frac{1}{2}$ million. At Peckham Rye alone bookings fell from 1,213,281 in 1902 to 526,273 in the year ending 30 November 1909. Orders were given to extend the electrification to London Bridge and Victoria, and the new service began on 1 December 1909 with doubled frequency and schedules cut from 36 to 24 minutes. By 1910 the South London had again reached 8 million and in 1922, 12 million.

Since then tube extensions offering direct services to West End and City and improved bus services have cut deeply into the regained traffic, and today four-car trains suffice at peak hours. In a 1960 survey it was found that between 7.0 and 9.0 a.m. only 71 passengers joined trains at East Brixton for Victoria and 46 for London Bridge. From Queen's Road (Peckham) the figures were 54 and 606 respectively.

So far 8·6 route miles had been equipped with overhead lines carrying alternating current at 6,600 volts, and extensions were put in hand immediately. On 12 May 1911 a service was inaugurated between Victoria and Crystal Palace, involving the conversion of 7·5 route miles of the old West End line from Battersea Park. In March 1912, to economize coal during a miners' strike, a service from London Bridge was started after the section between Peckham Rye and the Tulse Hill spurs had been electrified; the full service began on 1 June. On the same day trains were extended from the Palace to Norwood Junction and, empty, on to Selhurst car sheds. All this meant the conversion of a further 5·5 route miles.

Plans were now prepared for extensions to Cheam and Coulsdon North, the latter being the first step to Brighton. Standards were erected south of Balham along the main line, but war halted work until 1922.

By 1901 electric trams from Hammersmith had reached Hounslow, and Kingston soon after. Competition from these and from the rejuvenated District (p. 93) rapidly eroded the LSWR's suburban traffic. In 1908 the chairman complained that 1¼ million passengers had been lost to trams and buses in six months.

In 1913 the LSWR announced plans for electrification of lines on which traffic worth £100,000 a year had been lost. In contrast with the LBSCR it adopted the third rail system using direct current at 600 volts, but like the Brighton it used multiple unit trains instead of locomotives.

Work continued in spite of the war and a service between Waterloo and Wimbledon via East Putney was inaugurated on 25 October 1915. On 30 January 1916 the Kingston 'roundabouts' were converted, together with the Shepperton service, and on 12 March the trains over the Hounslow Loop. Electric trains ran to Hampton Court from 18 June and on 20 November down the New Guildford line to Claygate with pull-and-push connections beyond. But owing to shortage of rolling stock the Claygate service soon reverted to steam.

A total of 56·8 route miles had been converted. Timetables were arranged on a basis of regular intervals between trains, which became standard practice on 'Southern Electric'. In 1913, 25 million passengers had been carried on the services afterwards electrified. By 1918 the number had risen to 40 million and two years later to 52·6 million.

In south-east London there had been no real penetration by the Underground. But by 1908 trams were running through Woolwich to Abbey Wood and in 1911 a bus service began between Oxford Circus and Sidcup. The SE & CR services were hard hit, especially those on the Metropolitan Extensions and the North Kent. The Managing Committee had sought electrification powers in 1903 and in 1920 announced plans to reach Gillingham, Tonbridge and Redhill on a fourth-rail 1,500-volt D.C. system. But the necessary capital was not forthcoming.

'SOUTHERN ELECTRIC': FRUITION

The new Southern Railway took over in 1923 56·8 route miles of third-rail electrification from the LSWR and 24·6 of overhead from the LBSCR, to which must be added the 1·5 miles of the Waterloo and City Tube – 82·9 miles in all. The company pressed ahead, implementing its predecessors' plans and developing its own.

On the Western Section (the ex-LSWR lines) conversion of the remainder of the New Guildford line, together with those from Raynes Park to Dorking North and Leatherhead to Effingham, a total of 31·9 route miles, was completed on 12 July 1925. The area served was largely open country and still is one of discontinuous settlement. But between Raynes Park and Leatherhead is now built up and all stations have a considerable season-ticket traffic. At Dorking North 669 seasons had been sold in 1924, but by 1932 the figure had reached 2,737. Between 1927 and 1937 there was a tenfold increase in season-ticket holders at Motspur Park and Worcester Park.

On the Central Section (the ex-LBSCR lines) work was continued on the overhead extensions and on 1 April 1925 services were inaugurated over 18·25 route miles. The sections involved were from Balham Junction to Sutton via Selhurst, Selhurst to Coulsdon North, and Tulse Hill to Streatham Junction, together with necessary connecting spurs. Motor brake-vans sandwiched between two pairs of trailers were used, but this was still multiple unit, not locomotive, working.

There were no further extensions of the overhead system and on 9 August 1926 it was annnounced the Southern would standardize on the third rail. This LSWR system had already been adopted for the extensive conversions on the Eastern Section (the ex-SE & CR lines) where the Southern was desperately making up lost time.

The new services were inaugurated in three stages. The first covered 31 route miles and affected the services from Victoria and Holborn both on the main line and on the Catford Loop and those to Crystal Palace High Level. Working on the last-named began on 1 April 1925 for staff training and the full service on 12 July. At first 6 trains an hour were provided between Herne Hill and Shortlands. But over the years traffic and service frequencies have declined until in 1960 there were but two in off-peak hours. In a 1960 census 882 people joined up trains at Catford between 7.0 and 9.0 a.m., while at the adjoining Catford Bridge on the Mid-Kent the figure was 4,152. At Crofton Park and Nunhead, farther up the Catford Loop, the figures were 1,087 and 554 respectively. On the other hand traffic from the rebuilt St Mary Cray and Swanley stations has vastly increased.

The second stage was inaugurated on 28 February 1926 and covered the main line to Orpington, together with the Bromley North branch, the Mid-Kent to Addiscombe and the short spur to Beckenham Junction. The Hayes branch had been worked by an electric shuttle service since 21 September 1925 to provide crew training; 27·5 route miles were involved.

The final stage, 33·5 route miles, consisted of the four routes to Dartford, North Kent via Greenwich and via Blackheath, Bexleyheath and Loop lines. The full public service began on 19 July 1926. But a few electric trains had run during the General Strike and a full service had been operated to Charing Cross from 11 July. Cannon Street, however, had been closed for track alterations from 5 to 28 June, the commuters being left to walk from London Bridge.

Timetables were on a fixed interval basis, generally with 20-minute headways on ex-LCDR lines and with 30-minute ones on ex-SER lines. But in the mid thirties intervals were halved on the Mid-Kent, Bexleyheath and Dartford Loop services. By then new building had made these by far the busiest and peak-hour crowding was already serious.

As yet the main line from London Bridge to East Croydon was unconverted; it had not figured in Brighton plans because so much of the traffic was carried in SER trains. But now electric trains began running in steam schedules on 25 March 1928 to

Crystal Palace via Sydenham and to Caterham and Tadworth. Meanwhile work was going ahead laying third rail on the overhead routes and on extensions of these from Streatham Junction to Sutton via Mitcham Junction and on to Epsom Downs, and from Crystal Palace to Beckenham Junction. On 17 June 1928 interval electric services were inaugurated on these new routes. The Caterham and Tadworth trains were also put on an interval basis and the latter were projected on to Tattenham Corner. The A.C. trains were withdrawn gradually, the last running at 12.30 a.m. on the night of 21–22 September 1929. Eventually overcrowding on the services to East Croydon and beyond became as bad as the notorious North West Kent lines, while a very heavy commuter traffic grew up in the Sutton area.

So far the services in the Wimbledon and West Croydon area had lagged badly behind other sections and passengers were rapidly deserting them. They were therefore the next to be modernized. The old LSWR service from Wimbledon to the City was converted to electric traction on 3 March 1929. It had been suspended during the war, and was hastily reinstated in 1923 with the threat from the Tube extension to Morden, but had scarcely been flourishing. In 1928 receipts from Haydons Road station were £300. Four years after electrification, in 1933, they reached £5,000.

In 1910 a group of landowners had obtained powers for a 4·75-mile line from Wimbledon to Sutton, over which District trains would run. The powers lay dormant until 1922, when there were proposals to link the line with the Tube extension at Morden (p. 100). The Southern, sensitive to this thrust into its territory, admittedly the part with the worst services in the Inner Zone, strongly resisted the move. In the end it was agreed there should be no physical connection with the Tube and that the Southern should build and work the WIMBLEDON & SUTTON for which it obtained powers in 1924.

The line was opened to South Merton on 7 July 1929 and on to Sutton on 5 January 1930. It is worked by the electric service from Holborn projected on from Wimbledon to West Croydon. At St Helier the L.C.C. built a large estate (1960 population 30,692) and by 1939 private housing had spread over the rest of the district.

On 6 July 1930 the programme of improvements was completed when a self-contained electric service of increased frequency replaced steam pull-and-push trains on the West Croydon and Wimbledon. On the same date electric services were inaugurated to Windsor over the newly converted 12·75 miles from Whitton Junction through Staines.

In 1935 a short but very important extension came into use. The LCDR's Greenwich Park line had lain derelict since 1917, but in 1929 a connection was opened from it to Lewisham station, together with a curve thence from the Mid-Kent line to the main line. The remainder of the Greenwich branch was then torn up. The original purpose of the new line was to enable transfer freights from all parts of London to reach Hither Green, especially those coming via Ludgate Hill. Hitherto these had used the Union Street spur (p. 37) and had passed through the congested London Bridge High Level. But later the spur and the line from Lewisham to Nunhead were electrified and on 30 September 1935 a peak-hour service was started between the Bexleyheath and Loop lines and Blackfriars. Suspended during the war, it was reinstated in August 1946, most trains now running to Holborn.

It was an attempt to relieve the gross overcrowding on these lines, on which more trains could be run as far as Lewisham but not beyond, London Bridge being at saturation point. The time from Lewisham to Holborn, however, is 19 minutes as against 14 to Cannon Street, and there are no convenient underground connections at Holborn. Commuters therefore long preferred the discomforts of the quicker trains. But, particularly with the rebuilding of the City, loadings have steadily increased since about 1955.

On 30 September 1935 also the Woodside & South Croydon was reopened to local traffic and a service started between Charing Cross and Sanderstead. Because of the limited paths available over the London approaches, the Beckenham Junction trains were diverted to the new terminus. The Beckenham spur, however, is still in use, for Mid-Kent services are diverted to Beckenham Junction when Clock House station floods after heavy rain.

Finally a new line was opened from Motspur Park, on the Raynes Park–Epsom line, to Tolworth on 29 May 1938 and on to CHESSINGTON SOUTH on 28 May 1939. All of the four stations on the 3·75 miles are in the midst of entirely new communities, each with its own shopping centre. But for the war the line would have been built on to Leatherhead, but strict interpretation of the Green Belt here made it redundant.

By 1939 all the Southern's lines in Greater London had been electrified. For many years there were few changes in the basic pattern of services. Extra peak-hour trains have been put on where possible, and slack-period services have been pruned, especially after September 1958. Traffic from the Middle Zone has increased, while that from the Inner has remained remarkably constant. A continuing trend that is causing worry has been for an increasing proportion of the traffic to bunch up into the peak periods. On 10 July 1970 a completely revised time-table was inaugurated to increase peak capacity and reduce some off-peak services.

THE SOCIAL CONSEQUENCES OF ELECTRIFICATION

Electrification was the means of satisfying the social urge towards better and less congested housing which characterized the period since 1920 and which was achieved at the cost of increasing the journey to work and the proportion of total income spent on it. The Inner Zone emptied into the small semi-detached houses of the new Middle Zone. It was the amount of land required for this low density housing which resulted in the phenomenal spread of London.

In the Inner Zone there was much building of council flats and conversion of larger houses. But in all there was comparatively little rebuilding until the feverish activities of the later 1950's got under way. In the Middle Zone the L.C.C. laid out large estates at St Helier, Bellingham, Downham and Mottingham (1960 population 75,000) in connection with tramway extensions for the most part. But nearby railway stations were much used from the first, and especially after fare equalization, when the superior speed of rail became a marked advantage. But most houses were built on large estates by firms of speculative builders who invariably advertised their properties as being served by electric lines.

It would be tedious to detail the growth of all Greater London south of the Thames, so north-west Kent has been selected as typical. In 1925 the built-up area of south-east London extended no farther than Penge, Catford, Hither Green, Lee and Blackheath, though two prongs projected outwards for several miles. One of these linked Penge with Beckenham, Bromley and Bickley following the ex-LCDR main lines and consisting, as has been remarked on, of high-class housing. The other extended along Thames-side as far as Abbey Wood and was composed of small houses intermingled with factories, served more by trams than by the North Kent line. Outside the built-up area towns and villages were growing outwards from their centres, but were separated by wide stretches of farmland.

Today there is virtually no agricultural land up to the Cray Valley to the east and Farnborough, West Wickham and Selsdon to the south.

North-west Kent can be taken as the former Boroughs of Beckenham, Bromley, Bexley and Erith and the Urban Districts of Orpington, Chislehurst and Sidcup, and Crayford. Here housing densities are low, varying from 3 per acre in Orpington to 18·2 in Bexley. But the 1951 population numbered 449,230 and that of 1961, 478,555, or 28 per cent of the total for Kent. The 1931 figure was 232,801. The population had all but doubled in twenty years and more than doubled in thirty.

There has been no comparable growth of industry, and job ratios (the proportion of day-time jobs in the area to the resident working population) are low, from 29 in Bexley to 73 per 100 in Erith, so more than two persons in three of Bexley's working population are employed elsewhere, and even in industrial Erith one person in four. Many of these work in neighbouring industrial areas such as Woolwich, but about a quarter, and in the case of Beckenham 37 per cent, travel to Central London. Since rail has the virtual monopoly between the Middle Zone and Central London, the volume of traffic and extent of overcrowding is easily explained.

The former area of Chislehurst and Sidcup Urban District had a 1921 population of 16,920. In the year of electrification, 1926, the estimated number was 18,500, 9 per cent increase in

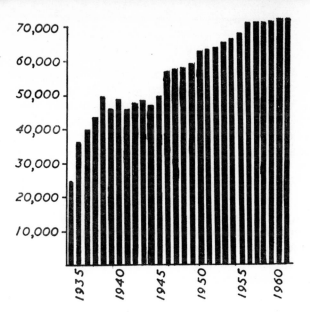

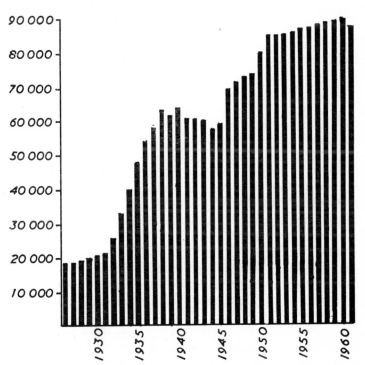

Fig. 9. Population growth in the south-eastern suburbs:
Above, Orpington. *Below*, Chislehurst and Sidcup.

five years. The 1931 census recorded 21,680, an increase of 17 per cent in the five-year period. But in the next five years the increase was one of *155 per cent*, and by 1939 the population had reached an estimated 61,670. During the war years there was a tendency to slight decline, but after 1945 growth was resumed and the 1961 population was 86,907, four times that of 1931.

There are a few factories, but otherwise there are only service industries and the 1951 job ratio was 56. Almost half the working population, 24,795 people, work outside the district. Of these many went to industrial Thames-side – 2,931 to Woolwich and 1,113 to Greenwich. But the majority, 8,955, went up daily to the Central Area, 24 per cent of the working population and 11 per cent of the total.

This phenomenal growth and social structure is typical of the Middle Zone. Until 1934 Orpington, despite its impressive six-platformed station and extensive yard, had but Civil Parish status. In that year the Urban District was created with a population of 25,000. By 1939 this had almost doubled and in 1961 was 80,277. In 1951, 25 per cent of the working population were employed in Central London.

In 1926 the population of Coulsdon and Purley numbered some 24,000. By 1936 it had more than doubled to 51,500 and by 1961 had reached 74,738. The 1951 job ratio was as low as 48, and 33 per cent of the working population travelled daily to Central London, 8,157 in all. In the same years Sutton and Cheam numbered 21,320, 52,530 and 62,940. The job ratio in 1951 was 55, and 26 per cent of the working population worked in Central London. Esher, in the south-west, had a 1926 population of 15,000 and one of 40,000 ten years later.

Thus villages mushroomed into large towns, with corresponding expansion of passenger traffic at local stations. In 1925, 1,097,000 tickets were sold at Sidcup, Welling and Bexleyheath. In ten years the increase was over fourfold and the figure stood at 4,754,000. Season issues swelled from 8,959 to 57,600. The 1933 figures for Sidcup alone were 800,000 ordinary and 22,000 seasons. In 1957 there were 2,950 season-ticket holders from Sidcup and 2,235 from Welling stations. In an average 1961 month 8,000 cheap day and 2,000 'off-peak' tickets to Central London were sold at Sidcup. In that year sales of 743,792 tickets and 55,772 seasons were recorded.

In 1924 Grove Park was in a semi-rural area and large numbers of first-class seasons were sold. In that year 71,133 passengers were booked and 1,088 seasons issued. Ten years later comparable figures were 917,585 and 12,041, a twelvefold increase. The Downham Estate (1960 population 25,464) was even then incomplete and by 1938 the harassed booking clerks were issuing 3,000 workmen's tickets daily. Since then social customs and fares structure have brought change. No longer do junior office workers crowd the 'last workmen's' train to while away the time in coffee-shops until their offices open. But the booking clerks of Grove Park now issue over 100,000 weekly seasons a year.

Again the list may be extended *ad nauseam*. But to preserve balance some examples have been taken from other sections and representative stations are shown in Table 5. In 1927 the three stations on the Epsom Downs branch sold 329,778 tickets and in 1935, 859,794. In the years 1927 to 1937 there was a threefold increase of season-ticket sales at Surbiton and New Malden. In 1937 over a million ordinary tickets and 45,607 seasons were issued at Surbiton alone (the 1913 figures were 700,000 and 19,000 respectively). In 1957 Twickenham had 2,135 season-ticket holders and Raynes Park 1,940.

TABLE 5

COMMERCIAL RESULTS OF ELECTRIFICATION -
BOOKINGS AT SELECTED SUBURBAN STATIONS

	1927		1937
		Seasons	
Malden	12,043		31,643
Surbiton	16,061		45,607
Motspur Park	2,061		12,808
Worcester Park	3,201		31,984
	1924		*1932*
Dorking North	669		2,737
	1927		*1935*
		Ordinary	
Banstead, Belmont and Epsom Downs	329,778		859,794

	1927		1934	
	Ordinary	Season	Ordinary	Season
Lordship Lane *	30,043	870	57,019	1,742
Beckenham Junction	277,338	5,345	394,804	14,680
Crofton Park	242,115	5,019	338,753	7,115
Bellingham	164,025	2,727	313,743	4,832
Ravensbourne	9,151	145	24,887	882
Orpington	272,060	2,677	403,451	13,378

	1928		1935	
Kenley	28,000	600	68,000	1,200

	1925		1935	
Woolwich Dockyard	85,272	537	99,138	517
Woolwich Arsenal	849,815	6,696	884,200	8,160

	1925		1934	
Eden Park	8,358	61	75,841	4,188
West Wickham	46,984	336	251,024	18,711
Hayes	21,856	159	177,424	5,831

	1924		1934	
Grove Park	71,133	1,088	917,585	12,041

		1938	1946	1961
Sidcup	Ordinary	733,010	772,163	743,792
	Seasons	21,523	25,509	55,772

* Now closed.

Throughout the twenties and thirties wage rates remained
almost stationary and thus with increasing length the cost of
the journey to work became an increased burden, especially
when coupled with the higher rentals of improved housing. But
nevertheless fares remained low. The 'quarterly special'
season-ticket rate from Sidcup to Charing Cross, 12 miles,
worked out at under 11d. per working day, while the workmen's
return from Charlton to Charing Cross was 7½d.

By 1949, 1 in 5 of Greater London's population rode to work
in public transport and the time for the return journey averaged
over an hour. But the rise in wages was much greater than the
rise in travel costs. In 1949 the average expenditure per worker
using public transport was 4s. 2d. a week in the County of
London south of the river and 5s. 6d. in the outer area. The
average weekly wage then was 119s. 4d. whereas in 1939 our
worker from Charlton would have spent 3s. 9d. a week getting
to Charing Cross out of a wage of 60s. or so. Increases in travel
costs since 1949 have probably done little to reverse this trend.

CHAPTER IV

Central London

Snow falls in the buffet of Aldersgate station,
Toiling and doomed from Moorgate Street puffs the train,
For us of the steam and the gaslight, the lost generation,
The new white cliffs of the City are built in vain.

JOHN BETJEMAN.

THE NORTH LONDON RAILWAY

COMPLEX in detail, railway development south of the Thames is comparatively straightforward in outline, but to the north there are two complications. First, an otherwise simple pattern of radiating trunk lines, each with but few branches, in the north-west and north, and the two compact systems of the Great Eastern and the Tilbury in the east have been overlaid and obscured by the elaborate system of London Transport spreading from a central ganglion. Secondly, there are at least two important routes which are peripheral rather than radial.

It has been said that London lacks a 'belt line'. But while there is no complete ring like the *Ceintures* of Paris, it must be remembered there is a regular freight service between every important marshalling yard from Hither Green right round to Ripple Lane (Barking). Only across the Thames in a direct line between those two is the ring incomplete. Over the southern part of the ring there is no single current or route. But several streams converge on the North & South Western Junction and West London lines and pass over them to Willesden. Thence the trunk stream passes over the Hampstead Junction line to Gospel Oak. Here it divides, one branch making for South Tottenham, Temple Mills and Ripple Lane yards, and the

73

Royal and Tilbury docks, the other making for the City and for Poplar and Millwall docks over the North London line.

From 1860 to 1910 this route, in whole or part, was one of London's principal arteries for passenger traffic. But while passengers are still carried over much of it, they create but minor cross-eddies in the great rivers of present-day passenger flow. On the other hand the constant procession of goods trains over any part of it bears witness to its continued importance as a freight route.

The second peripheral route, at one time of equal importance, but now somewhat decayed, is that from Paddington and King's Cross over the Metropolitan to Ludgate Hill and South London. We must therefore break with any attempt at chronology and deal with the North London Railway, the nucleus of the first route, and then with the Metropolitan Railway, the nucleus of the second.

The genesis of the North London lay in the desire of the London & Birmingham to reach the lower Thames. This diversion of traffic from west and north peripherally around London to waterside has been a feature of London's transport system, reflected in the New Road (Euston and City Roads) of 1756–7, the North Circular Road and Marple's unpopular 'lorry route'.

The East & West India Docks & Birmingham Junction Railway was incorporated on 26 August 1846 to build 8 miles of line from Camden to the West India Docks. The prospectus stated that exporters were complaining of delays to goods and that 'the expense of forwarding goods between Camden Town . . . and shipping on the river, now so expensive, may be reduced 50 to 70 per cent.'

The company emerged victorious from a three-cornered struggle, largely because it fitted in with the recommendations of the 1846 Commission on London Traffic set up to consider the nineteen Bills affecting Central London. The Commission decided the advantages of building railways right to the centre of London were overrated for long-distance travellers and unjustified for those from short distances. The southern termini might be sited close to the river as disturbance to property would be less. But the northern termini should be located along the New Road and a 'belt line' provided to link them.

The cumbersome title of the new company was changed to North London Railway on 1 January 1853. Nominally independent, it was popularly accorded precisely the degree of freedom now ascribed to the satellites of Eastern Europe. The LNWR subscribed 67 per cent of the capital and nominated six of the eighteen directors (the maximum number in office was usually only eleven to fourteen), while the Secretary's office at Euston was under the same roof as that of Captain Huish.

In the post-Mania slump money was tight and construction slow. Not until 26 September 1850 was the first section opened, the 5 miles from Bow Junction, on the London & Blackwall, to Islington. Some authorities say passenger traffic was not originally contemplated, but the 1846 Prospectus says 'income from Passenger Traffic will be very great both from suburban travellers and those making steamer connections from Brunswick Wharf'. In any case it was at first the only resource, and a 15-minute service was put on from Fenchurch Street. The extension to Camden Town (Camden Road 1853–70 and 1950) was opened on 7 December 1850 and on to Hampstead Road (Chalk Farm 1862, Primrose Hill 1950) on 9 June 1851. A junction with the LNWR had been laid in on 15 February 1851, but was not used for regular traffic.

Though the line was peripheral traffic was soon attracted. In October 1850, 97,531 passengers had been carried, while in 1853 the total reached 4·37 million. On 15 November 1851 the *Illustrated London News* described a journey over 'The Camden-Town Railway'. A picture of a different world, it makes strange reading.

Leaving Fenchurch Street, the train ran through the crowded and industrial East End, but at Stepney (1·75 miles) 'we began to breathe more freely, for we had left behind the region of smoke and gigantic chimneys' and were passing 'through the fields to Bow Common'. Soon after Bow station open country was entered again and 'passing onward through the verdant fields we came to the retired village of Homerton'. Then came Hackney, with its watercress beds, and Kingsland. 'In this district large tracts of land belonging to the Lord of the Manor ... are being laid out for building detached villas of a better class ', the visible results of the new railway. At Islington, too, Penton-ville Prison, a few years before set amidst fields, was 'nearly surrounded by houses'. Then, 'after passing several beautiful villas we arrived at Camden Town'.

The NLR's own lines were completed on 1 January 1852 by the opening of the line from Bow to Poplar, where connections were made to the dock lines by two branches. From the eastern branch at Prestons Road a connection was laid in to the Black-wall in 1852, but only after much pressure from the NLR. The other company, however, would not allow NLR passenger trains over its metals until agreement was finally reached in 1870. The NLR therefore opened its Poplar station in 1866 under the East India Dock Road bridge and terminated its trains there until they were extended to Blackwall in 1870. By then the steamer connections there were no longer a prize to be striven for. The service ceased in 1890 and the connection was severed.

The Docks Company leased a timber pond to the NLR, which converted it into a dock for the import of coal and the handling of lighter cargoes. Warehouses were provided and a large goods depot laid out and leased to the LNWR. Poplar Docks became one of the most important Thames-side railheads. In 1866 Harrow Lane sidings were laid out at Millwall Junction on the Blackwall Railway for exchange with the latter and with the dock lines. For the latter the rise of 1 in 34 of the western branch to the bridge over the Blackwall was avoided (Figure 16, p. 182) when the loop line was opened in 1875.

Freight traffic over the NLR started on 1 January 1852, worked by the LNWR. It was mainly merchandise to and from the docks, but some coal came off the LNWR, originating particularly from the Midland at Rugby. But the principal flow of coal was from Poplar Docks, whence it was worked by the shippers, the Northumberland and Durham Coal Company, with their own engines, a unique arrangement on a busy suburban line. The NLR bought out the rights and took over the locomotives in 1859, and in 1870 the LNWR took over the depots, converting some into general goods stations.

On 15th June 1855 the City Corporation, tired of congestion caused by animals driven through narrow streets to Smithfield Market, opened the Metropolitan Cattle Market off Caledonian

Road, Smithfield now dealing only in carcasses. In anticipation, the NLR opened a cattle terminal at Maiden Lane and the LNWR transferred its cattle traffic from Camden in April 1854. Caledonian Road passenger station had been opened on 10 June 1852. York Way, London's first freightliner terminal, opened in November 1965 on the site of Maiden Lane. On 7 November 1966 the A.C. electrification was extended thither.

The NLR laid out exchange sidings at St Pancras Junction, where a temporary connection was provided by the GNR in 1850 and a permanent one in 1853. A curve to the Midland was provided in 1867. The complex layout of this nodal point is shown in Figure 15 (p. 147).

All these connections brought local and transfer traffic to the NLR. Much was hauled by the company, but there were two features of operation shared with the LCDR: a number of 'foreign' companies, particularly the LNWR and the GNR, worked their own trains and also owned and staffed numerous goods depots along the route.

By 1861, 338,817 tons of minerals and 436,385 tons of goods were passing over the NLR. In 1871 the figures were 671,173 and 1,121,454 tons respectively. Traffic grew steadily until 1900, when the figures stood at 1·2 million and 2 million respectively, at which point it remained fairly stationary.

Meanwhile passenger traffic was also developing, nurtured by a policy of frequent services and cheap fares. In 1865 second-class fares averaged 0·4d. per mile. First and second only were provided, second-class carriages being used on the statutory Parliamentary trains.

In August 1853 a few NLR trains were extended from Hampstead Road over the LNWR to Willesden and thence to Kew. But this line with its primitive signalling was already congested. Accordingly the LNWR promoted the HAMP-STEAD JUNCTION RAILWAY from Camden Town to Old Oak Junction (Willesden). Opened on 2 January 1860, it was 6 miles long and had a 0·725-mile tunnel under the Hampstead heights. The line was absorbed by the LNWR in 1867 but the NLR provided the train service and shared in running the stations.

In 1861, 6·5 million passengers were carried by the NLR, but

at the general meeting of 26 February the chairman stressed
'the great disadvantage under which your line labours in
consequence of the extremely circuitous route'.

It was therefore decided to seek a more direct access to the
City. From a triangular junction at Dalston, where a new
station would be built, a triple line would lead southward for
two miles to Broad Street at the edge of the City. The line would
be carried on a viaduct over a very congested part of the Inner
Arc and some 4,500 people would be displaced. The NLR Act
of 1861 therefore included provisions for operating workmen's
trains. Rehousing clauses were not introduced until 1874 and
these were not really enforced until after 1885. As with other
lines, the NLR's progress towards Central London resulted in
even greater congestion and the workmen's fares chiefly
benefited the better-paid artisans.

The Broad Street extension was extremely costly. The LNWR,
being interested in a City goods depot as well as passenger
access, contributed heavily. To save the cost of land Broad
Street goods station is built on two levels. Passenger traffic began
on 1 November 1865, but the goods depot was not ready until 18
May 1868.

The extension was referred to as 'the happy afterthought',
for passenger traffic soon doubled, reaching nearly 14 million
in 1866. In 1871 quadrupling was completed between Dalston
and Camden Town and in 1874 a fourth line was provided into
Broad Street.

The train service had now assumed the form it would retain
almost unchanged for half a century. A 15-minute service ran
from Broad Street over the Bow line, first to Fenchurch Street
but later diverted to Poplar. Another, also at 15-minute
intervals, ran to Hampstead Road, calling at all stations, while
yet a third ran semi-fast to Camden, where connection was
made with the slow trains, before continuing over the Hampstead Junction to Willesden. From here alternate trains
traversed the NSWJR (p. 128) and the WLR (p. 125). The
LNWR ran local trains to Watford, but the short-lived 'City to
City' from Wolverhampton (1910–15) was the only long-
distance service.

The only other major change came with the opening of the

Canonbury Spur (p. 158) on 14 December 1874 for goods and
18 January 1875 for passengers, which connected Broad Street
with the GNR system. But this story is more properly dealt with
as part of the GNR's, for strategically it was a Cityward thrust
by that company and not a northward one by the NLR.

By 1870 the area traversed by the NLR's own line had been
completely built over, as was, during the next twenty years, that
traversed by the HJR, while there had been much building

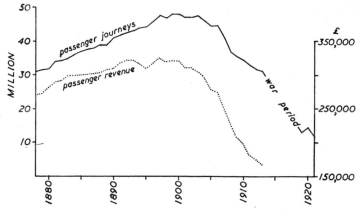

FIG. 10. Disaster for the North London: the effect of tramway and
Underground competition. (Based on company reports.)

beyond Willesden. The 14 million passengers of 1866 had
become 32·7 million in 1880. Thereafter the rate of increase
tapered off rapidly, but traffic increased steadily until 1896,
when 46·3 million passengers were carried.

The NLR had now reached its zenith, its traffic ceased to
grow and its arteries were becoming hardened. Though an
aesthetic joy, its little 4-4-0 tanks and their long rakes of
four-wheeled coaches were ill-equipped to face the coming
electric century. Such a train on a poster issued in 1909 to
counter the new Hampstead Tube is somewhat pathetic.

Tramway competition was mentioned for the first time at the
General Meeting of February 1872. But from 1900 it assumed
menacing proportions, particularly with electrification to
Hampstead in 1906 and Stamford Hill in 1907. The NLR were

helpless. 'To compete with halfpenny tram fares is impossible,' lamented the chairman. Nor was the NLR better able to meet the competition of the Hampstead Tube and Metropolitan's newly electrified 'Extension'.

At first the decline in receipts was more alarming than that in numbers. Between 1900 and 1905 there was a decline of 4 per cent in passenger numbers, but of 13·4 per cent in revenue. But after 1910 declining numbers assumed catastrophic proportions. The 21·4 million carried in 1913 were but 44·6 per cent of the 1900 figure and the 11·4 million in 1921 but 23·3 per cent.

In 1909 a common management with the LNWR was introduced and in 1922 the latter took over completely. All along the NLR Board had hesitated over electrification, and when it was finally carried out west of Broad Street it was as part of the LNWR's scheme (p. 122). Unfortunately, except a bare announcement that in 1921 there had been a 25 per cent increase in revenue due to electrification, statistical information of post-electrification trends is completely lost in the absorption into the LNWR. But the truth is the North London line never recovered its former glories.

THE NORTH LONDON LINE TODAY

Hampstead Heath dealt with huge crowds on bank holidays until the 1920's. As usual, the homeward rush was more concentrated than the outward and station officials would scan the skies anxiously, for a shower towards evening would bring an almost uncontrollable crowd. There was an ugly incident on the Easter Monday of 1892 when a thunderstorm brought in so many people that a crush developed on the staircase down to the eastbound platform and eight were killed.

Eastward of Camden Road there are four tracks, and freight activities are very conspicuous, though many depots have been closed. For the passenger the journey is redolent of decay. The large stations, with barn-like 'Italian warehouse' buildings and war damage unrepaired until after 1965, were all built to handle a traffic far in excess of the present, and four are closed.

Broad Street, gaunt and depressing, stands high above the street level. Originally there were seven platforms, but rearrangements in 1876 and 1891 increased the number under the two-arched roof to eight, and a ninth was added outside it in 1913. In the 1890's Broad Street was extremely busy, with 71 arrivals and departures between 9.0 and 10.0 a.m. alone. In 1902, 27 million passengers used it, more than twice the Cannon Street total, and in 1903, 102 trains arrived before 10.30 a.m. bringing more than 40,000 passengers, second only to the Liverpool Street figure. In 1960 only 41 trains arrived between 7.0 and 10.0 a.m. with about 6,400 passengers, 2,500 of them coming from the Great Northern line. Between 5.30 and 6.30 p.m., the busiest hour, the 4,000 passengers scarcely broke the brooding calm which contrasted mournfully with the scenes next door at Liverpool Street.

Without marked diurnal peaks, the Richmond service was reputedly among London's more profitable ones, but traffic declined after 1955 and the service was among the few in London marked for the Beeching Axe in 1963. Strenuous opposition by local authorities along the route resulted in a ministerial reprieve announced on 21 June 1965. A modest modernization scheme was started in 1967, and since 1963 there has been a 20-minute service throughout the day. The Watford service has operated only at peak hours since 1962; in 1961 there were 14 evening departures for former GN stations.

The Poplar service ceased on 14 May 1944, and east of Dalston the air of dereliction increases, especially around the shell of Devons Road sheds and works, but freight trains are frequent. The 1956 timetables showed 24 westbound goods trains passing Bow Junction daily from the Poplar direction. With the addition principally of trains from the Great Eastern line via Victoria Park, 75 trains passed Dalston Eastern Junction, while 81 passed on to the Hampstead Junction line.

THE METROPOLITAN

During the eighteen-fifties the streets were jammed with slow-moving horse traffic, and a bus journey was even more protracted than it is today. Thus schemes were propounded for railways connecting the northern termini and bringing the City within easy reach of northern and western suburbs. The

project finally reached fruition and was nurtured by Charles
Pearson, a City solicitor and the father of the Metropolitan, and
on 15 August 1853 the North Metropolitan Railway was incorporated to build a 3·5-mile line from Paddington to Farringdon
Street. The City Corporation and the GWR both subscribed,
the latter like all railway companies being interested in pene-
trating to the City.

The whole area was by then fully built up and the Metropolitan (the 'North' was dropped when the Company was
reincorporated by Act of 7 August 1854) was necessarily built
on the 'cut and cover' principle. Street lines were followed as
far as possible, to avoid demolishing property, a cutting was
dug and later covered over with brick arches. But even so there
was much destruction of slum property on the northern edge of
the City, the 'ill ventilated cul de sacs and dens of wretchedness
in the vicinity of Shoe Lane and Saffron Hill' (T. Hammond,
1835). George Godwin, editor of the *Builder*, estimated in 1864
that 1,000 dwellings housing 12,000 persons were destroyed in
making the open cuttings in the Fleet valley.

Physical connection was made with the GWR at Bishop's
Road, adjoining the north side of Paddington. The eastern
terminus was in part of the space vacated by the Cattle Market
(p. 76), alongside the rebuilt Smithfield Market. The GWR at
once leased the latter's basement as a goods station, opened on
3 May 1869 and closed from 30 July 1962.

The GWR had insisted on broad-gauge facilities, but was
amenable to mixed-gauge. Construction was slow and the
GWR became impatient, its meddling leading to cooling relations. Eventually the line was officially opened on 10 January
1863 and was worked by the GWR. Twenty-nine thousand
passengers were carried in the first three weeks, and traffic soon
expanded. The gas-lit rigid eight-wheelers rumbling beneath the
London streets were a tremendous novelty and the 15-minute
service made it a useful one. This extract from a diary kept by a
William Hardman gives a 'man-in-the-street's' impression:

26 January 1863 – Yesterday Mary Anne and I made our first
trip down the 'Drain'. We walked to Edgeware [*sic*] Road and
took first class tickets for King's Cross (6*d* each). We experienced

no disagreeable odour beyond the smell common to tunnels. The carriages hold ten persons, with divided seats, and are lighted by gas; they are also so lofty that a six footer may stand erect with his hat on.

Relations soon deteriorated further, and the GWR gave notice that they would cease to work the line after 30th September, but on 1st August peremptorily advanced the date to 10th August. Instead of capitulating the Metropolitan obtained rolling stock from the GNR, and as the discomfited GWR withdrew the trains came down the newly completed King's Cross connection to start the next day's service and maintain it until the Metropolitan's own stock was delivered.

On 1 October the GNR began a regular service to Farringdon Street, thus obtaining their foothold in the City. So delighted were the commuters on the first train that they drank the station buffet dry in their celebrations. On the same day through trains from GWR suburban stations also started running into Farringdon Street.

The overall success of the Metropolitan was so immediate that the idea of a circular line connecting City and West End rapidly developed, being recommended by a Parliamentary Committee in 1863, when a minor 'Railway Mania' peculiar to London occurred.

The first extension of the Metropolitan was of 0·75 mile to the more convenient Moorgate Street station opened on 23 December 1865. With a railhead within half a mile from the Bank of England traffic was growing fast. In 1865, 15 million ordinary tickets and 5,498 seasons were sold, but ten years later sales had swollen to 43·6 million and 32,941 respectively. In that year the mighty GWR issued 36 million and 13,575.

Meanwhile the circular line, invariably known as the Inner Circle, was beginning to take shape. On 29 July 1864 two Acts authorized an extension from Paddington to South Kensington and another from Moorgate Street to Minories. On 1 October 1868 the line from Praed Street Junction (just east of Bishop's Road) was opened to Gloucester Road. An end-on junction with the District was made at South Kensington and this section was opened on 24 December, the day the District was opened.

On 1 February 1875 trains began running into 1 and 2 platforms of the Great Eastern's Liverpool Street station. On 12 July a few yards of line were opened between Liverpool Street Junction and Bishopsgate (now Liverpool Street London Transport). The spur into the GER station was used at irregular intervals until 1904. The last train was an Aylesbury–Yarmouth excursion, reputedly the longest trip ever made by a Metropolitan train. The tunnel is now used as a staff canteen.

The reeking soot-laden atmosphere of a steam-worked underground is a fading memory which contemporary prints fail to convey. Staff reputedly found beards useful as filters, and E. L. Ahrons, as usual, must be permitted the last word: 'In the old days they [the Metropolitan and the District] provided a sort of health resort for people who suffered from asthma.'

The station interiors were magnificent, the cuttings being spanned by great glazed arches. The finest of all was perhaps Aldersgate with its 80-foot span. The glass disintegrated in the air raids and the frame was taken down in 1955. Rebuilding has caused the other roofs to go one by one, though portions remain at Paddington (Praed St), Bayswater and Notting Hill.

The bare bones of statistics are sometimes hard to clothe with flesh, and who, as opposed to how many, used the Metropolitan in mid-Victorian times is obscure. The Act for the Bishopsgate extension contained the usual provisions for workmen, but the line was never a great carrier. The Doré prints of troglodytic gnomes condemned by a merciless capitalism to pour off Metropolitan trains in hundreds on their way to their sweated labour is probably incorrect, for as usual destruction of slum property merely led to greater congestion near by. Besides, the line ran for such a short distance through the working-class area that the proletariat doubtless still walked. But on the other hand the volume of third-class traffic amounted to 74·7 per cent of all passengers carried in 1875 (the comparable District figure was 70 per cent).

THE WIDENED LINES

The connections with the GNR at King's Cross, which came into regular use on 1 October 1863, consisted of two single-line

STEAM SUBURBAN II

(12) *Commuting clerks of the early 1900's rode home in four-wheelers on the* GNR. *Here a train from Moorgate and King's Cross climbs past Holloway station.*

(13) *But the wealthy commuters on the* LSWR *were provided with the latest bogie coaches. A train of two four-coach 'bogie block' sets from Waterloo approaches Surbiton.*

(14) *The* LT & SR *also had the reputation of providing very good rolling stock. This train is from Ealing and is of the special coaches for that service.*

THE INNER CIRCLE

(15) *This contemporary engraving gives an excellent impression of the 'cut and cover' method employed in building the original Metropolitan Railway. One is looking down Pentonville Road with Euston Road on its original line in the background. King's Cross station may easily be seen, but St Pancras was not yet built.*

(16) *The arched roof of Notting Hill Gate in this 1868 view is typical of the Metropolitan stations. Note the signal and signal box.*

tunnels, the East Branch, from the GNR up side, and the Hotel Curve, to the GNR down side. A west-facing connection from the East Branch was never regularly used and was taken out during the building of the double-track tunnel from the Midland, opened on 13 July 1868. A junction with the LCDR was opened at West Street, hard by Farringdon, on 1 January 1866, and a triangular layout, under Smithfield Market, was completed by a spur from Aldersgate Street to the LCDR, opened on 1 September 1871.

To handle the heavy traffic, passenger and freight, which would use these connections, particularly as they formed the only north–south route across the City, the double track of the Metropolitan would be insufficient. A second pair of tracks, always known as the Widened Lines, was therefore provided by that company between King's Cross and Moorgate, burrowing under the Inner Circle at Ray Street, just west of Farringdon.

The Widened Lines, sanctioned in 1861, went into use between Farringdon and Aldersgate on 1 March 1866, being extended to Moorgate on 1 July and westward to King's Cross on 27 January for goods and 17 February 1868 for passengers. It was intended to carry the new tracks even farther west, but only a short tunnel was ever built. It lay unused until 15 March 1926, when a single line connection was laid through it from the Outer Rail of the Inner Circle to the eastbound Widened Line. This allowed eastbound Metropolitan trains to reach Moorgate without crossing the Inner Rail at that station. This practice, the only use ever made by the Metropolitan services of the Widened Lines, ceased on 27 April 1935, after which the tunnel was incorporated in the re-sited King's Cross station (Inner Circle). Mixed-gauge was at first provided on the Widened Lines, but authorities differ as to whether the King's Cross–Farringdon section was ever used by GWR broad-gauge trains.

Goods stations were opened by the GNR at Farringdon (closed 16 January 1956) and by the Midland at Whitecross Street (closed 1 March 1936). Derelict since the City was blitzed in 1940, they became redundant since numerous bombed-out 'soft goods' firms did not return to the rebuilt City.

The Chatham and the GNR began a reciprocal through service on 1 January 1866. This was in addition to the latter's

METROPOLITAN EXTENSION.—South Eastern and Chatham.

Miles	Up. Midland Station,	mn	mn	mn	mrn	mrn	mrn	f	mrn	mrn	mrn	d	mrn	a	mrn	f	mrn	mrn	b c	mrn	mrn	f	mrn	mrn
	Kentish Town.....dep.	....	....	....	3 cl. Workmen's Train.	Workmen's Train.	3 cl. Workmen's Train.	....	Workmen's Train.	....	6 14	7 3	....	7 29	....	7 48	....	8 3	8 20	8 29	....	8 39	....	8 48
—	**York Road** (G.N.) .. "	....	....	....				....		....	....	7 25	....	7 36	....	....	....	8 14	8 21	8 31	....	8 40	....	8 57
3	**King's Cross** (Met.).. "	....	....	....				....		....	6 46	7 28	....	7 39	....	....	....	8 17	8 27	8 37	....	8 46	....	9 4
4	**Farringdon Street.. "**	....	....	....				....		....	6 50	7 32	....	7 43	....	....	....	8 21	8 31	8 41	....	8 50	....	9 8
3¼	**Moorgate Street.... "**	....	....	....				....		....	7 13	....	7 35	....	7 50	8 2	....	8 27	....	8 47	....	8 55	....	9 10
3¾	**Aldersgate Street.. "**	....	....	....				....		....	7 15	....	7 37	....	7 52	8 4	....	8 29	....	8 49	....	8 57	....	9 12
4¼	Snow Hill............	....	....	....				....		....	7 17	7 35	7 39	7 46	7 54	8 6	8 12	8 31	8 34	8 51	....	8 59	9 8	9 15
—	**Holborn Viaduct......**	....	....	....				615		6e50	....	....	....	....	....	....	....	....	....	....	....	....	....	....
4½	**Ludgate Hill..........**	245	315	415	5 0	5 48	6 0	618	6 47	6 56	7 21	7 37	7 43	7 53	7 58	8 11	8 16	8 35	8 39	8 55	9 1	9 5	9 11	9 23
—	**St. Paul's..........**	....	....	....	....	....	....	....	....	....	....	....	....	....	....	....	....	....	....	....	....	....	....	....
5½	Borough Road.........	....	....	....	5 5	....	6 4	....	....	7 1	7 25	....	7 47	7 58	8 4	....	8 20	....	8 43	9 0	9 6	....	....	9 29
6	Elephant and Castle...	250	319	419	5 7	5 52	6 6	623	6 51	7 3	7 27	....	7 49	8 0	8 6	8 16	8 22	8 41	8 45	9 3	9 9	9 12	9 18	9 32
6½	Walworth Road........	253	322	422	5 10	5 55	6 9	626	6 54	7 6	7 30	....	7 52	8 3	8 9	....	8 25	8 44	8 48	9 6	9 12	....	9 21	9 35
7¼	Camberwell New Road..	256	325	425	5 13	5 58	6 12	629	6 57	7 9	7 33	....	7 55	8 6	8 12	....	8 28	8 47	8 51	9 9	9 15	....	9 24	9 38
8	Loughboro' Junction...	259	328	428	5 16	6 0	6 14	632	6 59	7 12	7 36	....	7 58	8 9	8 15	8 22	8 30	8 50	8 54	9 12	9 18	9 18	9 27	9 41
8½	Brixton & S. Stockwell	3 2	....	....	5 19	6 3	6 17	....	7 2	7 15	7 39	....	8 1	8 14	8 19	....	8 33	8 53	8 57	9 15	9 22	....	9 30	9 44
9¼	Clapham & N. Stockwell	3 5	....	....	5 23	6 7	6 20	....	7 5	7 18	7 42	....	8 4	8 17	8 22	....	8 36	8 56	9 0	9 18	9 25	....	9 33	9 47
9¾	Wandsworth Road.....	3 7	....	....	5 26	6 10	6 23	....	7 7	7 20	7 44	....	8 6	8 20	8 24	....	8 38	8 58	9 2	9 20	9 27	....	9 35	9 49
—	**Clapham** Junc. ..arr.	....	....	....	....	....	....	....	....	....	....	....	....	....	8 29	....	....	9 5	....	....	....	....	....	9 54
10½	Battersea Park Road...	310	....	....	5 29	6 13	6 26	....	7 10	7 23	7 47	....	8 9	8 23	....	....	8 41	....	9 5	9 23	9 30	....	9 38	....
11	Grosvenor Road........	314	....	....	5 32	6 18	6 29	....	7 12	7 25	7 49	....	8 11	8 25	....	....	8 43	....	9 7	9 25	9 34	....	9 40	....
11½	**Victoria..........arr.**	317	....	....	5 39	6 21	6 34	....	7 17	7 30	7 54	....	8 16	8 30	....	....	8 48	....	9 12	9 30	9 36	....	9 45	....

Week Days—*Continued below.*

Up. Midland Station,	mrn	mrn	d	mrn	b	mrn	mrn	a	mrn	b	a	mrn	b c	mrn	d	mrn	a	b	aft	aft	a	aft	aft	aft
Kentish Town dep	Except Saturdays.	9 9	....	9 25	9 52	....	9 58	1013	....	1042	1052	11 8	1132	....	....	1149	1149	1219	....	1236	....	1257	....	Sats. only.
York Rd. (G.N.) "		9 16	9 36	....	9 45	9 55	....	1020	1029	....	11 9	1118	....	....	1159	....	1211	1220	....	....	1256	....	....	
King's C. (Met.) "		9 19	9 39	9 32	10 1	9 58	10 7	1023	1032	1053	1112	1121	1139	....	12 2	1159	1214	1226	....	1243	1259	1 5	....	
Farringdon St.. "		9 23	9 43	9 36	10 5	10 2	1011	1027	1036	1057	1116	1125	1143	....	12 6	12 3	1218	1230	....	1247	1 3	1 9	....	
Moorgate St. .. "		9 27	....	9 45	....	10 7	1019	....	1042	....	....	1126	....	1155	....	12 8	....	....	1244	1252	....	1 13	1 24	
Aldersgate St.. "		9 29	....	9 47	....	10 9	1021	....	1044	....	....	1128	....	1157	....	1210	....	....	1246	1254	....	1 15	1 26	
Snow Hill.........		9 32	9 45	9 50	10 7	1011	1023	1029	1046	11 0	1119	1130	1145	1159	12 8	1212	1220	1232	1248	1256	1 5	1 18	1 28	1 36
Holborn Viaduct..	....	....	....	....	....	....	....	....	....	....	....	....	....	....	....	....	....	....	....	....	....	....	....	....
Ludgate Hill.....	9 33	9 37	9 48	9 55	1011	1016	1027	1033	1051	11 5	1123	1134	1150	12 3	1211	1216	1224	1236	1252	1 1	1 9	1 23	1 32	1 40
St. Paul's.........	....	....	....	....	....	....	....	....	....	....	....	....	....	....	....	....	....	....	....	....	....	....	....	....
Borough Road	9 37	9 42	....	9 59	1015	1021	1031	1038	1055	11 9	1128	1139	1154	12 8	....	....	1229	1240	1257	1 6	1 13	1 28	1 36	1 45
Elephant & Castle.	9 39	9 44	....	10 1	1017	1023	1033	1040	1057	1111	1130	1141	1156	1210	....	1222	1231	1242	1259	1 8	1 15	1 30	1 38	1 47
Walworth Road...	9 42	9 47	....	10 4	1020	1026	1036	1043	11 0	1114	1133	1144	1159	1213	....	1225	1234	1245	1 2	1 11	1 18	1 33	1 41	1 50
Camberwell Nw Rd	9 44	9 50	....	10 7	1023	1029	1039	1046	11 3	1117	1136	1147	12 2	1216	....	1228	1237	1248	1 5	1 14	1 21	1 36	1 44	1 53
Loughboro' Junc..	9 47	9 53	....	10 9	1025	1032	1042	1049	11 6	1119	1139	1151	12 5	1219	....	1231	1240	1250	1 8	1 17	1 24	1 39	1 46	1 56
Brixton & S. S.....	9 50	9 56	....	1013	1028	1035	1045	1052	11 9	1121	1143	1153	1210	1222	....	....	1243	1253	1 11	Except Saturdays.	1 27	1 42	1 49	1 59
Clapham & N. S...	9 53	9 59	....	1016	1031	1038	1048	1055	1112	1124	1146	1156	1213	1225	....	....	1246	1256	1 14		1 30	1 45	1 52	2 2
Wandsworth Road	9 55	10 1	....	1018	1033	1040	1050	1057	1114	1126	1149	1158	1215	1227	....	....	1248	1258	1 16		1 32	1 47	1 55	2 4
Clapham Jn. arr.	....	....	....	....	....	1045	....	....	....	....	....	12 3	....	....	....	....	....	....	....		....	1 52	....	2 10
Battersea Park Rd.	9 58	10 4	....	1021	1036	....	1053	11 0	1117	1129	1151	....	1218	1230	....	....	1251	1 1	1 19		1 35	....	1 58	....
Grosvenor Road...	10 1	10 6	....	1023	1038	....	1055	11 2	1119	1131	1153	....	1220	1232	....	....	1253	1 3	1 21		1 37	....	2 0	....
Victoria......arr.	10 5	1011	....	1028	1043	....	11 0	11 7	1124	1136	1158	....	1225	1237	....	....	1258	1 8	1 26		1 42	....	2 5	....

Week Days—*Continued on page 229.*

Up. Midland Station,	b	aft	a	aft	aft	d	aft	a	aft	aft	aft	a	b	d	aft	aft	aft	aft	b	a	aft	aft	a	aft	aft
Kentish Town dep	1 25	1 38	....	Saturdays only.	1 51	....	....	2 15	2 34	....	Sats. only.	2 53	3 17	....	....	Saturdays.	3 30	3 53	4 21	....	4 32	4 45	4 55	....	....
York Rd. (G.N.) "	....	1 27	1 52		1 59	2 23	....	2 32	....	....		3 9	....	333	....		3 53	4 14	....	4 33	4 39	4 52	5 8	5 12	5 22
King's C. (Met.) "	1 33	1 45	1 55		2 3	2 26	....	2 35	2 41	....		3 12	3 26	336	....		3 56	4 17	4 28	4 36	4 42	4 55	5 11	5 15	5 25
Farringdon St.. "	1 37	1 49	1 59		2 7	2 30	....	2 39	2 45	....		3 16	3 30	340	....		4 0	4 21	4 32	4 40	4 46	4 59	5 15	5 19	5 29
Moorgate St. .. "	....	1 52	....		2 12	....	2 33	....	2 47	3 5		....	....	....	340		4 5	4 26	....	....	4 53	5 4	....	5 26	5 34
Aldersgate St.. "	....	1 54	....		2 14	....	2 35	....	2 49	3 7		....	....	....	342		4 7	4 28	....	....	4 55	5 6	....	5 28	5 36
Snow Hill.........	1 39	1 56	2 2		2 16	2 32	2 37	2 42	2 52	3 9	3 12	3 19	3 34	342	345		4 9	4 30	4 34	4 43	4 57	5 8	5 17	5 30	5 38
Holborn Viaduct..	....	....	....		....	....	....	....	....	....	....	....	....	....	....		....	....	....	....	....	....	....	....	....
Ludgate Hill.....	1 44	2 0	2 7	2 16	2 21	2 35	2 40	2 46	2 56	313	3 17	3 22	3 39	345	350	4 2	4 15	4 34	4 38	4 47	5 1	5 11	5 20	5 34	5 42
St. Paul's.........	....	....	....	....	....	....	....	....	....	....	....	....	....	....	....	....	....	....	....	....	....	....	....	....	....
Borough Road	1 49	2 4	2 12	....	2 26	....	....	2 51	3 0	317	3 21	3 26	3 43	....	355	4 6	4 19	....	4 43	4 52	5 6	....	5 25	5 38	....
Elephant & Castle.	1 51	2 6	2 14	2 21	2 28	....	2 44	2 53	3 2	319	3 23	3 28	3 45	....	357	4 8	4 21	....	4 45	4 55	5 8	....	5 27	5 40	5 45
Walworth Road...	1 54	2 9	2 17	2 24	2 31	....	2 47	2 56	3 5	322	3 26	3 31	3 48	....	4 0	411	4 24	....	4 48	4 58	5 11	....	5 30	5 43	5 48
Camberwell Nw Rd	1 57	2 12	2 20	2 27	2 34	....	2 50	2 59	3 8	325	3 29	3 34	3 51	....	4 3	414	4 27	....	4 51	5 1	5 14	....	5 33	5 46	5 51
Loughboro' Junc..	2 0	2 14	2 23	2 30	2 37	....	2 53	3 2	3 11	328	3 31	3 37	3 54	....	4 6	416	4 30	4 43	4 54	5 4	5 17	5 22	5 36	5 49	5 53
Brixton & S. S.....	2 3	2 17	2 28	....	2 40	....	2 56	3 6	3 14	331	3 34	3 40	3 57	....	4 9	....	4 33	4 47	4 57	5 7	5 20	5 25	5 39	5 52	5 56
Clapham & N. S...	2 6	2 20	2 31	....	2 43	....	2 59	3 9	3 17	334	3 37	3 43	4 0	....	412	....	4 36	4 50	5 0	5 10	5 23	5 28	5 42	5 55	5 59
Wandsworth Road	2 8	2 22	2 34	....	2 45	....	3 1	3 11	3 19	336	3 40	3 45	4 2	....	414	....	4 38	4 52	5 2	5 12	5 25	5 30	5 44	5 57	6 1
Clapham Jn. arr.	....	2 27	....	....	....	....	3 6	....	....	341	....	....	....	....	....	....	....	....	....	....	5 30	....	....	6 2	....
Battersea Park Rd.	2 11	....	2 37	....	2 48	....	....	3 14	3 22	....	3 43	3 48	4 5	....	417	....	4 41	4 54	5 5	5 15	....	5 33	5 47	....	6 4
Grosvenor Road...	2 13	....	2 39	....	2 50	....	....	3 16	3 26	....	3 47	3 50	4 7	....	419	....	4 43	4 56	5 7	5 17	....	5 35	5 49	....	6 6
Victoria......arr.	2 18	....	2 44	....	2 55	....	....	3 21	3 29	....	3 50	3 55	4 12	....	424	....	4 48	5 1	5 12	5 22	....	5 40	5 54	....	6 10

a Run through from King's Cross (G.N.) to Victoria; change at Aldersgate Street by other Trains. **b** Through Trains from Kentish Town on Midland Line. **c** Midland Trains, 1 & 3 class. **d** Through Trains from G. N. Line. *e* Except Mondays; starts from Snow Hill on Mondays. **f** Run to the Crystal Palace Line Platform at Loughboro' Junction, and the Main Line Platforms at Borough Road, Elephant and Castle, Walworth Road, and Camberwell New Road.

☞ For **other Trains** between Moorgate Street, Ludgate Hill, &c., and Loughborough Junction, see pages 230, 231, and 234, from Brixton and Clapham to Victoria, see pages 232 to 234. For L. & S. W. Trains from Ludgate Hill to Wandsworth Road, see page 128.

*** Passengers from Metropolitan Line change at Aldersgate Street.

The former importance of the Metropolitan Extension of the LCDR both as part of the north–south through route over the Widened Lines and for inner suburban traffic is shown by this extract from *Bradshaw* of June 1904. Before they were killed by competition from Tubes and trams, services were intensive, routes complex and stations closely spaced.

Moorgate service, while the former began running into Moorgate over the Aldersgate spur on 1 September 1871. The Midland ran trains to Moorgate from 13 July 1868 and from 1 June 1869 through to the Chatham.

In the 1880's there were about 200 trains a day over the Widened Lines into Moorgate and 100 southbound through Snow Hill. The latter ran from stations on the Northern Heights (p. 162) and from Kentish Town to such points as Victoria, Herne Hill and Woolwich (SER). In 1902 there were 109 northbound trains through Snow Hill and 521 arrivals at Moorgate, including those on the Inner Circle. A count on a 1903 day revealed 9,887 passengers from GNR stations arriving before 10.30 a.m., 7,018 from Midland, 4,816 from SE & CR and 20,771 from Metropolitan stations.

But the great days of the Widened Lines were passing. By 1901 the City & South London Tube was operating through the City, while the new motor-buses and the Kingsway tram-tunnel were soon to speed up road journeys.

The GN–SE & CR service ceased from 1 October 1907 and its Midland counterpart from 1 July 1908. SE & CR trains continued to Moorgate until 1 April 1916, after which the Aldersgate curve was abandoned and the north–south passenger link over the Widened Lines severed.

The City services of the GNR and Midland also suffered, partly from northward extensions of the City & South London, but mainly from the Great Northern & City Tube, which diverted GNR passengers at Finsbury Park, and from trams. After the first world war they ran in peak hours only and in 1930, 20 trains a day entered Moorgate from the ex-Midland line and 59 from the ex-GNR. Nineteen of the latter came from High Barnet, and of course all traffic from there was diverted to the Northern Tube in 1940.

Suspended for long periods during the war, an even sparser service was finally restored in 1945. In 1960 there were 16 trains from the GN line and 2 from the Midland. The ER introduced diesel traction in 1959 and the LMR shortly after.

Quite apart from the brief period it operated the Metropolitan, the GWR also used the line from the opening for a service from its suburban stations to the City, for Paddington was so remote, some connection thither was vital if the company were to create any suburban traffic at all. The last broad-gauge trains ran on 14 March 1869. Eventually the narrow-gauge trains were extended to Liverpool Street and certainly after that date used the Circle Tracks and not the Widened Lines. From electrification in 1907 Metropolitan locomotives hauled the GWR coaches eastward from Bishop's Road. In the 1930's there were 5 eastbound trains in the morning and 2 westbound in the evening, but they ran for the last time on 15 September 1939.

Moorgate was the largest Metropolitan station, with two Inner Circle platforms, two electrified and three non-electrified bays. The last-named may now deal with but a trickle of peak-hour traffic, but Moorgate remains a key point on the Circle and Northern lines. During a census made in November 1959, 15,465 passengers entered the station between 4.30 and 7.0 p.m., 3,350 between 5.31 and 5.45.

TABLE 6

THE PEAK HOUR
PASSENGERS LEAVING SELECTED STATIONS

Station	Census Date	Peak p.m.				Off peak
		5.1–5.15	5.16–5.30	5.31–5.45	5.46–6.0	6.46–7.0
Liverpool Street	4 Oct. 60	7,612	12,960	12,887	10,216	712*
Fenchurch Street	4 Oct. 60	2,300	2,429	2,666	2,174	549
Baker Street	Nov. 59	1,943	1,881	2,953	2,223	474
Moorgate	Nov. 59	2,686	2,547	3,350	2,079	340

* 2.16–2.30 p.m.

The Widened Lines were a vital north–south freight link. The 1951 B.T.C. Committee on Electrification reported an average of 51 southbound trips daily and the banking engine maintained at Farringdon to assist trains up to Ludgate Hill is kept constantly busy. The use of diesel locomotives has meant fewer trips but heavier loads, less congestion but increased use of this route. There are also proposals to restore it as a passenger route.

THE DISTRICT

The southern part of the Inner Circle, from Minories to South Kensington, was allocated to a new company incorporated on 29 July 1864. This was the Metropolitan District Railway, invariably known as the District to distinguish it from its neighbour. Also built by the 'cut and cover' method, the first section was opened between South Kensington and Westminster Bridge on 24 December 1868. That on to Blackfriars went into service on 30 May 1870 and thence to Mansion House on 3 July 1871.

All parties assumed that the District would be absorbed by the Metropolitan, and indeed to the impartial observer such a measure would appear a necessity to ensure efficient working of the Inner Circle. It was a curious analogy with the early relations between the South Eastern and East Kent Companies (*see* Vol. II, Chap. III), and the only rational explanation of subsequent events was that the two Boards were bent on pursuing this analogy.

In 1866 the Metropolitan agreed to work the District for 45 per cent of the takings. But this was not regarded by the latter as satisfactory and it gave a year's notice of termination of the agreement from 1 July 1871. The Metropolitan directors resigned from the District Board and none other than J. S. Forbes, General Manager of the LCDR, was invited to join and in 1872 he became chairman. The Metropolitan, in the throes of financial crisis, turned to Forbes's inveterate antagonist, Sir Edward Watkin, chairman of the South Eastern and already known for his dislike of Forbes. A character sketch of these men appears in Volume II, pp. 42–3.

THE INNER CIRCLE

The bad farce being played out in the fields of Kent was now transferred to the sulphurous catacombs beneath the London streets. But, though respectively controlled by two personal enemies, the two London companies were locked in indissoluble wedlock sealed by the ring of the Inner Circle.

Even before Watkin's advent the Metropolitan had, until only a week before the District were due to take over their own working, refused to countenance the obvious course of both companies' trains running over the other portion of the Circle. Then, revenue during the early seventies was disappointing for the District and an amalgamation was sought with the Metropolitan. The latter resisted the move, urged on by Watkin, waiting as over-confidently for the District to collapse as he did for the LCDR.

Meanwhile the Circle remained uncompleted between Bishopsgate and Mansion House, 1·5 miles. The powers were in existence and public clamour was loud, but the Metropolitan delayed completion by every means possible and the District consistently dragged its feet. Eventually a Metropolitan Inner Circle Completion Railway Company was floated by independent City interests and incorporated on 7 August 1874. The Metropolitan were compelled to complete the line to Aldgate, opened on 18 November 1876. But capital for the independent company was not forthcoming, due to Watkin's intrigues, the *Railway News* being on sufficiently safe ground to accuse him openly.

But even Watkin realized that he must eventually give way, and on 11 August 1879 the Royal Assent was given to the Metropolitan & District (City Lines and Extensions) Act. This provided for the taking over jointly of the Completion Company's powers. Parliament, well aware of their nonsensical rivalry, laid statutory obligations on the companies to maintain the Circle service.

The Metropolitan now rushed forward the completion of its works and opened the line from Aldgate to Tower Hill (closed 1884, reopened 1967) on 25 September 1882. Watkin meanwhile delayed work on the joint line by getting the SER to raise difficulties about its passage under Cannon Street station. But these moves failed in their objective. The Metropolitan were forced to sell a half share of the new line to the District and failed to saddle the latter with half the deficit involved through premature opening. The City Lines were opened on 6 October 1884 and at last the Inner Circle was one in fact as well as name.

The rivals bickered on, quarrelling first over the interpretation of the City Lines Act with regard to interest charges, a round won by the Metropolitan. Then, in 1885, there was a dispute over through bookings from stations on the City Lines and on the Tilbury (via Fenchurch Street and Mark Lane) to South Kensington in connection with an exhibition. This spread to other bookings and lasted until 1888, the District emerging partially victorious.

The District, without statutory authority, built 11 chains of double line on its own land to allow through running alongside Metropolitan metals from Gloucester Road to Kensington High Street. The motive was to divert its Inner Circle trains over this, the 'Cromwell Curve', to gain extra mileage. But to use the curve, trains on the inner rail had to cross the outer rail twice. The practice was indefensible and lasted only from 1 October to 10 November 1884. But the dispute dragged on until 1903, when the courts ruled the Cromwell Curve not to be part of the Inner Circle and the District was unable to claim mileage for using it.

TRAIN SERVICES ON THE INNER CIRCLE

The Inner Circle filled a real social need, providing inter-terminal connections, transport from the residential areas of Paddington and Kensington to Central London, and rapid communication between City and West End. Thus much of its traffic was local. But the great increases which came over the years were mainly from suburban services coming on to the Circle from extensions of the two companies. Thus, while there has always been a basic circular service, these trains were by no means the only ones using the Circle, and are now in the minority.

In 1875, 43·6 million ordinary tickets were sold by the Metropolitan and 25·9 million by the District. Ten years later the figures were 67·4 million and 38·9 million respectively, while in 1895 they were 73·7 million and 40·9 million, not including a million at the City Lines stations. Between 1875 and 1895 season-ticket journeys over the District had increased from 1·5 million to 4·4 million.

The Metropolitan was part of the Watkin Empire, which embraced the Manchester, Sheffield & Lincolnshire and the SER, and had yearnings to become a trunk line. Between 1868 and 1892 it reached out beyond the Chilterns (p. 136) and it dabbled in freight traffic. The District's ambitions were more limited, extending only to Guildford, and in fact its ultimate bounds were but Uxbridge and Upminster and these were reached only by running powers.

By 1903 an average of 28,800 passengers a day were arriving at Moorgate from Metropolitan stations before 10.30 a.m. At Mansion House equivalent numbers were 17,000 from stations to the west and 6,000 from those to the east, and 381 trains a day were arriving at the station. The Inner Circle was choked with traffic, delays were frequent and on the District extra peak-hour services were impossible. But at the same time it was suffering competition from buses and trams, while tube promotion was causing anxiety.

Watkin had retired in 1894 and the breach with the District was slowly healing. But Forbes's influence was stultifying. Because of him the District were reluctant to modernize, and the Metropolitan were unable to pursue an independent course, though they had obtained electrification powers in 1882. By 1900 both were suffering severely from hardened arteries. Stock was antediluvian, mostly four-wheelers on the District and rigid eight-wheelers on the Metropolitan, and operating methods were unchanged since the seventies. 'Sewer Rats' was the City's name for commuters coming in by Inner Circle or Widened Lines.

But in that year the two companies at last combined to equip the 0·75 mile of District line between Earl's Court and High Street with D.C. traction on the fourth-rail system. An experimental shuttle service was operated for six months. Later, a joint committee recommended overhead electrification at 3,300 volts A.C.

By then a new figure had entered the scene, an American financier, Charles Tyson Yerkes. United States money was then available for investment in British railways when native capital was short, and Yerkes was over to see what fields there were to conquer. Through Sir Robert Perks, a solicitor with District interests, he secured control of that company in 1901. He represented the twentieth century better than Forbes and the latter was forced to resign his position of chairman. He died in 1904 and the *Railway Times* wrote an epitaph: 'It is doubtful whether any company, in the long run, benefited materially from his services.'

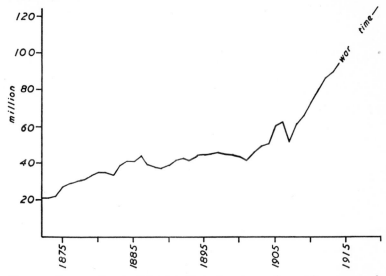

FIG. 11. Success for the District. Note the stagnation 1885–1901 and the expansion in the years following the 1903–5 electrification. (Based on Board of Trade railway returns. No returns were made in the war years. After 1920 the returns are merged in London Electric Railways.)

Yerkes, with his American experience, backed fourth-rail D.C., a method already widely used for suburban electrification in the United States. The Metropolitan were unwillingly forced to follow suit. The first regular services were on the Harrow and Uxbridge line, but on 1 July 1905 the District inaugurated an electric service between Ealing and Whitechapel, using the southern section of the Circle. By 24 September all the Circle steam trains had been replaced and by 5 November 1906, with the electrification of the Hammersmith & City services, nearly all passenger trains over the Circle were so worked.

Electrification brought new life, and sufficiently early to

meet the competition from electric trams and tubes. But though figures rose over the critical years between 1905 and 1914 it must be remembered that the period was one of route extensions and increased building in the outer suburbs.

The District's traffic had tended to stagnate between 1885 and 1901, but from then until 1905, for the reasons just given, passenger journeys (including those of season-ticket holders) climbed from 42·2 million to 51·5 million. In 1908 they reached 61·1 million, an increase of 18·8 per cent over the first three years of electric working. The 1908 revenue was 26·2 per cent up on that of 1905, but this was due to longer journeys.

Today the southern part of the Inner Circle is one of the busiest sections of the London Transport system, with 24 trains per hour on each rail. At peak hours this is increased to 36 and no sooner has a train cleared the platform than the following one is running in. Besides Circle trains there are services from Richmond, Wimbledon and Ealing in the west and Barking and Upminster in the east. On the northern part the basic service is one of 16 trains an hour on each rail, 8 on the Circle service and 8 on that between Hammersmith and Whitechapel. At peak periods this is augmented between Baker Street and the City by services to and from the 'Extension' line and 32 trains an hour each way pass King's Cross.

THE EAST LONDON LINE

Between 1824 and 1843 Marc Brunel built a tunnel for pedestrians under the Thames between Wapping and Rotherhithe. A remarkable feat for the time, it was, however, little used and in 1865 the East London Railway was incorporated to take it over as part of a rail route linking the GER with the Brighton and the South Eastern.

It was opened with double track through the tunnel from Wapping to New Cross (Gate) on 7 December 1869. At the latter was a separate station, but this was closed in 1886 and East London trains used the easternmost platform of the Brighton's station. On 13 March 1871 a spur was opened from Rotherhithe to the South London line at Old Kent Road. In 1876 spurs were provided to the up side at New Cross Gate and to both sides of the SER at its New Cross station. On 10 April that year the line was opened between Wapping and Shoreditch, where there was a junction with the GER to allow through running into Liverpool Street.

The LBSCR worked a service from the start, eventually running between Liverpool Street and Croydon. On 1 April 1880 the SER inaugurated a service between Addiscombe and Liverpool Street. There were also some through services, never very popular, between Liverpool Street and Brighton from 1876 to 1884.

The City Lines Act of 1879 authorized a connection between the Inner Circle and the East London. This was to be owned jointly by the Metropolitan and the District and was to run from a triangular junction at Aldgate to a point just south of Whitechapel station. In 1884 the north curve at Aldgate was vested solely in the Metropolitan. On 6 October 1884 both companies started through services to New Cross and New Cross Gate, the SER withdrawing its trains. In 1886 the GER started running trains. After the Circle was electrified Metropolitan and District trains were withdrawn. But in 1913 fourth-rail electrification of the East London was completed between the New Cross stations and Shoreditch. The service on the Old Kent Road spur had ceased in 1911. The Metropolitan now provided all the trains, running through from South Kensington via Baker Street and later from Hammersmith.

Since 1941 the connection at Whitechapel has been unused except for stock movements. The East London is now operated by a self-contained service between New Cross and New Cross Gate and Whitechapel, extended to Shoreditch at peak periods. The basic intervals are three trains an hour from each southern terminus and six from Whitechapel.

The line is the second of the four north–south cross London connections to be mentioned, but was of limited importance as the northern junction faced Liverpool Street. In 1960 there were three freight and a parcels trip to New Cross Gate and occasional seaside or football excursions. It ceased to function as a through route after 18 April 1966.

After a complex history of ownership and management the line was vested in London Transport after nationalization.

CHAPTER V

The Tubes

London knew how to use new means of transport.

S. E. RASMUSSEN.

THE steam-operated urban lines had failed to divert much of the rapidly growing traffic which threatened to choke the Central London streets and which led to the 1905 Royal Commission. In 1901 all railways in Greater London conveyed 357 million local passengers, while there were 811 million journeys by horse-tram and bus. But the Inner Circle and other lines were already working to capacity and some more efficient means of urban rail transport was needed.

The 'cut and cover' method had become much too costly. Deep tunnels, bored without disturbance to buildings and main services – 'tubes' in short – were the only answer. Their full success depended on a favourable combination of circumstances: the existence of a soft but water-tight stratum of London Clay; the invention by a South African engineer, J. H. Greathead, of a 'shield' which made the boring of a tube through the clay economically possible; the perfecting of the only practicable form of traction, electricity; and the provision of capital for works which even in 1900 would cost well over £250,000 a mile. Fortunately all these coexisted around 1900.

THE CITY & SOUTH LONDON

London's first tube was the Tower Subway beneath the Thames. Built by Peter Barlow, assisted by Greathead, it was opened in 1870. A small cable car on 450 yards of 2 foot 6 inch track was used at first, but the tunnel soon became a footway.

This was closed in 1894 when Tower Bridge was opened and the tunnel is now used for hydraulic power mains.

The Tower Subway was followed by numerous schemes, notably for providing Waterloo with better connections to the West End. However, capital was not forthcoming until Greathead

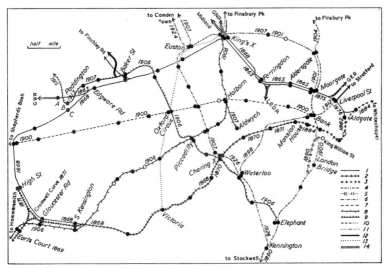

FIG. 12. The Underground lines of central London: 1, Metropolitan. 2, Metropolitan District. 3, Metropolitan & District Joint (City Lines). 4, City & South London. 5, City & South London (abandoned). 6, Charing Cross, Euston & Hampstead. 7, Central London. 8, Great Northern, Piccadilly & Brompton (Piccadilly). 9, Baker Street & Waterloo (Bakerloo). 10, Great Northern & City. 11, Waterloo & City. 12, London Transport. 13, The Victoria Line. 14, Main Line connections: A, Bishop's Road. B, Paddington (Bakerloo). C, Praed Street.

floated the City of London & Southwark Subway Company, which obtained powers in 1884 for a cable-worked tube from King William Street, the City approach to London Bridge, to the Elephant and Castle. Work started on the 1·25-mile line in 1886.

It was soon decided that an extension of 1·75 miles to Stockwell was necessary and powers were obtained in 1887. Next year the directors announced that electric traction would be used, and in 1890 another Act authorized a short extension to Clapham

Common. Then as now this was a great local traffic centre where routes from the outer suburbs converged and where traffic for the City could be diverted underground. By the same Act the company became the City & South London Railway.

Public service between King William Street and Stockwell began on 18 December 1890. The gauge was standard, but the tunnel diameter was only 10 feet 2 inches north of the Elephant and 4 inches wider to the south. There were four intermediate stations and at first a uniform fare of 2d. was charged. Though this was soon abandoned, the single class remained a characteristic of the tubes. In contrast first class lasted on the Inner Circle until 1940.

King William Street proving inconvenient, powers were obtained in 1893 for a northward extension from The Borough to The Angel. The new line was opened as far as Moorgate on 25 February 1900, when the King William Street appendix was closed. The Clapham Common extension went into service on 3 June 1900 and on 17 November 1901 The Angel was opened. In 1903 an extension from there to Euston via King's Cross was authorized and opened on 12 May 1907, bringing the route mileage to 7·26.

On the first day, 10,000 passengers passed the King William Street turnstiles and by early 1891, 15,000 a day were using the new line. By 1901, 13·4 million were carried over 6·9 miles of route and in 1911, 26·2 million over the full 7·26 miles. In 1905 the District, with 18 miles and running powers over as much again, was carrying 51·5 million. But road competition kept fares very low and dividends were disappointing.

Diminutive locomotive-hauled trains were used until the line was rebuilt between 1922 and 1924 to allow standard tube stock to run through over new connections at Camden Town and Kennington with the Hampstead Tube (p. 100). The section from Kennington to Euston has a 2½-minute through service at peak periods, but otherwise a six-minute shuttle service suffices.

THE CENTRAL LONDON

Shepherd's Bush is a traffic node on the west of Central London similar to Clapham Common in the south, and there were a number of projects to connect it by tube with the City along the busy artery of Oxford Street. The Central London was ultimately successful and was incorporated on 5 August 1891 to build a line from Wood Lane, just beyond Shepherd's Bush, to the Bank. Next year a short extension to Liverpool Street was authorized.

On 30 July 1900 the Shepherd's Bush–Bank section was opened and was extended to Wood Lane on 14 May 1908 and Liverpool Street on 28 July 1912. At first locomotives were used, but the vibration caused their replacement by multiple units, the standard method of tube operation ever since. A uniform fare was charged only for the first few years, but it remained 'The Twopenny Tube' to Londoners for decades. In 1901, the first full year of working, 41·2 million passengers were carried, and in 1904, 44 million. It was a more profitable venture than the c & slr.

THE HAMPSTEAD TUBE

The initial success of the c & slr resulted in a wave of tube promotion. The clr's Bill was presented in 1891 and next year there were a further six. One, incorporating the Charing Cross, Euston and Hampstead Railway, received the Royal Assent on 24 August 1893.

Money for the Hampstead tube was slow to be subscribed and no progress was made until Yerkes arrived in London and bought the powers for £100,000 in 1900. R. D. Blumenfeld, then editor of the *Daily Express*, remarked that Yerkes believed that by 1920 people would travel 20 or more miles to work by electric train and that the horse-bus was doomed. He added, 'Although he is a very shrewd man, I think he is a good deal of a dreamer'.

From now on we are in the familiar world of the holding company and the take-over bid. On 15 July 1901 Yerkes founded the Metropolitan District Electric Traction Company Ltd with money from Speyer Brothers, a New York financial house. With this firm the District and the Hampstead Tube were controlled. It was reconstituted the next year as Underground Electric Railways Company of London Ltd.

Work began on the Hampstead line in September 1903, the tunnels being built to a bore of 11 feet 8¼ inches, the tube standard. It was opened to public traffic throughout from Strand (beneath the forecourt of Charing Cross Station) to Golders Green, together with the branch from Camden Town to Highgate (now Archway), on 23 June 1907.

The line emerged into daylight to terminate in the fields bordering the Finchley Road. Most people were unimpressed by the wisdom of this move, but it is said a syndicate had already been formed to buy up the turnip fields before the announcement of the new line had affected land values. Thus at Golders Green first began the typical pattern of twentieth-century suburban development, the arrival of an electric railway in some untouched rural area, soaring land values, semi-detached villas and chain stores.

In 1908, 2·4 million passengers used Golders Green station and the population of Hendon Urban District was 29,000. In 1921, 12·6 million people passed through the station and Hendon now housed 56,000. After that passenger use levelled off, but consequent on the tube extensions of 1923–4 the population of Hendon grew to 72,000 in 1926. The 1961 figure was 151,500.

Golders Green station is typical of those on tube extensions in that its forecourt became a terminus of local bus routes. Road and rail co-ordination was begun, but with few exceptions has not been pursued to the logical conclusion of through fares to encourage passengers off the roads of Central London.

On 6 April 1914 the short extension from Strand to Charing Cross (Embankment) was opened to increase interchange facilities with the District and Bakerloo lines. In 1959 exchange traffic here amounted to 30·9 million out of a total passenger use of 49 million. On 20 April 1924 the connection with the City & South London at Camden Town went into use together with the complex non-conflicting junctions. On 13 September 1926 a southward extension from Charing Cross through Waterloo linked with the C & SLR at Kennington, and on the same day the 5-mile line from Clapham Common to Morden was opened.

The two tube systems were now completely integrated,

TUBE EXTENSION AND SUBURBAN SPRAWL

(17 and 18) *The great speed of suburban development in the inter-war years is vividly illustrated in these aerial photographs of Edgware. The upper view shows the terminus under construction; the lower was taken some three years after it was opened in 1924. The ex-GNR station can be distinguished in the left foreground with the Underground station and car-sheds behind.*

(19) *The first train (19 November 1923) from Hendon Central, on the Edgware Line, also left from now-forgotten rural surroundings.*

PADDINGTON

(20) *Brunel's original terminus was in the arches of the Bishop's Road overbridge. J. C. Bourne's print gives a good impression of its rural location on the far outskirts of London.*

(21) *'A unique work of art', as it has been called, Brunel and Wyatt's roof of the 1854 station still survives, though the low platforms have been raised. The deserted station sleeps through the peace of Good Friday 1900.*

(22) *A turning point in the Paddington story. The last Broad Gauge train for Cornwall leaves on 20 May 1892.*

though the c & sl Company survived until 1932, and they became the Morden–Edgware line, renamed the Northern Line in 1937. The original names of all the other underground lines have stubbornly survived vulgarly and officially till this day.

The Bakerloo is said to have originated in the wish of Westminster business men to enjoy the last hour's cricket at Lord's without leaving their offices unduly early. In any case there was an urgent need for a north–south connection across the West End. To meet this the Baker Street and Waterloo was floated during the 1892 tube boom and was incorporated on 28 March 1893 to build a 3-mile line. Waterloo would at last be in direct contact with the West End, but the lswr did not back the project as it had backed the Waterloo & City. As yet the West End was not such an important goal for commuter traffic. At Baker Street connection would be made with the Metropolitan's 'Extension', offering passengers on that line a direct route to the West End.

Money was short until provided by the London & Globe Finance Corporation and work did not begin until 1898. On 6 August 1900 powers were obtained for extensions to Paddington and to the Elephant, a distance of a mile in each case. But in January 1901 London & Globe failed. So the works lay derelict until in the following year Yerkes bought the interests for £360,000.

On 10 March 1906 the line between Baker Street and Kennington Road (now Lambeth North) was officially opened, and the short extension to the Elephant came into use on 5 August. Traffic was disappointing at first with only 20–30,000 passengers a day, but eventually picked up.

In contrast to the Northern Line there have been no further southward extensions, though local authorities have urged one to Camberwell and Lewisham. As late as 1960 the matter was referred to the Transport Users' Consultative Committee, which made an adverse report on the grounds of a declining population in the area and of the adequate facilities provided by

Southern Electric and buses. This would not be wholeheartedly endorsed by local residents and the project is still live.

The northern end of the Bakerloo was extended to Marylebone on 27 March 1907 and to Edgware Road on 15 June. Paddington was not reached until 1 December 1913, by which time the tubes and Inner Circle served all the main-line termini except Holborn and Fenchurch Street, and save in Clerkenwell no part of Central London was more than a quarter of a mile from an Underground station.

G. H. F. Nichols of the *Evening News* coined the line's portmanteau title, and Bakerloo the line has been ever since, even out at Watford and Stanmore. G. A. Sekon, who disliked the American invasion of London's transport, inveighed vainly against the word in the *Railway Magazine*: 'Some latitude is allowable perhaps to halfpenny papers . . . [but] to adopt its gutter title is not what we expect from a railway company.'

THE PICCADILLY

The Brompton & Piccadilly Circus Railway was incorporated on 6 August 1897 to build a 2-mile line from Piccadilly to Earl's Court. At the same time the District, for which some humorist in the advertising department had coined the title 'The Daylight Route', its sulphurous murk becoming ever more congested, obtained powers for a deep-level electric line between Earl's Court and Mansion House. In 1899 the smaller company were empowered to make connection, but nothing further was done about either project.

The Great Northern & Strand Railway was incorporated on 1 August 1899 to construct a tube from Wood Green Station via Finsbury Park to a terminus under the Strand at King's College. The GNR lent a benevolent interest but no financial aid. Like the LSWR, it was more concerned with City traffic, then the greater prize.

In 1901 both tube companies came under the control of the Yerkes Group, which sought powers to connect them physically and to abandon the section north of Finsbury Park. On 8 August 1902 they were merged, and by Act of 18 November became the Great Northern, Piccadilly & Brompton legally and the Piccadilly for everyday usage. The same Act authorized the transfer of the District's deep-level powers west of South Kensington.

The Piccadilly was opened throughout from Finsbury Park to Hammersmith (p. 134) at a formal ceremony on 15 December 1906. Between South Kensington and Earl's Court it was on the line of the District's deep-level scheme and at the former station the junction tunnels were built. But electrification of the District made further work redundant.

The merging of the original schemes left a curious vestigial appendix in the last ¼-mile of the GN & Strand between Holborn and Aldwych (Strand to 1915). This was opened on 30 November 1907 and has always been worked by a shuttle service of a single 2-car train. Used in the second world war as an air-raid shelter, it reopened on 1 July 1946. It now works only at peak hours, about a million passengers a year using it.

THE GREAT NORTHERN & CITY

The Great Northern & City originated in yet another effort by the GNR to develop suburban traffic north of Finsbury Park while avoiding congestion to the south (p. 157). It was in effect a cityward thrust by the GNR in the same way as the Waterloo & City was by the LSWR.

The company was incorporated on 28 June 1892 to build from a junction on the Canonbury Curve (from Finsbury Park to the NLR) to Moorgate. Through running was envisaged (a scheme by no means dead even in 1961) and the tunnels were 16 feet in diameter. As usual subscriptions were slow and work was not begun until August 1898.

The companies then fell out over through running. The quarrels were resolved, but the Canonbury Junction was not proceeded with. Instead the GNR built a terminus under its Finsbury Park station and leased it to the GN & CR. To this day the latter has no physical connection with the outside world except through a siding from its depot at Drayton Park.

The line was opened on 14 February 1904, and 306,992 passengers were carried in the first fortnight, a figure regarded as satisfactory. Lack of through running has always been regretted, but traffic increased after 31 December 1904, when the GNR introduced 'three route' seasons from its suburban stations, to Moorgate either over the GN & CR or over the Widened Lines, and to Broad Street.

The Metropolitan, anxious to strengthen its position vis-à-vis Underground Electric Railways, took over the line from 1 July 1913. Large-size stock was used until 13 May 1939, when it was replaced by standard tube trains. From 4 October 1964 services were cut back at Drayton Park to allow the tracks beyond to be taken over by the Victoria Line (p. 108). Passengers from ex-GN stations have two changes. With little intermediate traffic, the line's utility is much reduced.

UNDERGROUND

Up to 1914, with the exceptions of Golders Green and of South Kensington to Hammersmith, the tubes were concerned very much more with urban than suburban traffic. Each line maintained a 'rapid transit' shuttle service beneath city streets for short-distance passengers. During the 1920–60 period extensions converted them into suburban railways with a vast commuter traffic superimposed twice daily on to their urban traffic and thereby bringing new operating problems. The original Central Line was 6·5 miles beneath crowded streets from Shepherd's Bush to the Bank. Today it is possible to board a tube train at the lonely wayside station of Blake Hall in the heart of rural Essex and travel 36 miles by Central Line to the western outpost of Greater London, West Ruislip.

Yerkes died on 4 December 1905 and Edgar Speyer of Speyer Brothers succeeded him as chairman of Underground Electric. But much surprise was caused by the appointment as deputy and general manager (and also chairman of the District) of Sir George Gibb, general manager of the mighty North Eastern. It was proof that the Yerkes Empire was more than a mere group of bankrupt local lines.

But a new star was in the ascendant. Few men have left an indelible mark of their personalities on London's railways. We can single out here as exceptions Charles Pearson, father of the first underground line, Watkin and Forbes, whose mutual hatred quartered South London with such a network of lines that when these were electrified they kept the tubes out, and Yerkes himself. But the greatest of all was Albert Stanley, First Lord Ashfield, creator of London Transport.

Stanley was born Albert Knattries at Derby in 1874 of parents *en route* from Central Europe to the U.S.A. He returned to England Albert Stanley in 1907 to become general manager of the District after a successful career in United States tramways. On Gibb's retirement in 1910 he took over his offices.

In July 1907 Gibb had established the London Passenger Traffic Conference to co-ordinate fares and services of companies outside as well as within the Yerkes Group. When Stanley assumed office in 1910 he introduced the famous UndergrounD symbol used by all members of the Conference and the surrounding lozenge which still encloses 'London Transport'.

On 1 July 1910 the Piccadilly, financially the most successful, became the London Electric Railway and absorbed the Hampstead and Bakerloo companies. The change had no significance for the travelling public. For them it was the UndergrounD Group that mattered, for it was this group which co-ordinated fares, provided through bookings and built the magnificent exchange stations, Charing Cross, Leicester Square, Piccadilly and Oxford Circus among them.

Through the Common Fund Act of 1915 UndergrounD controlled London Electric Railways, the District, the Central London, the c & slr, most of the private tramway companies and the London General Omnibus Company, though all retained their legal identity. Headquarters were at 55 Broadway, which eventually became a skyscraper block over the Inner Circle station of St James's Park.

Only three large concerns stood aloof, the Metropolitan, the L.C.C. tramways and the Tilling bus group. But the UndergrounD, successfully controlled by Stanley, demonstrated the practical advantages of monopoly in city transport. It was thus the germ of one of the brain-children of the 1929–31 Socialist administration, the London Passenger Transport Board.

LONDON PASSENGER TRANSPORT BOARD

The L.P.T.B. was set up by the 1933 Act and was an example of the device of exercising monopoly through a public corporation. A board under the chairmanship of Lord Ashfield was appointed to control all road services and all underground rail services within an area of 1,986 square miles with an estimated population of 9·5 million. Only the suburban services of the main-line companies were excluded. In all the Board took over five railway companies, fourteen municipal tramways, three tramway companies and sixty-one bus companies. The Board's nominal capital was £109·8 million. In 1934 it owned 174 route miles of railways, with 3,072 electric cars, 84 locomotive-hauled coaches and 51 electric and 38 steam locos. In that year 315·8 million passenger journeys originated on L.P.T.B. railways and 525 million local journeys on main-line railways in the London Transport Area.

This was much larger than Greater London as we have defined it, though all London Transport railways are covered here. The scope of the constituent companies was also wider than the carriage of passengers. So we find the Board in its early days engaged in the carriage of freight – 3 million tons of goods and coal and 56,000 head of cattle in 1934. In places its activities were rural rather than urban. Steam-hauled trains waiting while their guards opened level-crossing gates contrasted rather oddly with the automation of the tubes.

All passenger bookings made between places within the Transport Area were pooled and divided in the proportions announced by the London Passenger Transport Arbitration Tribunal on 11 June 1935. The L.P.T.B. received 62 per cent (including road services) and the Southern 25·6 per cent. Even the extensive LNER suburban services brought their owners but 6 per cent. The LMS, then the owners of the Tilbury line, got 5·1 per cent and the GWR 1·3 per cent.

The L.P.T.B.'s main task was to weld the diverse constituents into a single co-ordinated system. Its secondary task was to raise capital for extensions into suburbs, particularly in the north-east, which had outgrown the existing transport system. But in addition numerous stations in Central London were rebuilt and all experienced considerable increases of traffic. The 9 million passengers passing through Leicester Square in 1907 grew to 27 million in 1935 and 32·4 million in 1959.

TABLE 7

TRAFFIC AT SOME PRINCIPAL INTERCHANGE
TUBE STATIONS – 1959
(*Figures in millions*)

	Originating and terminating	Exchange	Total
Bank and Monument*	22·7	14·7	37·4
Charing Cross	18·2	30·9	49·1
Leicester Square	16·8	15·6	32·4
Oxford Circus	27·1	13·2	40·3
Piccadilly	30·6	11·0	41·6

* Excluding Waterloo and City traffic.

At the eight stations in Table 8 there was a 10 per cent increase in originating journeys to 28·6 million in 1959 over 1938.

TABLE 8

GROWTH OF TRAFFIC AT REPRESENTATIVE TUBE STATIONS

	Millions of tickets issued, 1959	Percentage increase, 1938–1959	Percentage increase, 1931–8
Chancery Lane	2·7	−12	18
Green Park	3·0	40	41
Holborn*	5·0	−17	12
Hyde Park Corner†	1·6	13	33
Knightsbridge‡	3·3	25	24
Leicester Square	6·8	21	13
Marble Arch	4·4	36	48
Warren Street	1·8	−3	33
TOTALS	28·6	10	23

* Includes British Museum traffic in 1931.
† Includes Down Street traffic in 1931.
‡ Brompton Road traffic in 1931.

LONDON TRANSPORT

Under the terms of the 1947 Transport Act, the property and functions of the L.P.T.B. were vested in the British Transport Commission and administered by the London Transport Executive. The latter's first chairman was Lord Ashfield, who died in 1952. By 1959 rail journeys had risen to 669 million, a 116 per cent increase over 1934. Road journeys numbered 2,765 million.

Services withdrawn and lines closed by London Transport between 1933 and 1970 were negligible compared with the opening of new lines. But in spite of embarrassing traffic increases the only line opened in Central London between 1926 and 1968 is the tube from Liverpool Street to Stratford of 1946.

The tube system, particularly because of new traffic generated by constant extensions, was rapidly becoming overloaded on the sections within Central London. There were also some gaps in it. The planning schemes for Greater London therefore recommended radical improvements in the railways, most of them visionary rather than practicable. The B.T.C. were asked by the Minister of Transport to examine these proposals and a London Plan Working Party was set up in 1948. It suggested the construction of 49·25 miles of tube (the total then in operation was 66·75) as a first priority. These were in five 'routes', but only one, 'Route C', has yet come to fruition.

Now known as the 'Victoria Line', it was planned to run between Walthamstow and Victoria via King's Cross. Its purposes are to put north-east London on the one hand and Victoria on the other in closer and more convenient touch with the West End, to supplement the overcrowded Central Line, and above all to encourage more traffic off the streets.

London Transport obtained the necessary powers in 1955, but claimed the expected traffic would not cover interest charges, that the tube was a social necessity and that the Government should guarantee the interest. This the Government were reluctant to do, its policy being to count the economic and not the social cost of public transport. But on 20 August

1962 it approved and London Transport put the work in hand immediately.

The Victoria Line opened for public traffic in three stages, from Walthamstow to Highbury on 1 September 1968, to Warren Street on 3 November and on to Victoria on 7 March 1969. At all but one of the 12 stations there is interchange with LT or BR lines. The line's principal feature is the high degree of automation, including the automatic driving and control of its one-man crewed trains.

In 1966 the publication of the White Paper on Transport Policy indicated a move to the recognition that public transport investment should be justified on social as well as economic grounds in the same way as road improvements. The 1968 Transport Act gave powers to the Minister of Transport to make 75 per cent grants towards rail construction on the same terms as for road programmes, instead of merely guaranteeing loan interest. With grant-aid, the Victoria line was pushed on to Brixton, the civil-engineering work being finished in 1970. In November 1968 the London Transport Board announced it was seeking powers for a 'Fleet Line', crossing the Central Area from Baker Street to Fenchurch Street via Strand and Cannon Street, with possible extension to Lewisham.

Under the 1962 Transport Act the British Transport Commission was dissolved, and on 1 January 1963 an independent London Transport Board took office. But in subsequent years there was a growing recognition that in the planning process the factors of land use, roads and public transport were inseparable. This led to the London (Transport) Act of 1969, under which the Board was dissolved and the railways and 'red' buses vested in the Greater London Council and operated by a London Transport Executive. The 'green' buses and Green Line coaches were taken over by the National Bus Company.

It is too early to pass judgment, but at the time of writing it would appear the G.L.C. is more concerned with its road programme than with long-term consideration of the part rail transport must play in Greater London.

CHAPTER VI

Main Lines and Middlesex

Stanmore . . . looks over a country of little variety, though rich.

WILLIAM COBBETT.

THE GREAT WESTERN RAILWAY

IN 1835 London ended abruptly at Marble Arch. Beyond on the clay plain were large farms and a few small villages. In contrast, among the orchards and market gardens of the Thames gravels, a line of towns and high-class suburbs stretched out to Hounslow.

Through this area ran the Great Western Railway, incorporated on 31 August 1835 to connect Bristol with London. The Act envisaged the new company making a junction with the London & Birmingham at Kensal Green and sharing Euston. This was rendered impracticable by the GWR's subsequent decision to employ a gauge of 7 ft o¼ in. But the L & B had proved difficult, refusing security of tenure.

Instead a site was selected near Paddington village, in anticipation of Parliament sanctioning the change, which it did by Act of 3 July 1837. The line was opened to Maidenhead on 4 June 1838 and by 30 June 1841 through to Bristol. There were only a few large houses near the railway yards, but the neighbourhood became built over in the eighteen-fifties with large terrace houses interspersed with Gothic churches.

The small villages of Acton and Ealing were the only ones anywhere near the line, and West Drayton, 13¼ miles out, was the first station. Ealing and Hanwell stations (opened December 1838) were amidst fields and Hayes was reputedly the most backward part of Middlesex, where 'dirt, ignorance and darkness reign supreme' (*Hayes Past and Present*, E. Hunt, 1861). But new settlements soon began to grow up round all the stations as they were opened.

Of these Ealing is still characterized by its solid Victorian villas. Its 1841 population was 8,407. Growth was slow until 1871, when the numbers were 18,189. But with the service to the City over the Metropolitan begun in 1863 the town became more convenient to live in. In 1901 the inhabitants numbered 47,510.

But, though it had introduced season tickets in 1851, the GWR made no consistent effort to develop suburban traffic. An Ealing policeman told the L.C.C.'s inquiry of 1892 into workmen's services that he had to call numerous artisans at 3.30 a.m. to enable them to walk the four miles to Shepherd's Bush, the nearest station issuing workmen's tickets.

Most of the area served became extensively built over only during the present century and mainly because of tram and underground extensions. Ealing's population grew fivefold between 1901 and 1951. Hayes and Harlington grew from under 5,000 in 1911 to 67,912 in 1961.

Local employment opportunities are numerous. In 1952 there were 593 industrial firms in Acton employing 38,400 workers, in Ealing 507 employing 21,800 and in Hayes 148 employing 26,800. Thus job ratios are high, 182 in Acton, 86 in Southall and 121 in Hayes, and numbers working in Central London are small by South London standards, 15 per cent of Acton's working population, and only 7 per cent of Southall's and 4 per cent of West Drayton's.

It follows that even at peak hours station-to-station traffic is heavier than that to and from Paddington. In addition, although the majority of the factories use road transport, freight and parcels traffic looms large. In 1952 at the three adjacent stations of Southall, Hayes and West Drayton 89,500 tons of merchandise were forwarded and 318,000 tons received, as well as 401,000 tons of coal.

In 1871 the line was widened between Paddington and Westbourne Park and stations opened there and at Royal Oak. In 1878 a flyunder for the Hammersmith and City trains went into service west of Royal Oak. At least four lines were provided out to Southall by 1 October 1877 and on to West Drayton by 25 November 1878, the new lines being narrow-gauge only.

PADDINGTON

The original terminus was on the site of the present goods station. In 1839 there were 14 daily departures, but subsequent growth of traffic led to the building of the present Paddington. The departure side was opened on 16 January 1854 and the arrival side on 29 May. There were three departure and three arrival platforms, the two groups being separated by five sidings. In the middle years of the century trains were few and far between. In 1855 there were 20 daily departures, of which 9 called at the four intermediate stations to West Drayton.

The first narrow-gauge train left Paddington for the Birmingham line (via Oxford) on 1 October 1861. T. H. Wright (locomotive superintendent, Neath) said: 'Some of the Broad Gauge bigots wondered whether the train would reach its destination.' It did, only three minutes late, and carried with it the death sentence of the broad gauge.

On 10 January 1863 Bishop's Road station was opened on the north side. It was used by the frequent Metropolitan service, the Hammersmith & City trains after 1864, and a few of the GWR's infrequent suburban trains, including of course those to the City.

In June 1878 an additional arrival platform (No. 9) came into use. The central carriage sidings were also replaced by extra platforms in 1884 and 1893. After 1870 broad-gauge services began to decline. Of the 48 departures in 1878 (18 for beyond Maidenhead) there were 7 broad-gauge departures for Bristol and beyond, which included two of the most famous trains of mid-Victorian England, the *Flying Dutchman* and the *Zulu* (the title was later transferred to the 6.10 p.m. for Birmingham). There was also a solitary return trip from Windsor, said to have been retained in deference to Daniel Gooch, who lived there. But the broad gauge was long a-dying in the West and in June 1884 there were still 6 passenger and 2 freight departures. Then, as now, there were 'Ocean Specials' from Plymouth and seasonal broccoli and potato trains from Cornwall, and these were broad gauge.

The inevitable did not come until 1892. Friday, 20 May was the sad day ending Brunel's large vision. The last departure was the 5.0 p.m. for Plymouth, hauled by 4-2-2 *Bulkeley*, which returned with the last up train, 'The Mail', which arrived early next morning.

By 1903, 39 suburban (only 9 before 10.30 a.m.) and 64 main-line trains were arriving daily at Paddington and Bishop's Road and 9·2 million passengers used the stations. In 1909 work began on platforms 10, 11 and 12 under a new roof span, the work being completed in 1916. In 1933 platforms were lengthened, Bishop's Road was incorporated and colour-light signalling installed.

The station's Eastbourne Terrace façade is dreary in the extreme, in spite of its being the front and not the side. Paddington's glory is its great triple-arched roof, the result of a partnership between M. Digby Wyatt, the architect, and Brunel. It is, as Christian Barman says, 'a unique work of art, remarkable for many qualities'. Mid-Victorian Paddington is immortalized in W. P. Frith's painting, 'The Railway Station', of 1862. But though broad-gauge trains, crinolines and top hats have gone, the roof survives unchanged to echo the roar of diesel engines.

Prior to re-signalling in 1967–8 platforms 1–4 dealt with main-line departures, 5–7 were normally used by outer suburban trains, 8–11 were the main-line arrival platforms and 12 was normally used for parcels trains. At the through platforms of the former Bishop's Road, London Transport trains on the Hammersmith line use 13 and 16 and suburban trains to and from Slough 14 and 15. After that date all platforms were used for arrivals and departures, while LT trains, now segregated, used 15 and 16. In 1960, 104 trains left daily for places beyond Reading and 76 for there or nearer, the 180 trains carrying about 32,000 passengers, an average of 177 per train.

All London termini have their individualities, but Paddington is unique. Waterloo is brash and parvenu, but Paddington is an aristocrat, and not at all a decayed one. In 1961 it was stated that Paddington alone of London stations was never short of platform staff – tipping was so lavish.

Suburban traffic increased after 1930 and by 1952 there were 33 arrivals before 10.30 a.m., but this is small by London standards; during the busiest evening hour only 10 trains leave with 6,000 passengers, and commuters ride in comfort out to their Thames-side villas. Holiday traffic is very heavy and business men travel to industrial Bristol and South Wales. But it is for the grassy western shires and their cathedral cities one really feels the trains are bound, carrying archdeacons, colonels' widows, and 'Backwoods Peers' returning thankfully from brief visits to the Lords.

THE GREAT WESTERN & GREAT CENTRAL JOINT LINE

Fierce competition with the LNWR for the Birmingham traffic led the GWR to shorten its lengthy route through Oxford. The Great Central wanted an alternative access to London, since the Metropolitan's line was congested and heavily graded (p. 139). They made common cause, and in 1897 obtained powers for a line from Old Oak Common through the Chilterns to High Wycombe and beyond. As far as Northolt Junction, where the line from Marylebone would join, it would be owned by the GWR, but beyond by the GW & GC Joint Committee, incorporated by Act of 1 August 1899.

In 1903 the new line was used for a service out to Park Royal during the Royal Agricultural Society's Show. Next year a regular service of auto trains was started between Westbourne Park and Greenford, but through GWR goods traffic did not start until 4 April 1910 and passenger traffic on 1 July.

In 1905 Old Oak, 3·5 miles from Marble Arch, was on the edge of London and beyond the line traversed '23 miles of verdant tranquillity', thus being used almost solely for long-distance traffic. In that year the Royal Agricultural Society abandoned their new permanent show ground at Park Royal, and during the first world war factories were erected on it by the Ministry of Munitions. Between the wars these were converted to civilian use and a large industrial estate grew up. In 1952 B. A. Bates found there were 302 plants, of which Guinness's brewery is the best known, employing 31,680 workers, making it 'the most important industrial area of

London'. In that year Park Royal goods depot handled 246,000 tons of merchandise and 100,000 tons of coal. Still important for wagon-load traffic, in 1968 it became a freightliner terminal. At Greenford 75,000 tons of raw materials were received annually by rail for glass bottle manufacture.

Brentham Garden City Estate dates from 1911, but in no other area a comparable distance from London was development so slow. In the hamlet of West End (Northolt) only three houses were built between 1837 and 1935. It was not until the late 1950s that most of the area out to West Ruislip had become built over.

The GWR provided a number of halts in addition to Greenford and West Ruislip stations and served them by infrequent auto trains right up to 1947, in spite of the rising tide of suburban development after 1935. But, as part of the 1935 scheme to improve transport in London (p. 187), the GWR were to build an extra pair of tracks from Acton on the Ealing and Shepherd's Bush line (p. 116) to Denham for the exclusive use of Central Line tube trains.

After war's delays, the widened lines were opened to Greenford on 30 June 1947 and on to West Ruislip on 21 November 1948. The section to Denham was not proceeded with. Tube trains handle all traffic east of West Ruislip, while the growing traffic beyond has been concentrated on Marylebone. Since 1967 main line traffic is greatly reduced.

BRANCHES

The HAMMERSMITH & CITY, 2·5 miles, was opened on 13 June 1864 by the GWR as a double line of mixed gauge from Green Lane Junction (the site of Westbourne Park) to the growing high-class suburb of Hammersmith. Skirting the newly built-up area, the only intermediate stations were Notting Hill (Ladbroke Grove) and Shepherd's Bush. A good service of through trains to the City made the district popular and Latimer Road (1868) and Goldhawk Road (1914) were opened to serve neighbourhoods which were fully built up by 1890. On 1 July 1864 a spur was opened from Latimer Road Junction to the West London line at Uxbridge Road Junction.

Improved relations with the Metropolitan led to the line's being vested jointly in the two companies from 15 July 1867. Thereafter the Metropolitan provided the basic service, broad gauge being removed beyond Latimer Road Junction in August 1868 and to the West London in March 1869. The H & C then became virtually a branch of the Inner Circle, though the GWR ran some through trains, notably a Paddington –Brighton service in 1906–7. On 5 November 1906 the line was electrified, jointly owned stock being used.

There are now 8 LT trains an hour each way between Hammersmith and Whitechapel (Barking at peak periods). The district served has much decayed, and some of the worst slums in London may be seen from the train windows.

The EALING & SHEPHERD'S BUSH railway, 4 miles 15 chains, was authorized in 1905. The scheme envisaged a branch from the main line at Ealing Broadway to Shepherd's Bush, with a suburban terminus there including exchange facilities with the Central London Tube. There would also be a connection with the Northolt line at North Acton junction and with the West London just north of Wood Lane.

Probably as a result of the decision to enlarge Paddington, the terminus project was abandoned. The new line was cut back to Wood Lane, the Central London obtaining powers in 1911 for a short extension to an end-on junction with it. The Ealing & Shepherd's Bush was opened for goods on 16 April 1917. Tube trains were projected over it on 3 August 1920, then running through open country which has since been fully built up and largely industrialized.

The line starts from two bay roads in Ealing Broadway and was quadruple from North Acton Junction to White City, the northern pair not being electrified. The latter were used by through freight trains and by milk trains for Wood Lane. The lines were closed on 9 March 1964, trains being diverted. Wood Lane was superseded in 1947 by the new White City station. From Marble Arch there is a six-minute service to North Acton, whence alternate trains go to Ealing and to West Ruislip. Three times as many trains run in peak periods.

The GREENFORD LOOP was authorized in 1897 as a 1·5-mile double line with a triangular junction at each end from

WILLESDEN JUNCTION

(23) *The tiny roadside station opened on Acton Lane in 1841 or 1842.*
(24) *Willesden Junction about 1880. This is the station opened on the present site in 1866 and rebuilt in 1894.*

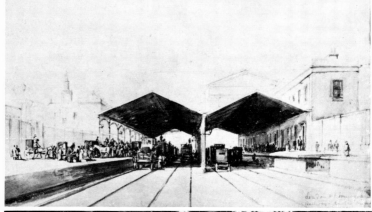

EUSTON

(25) *The propylaeum, flanked by two hotel blocks, formed a dignified entrance to the new terminus. The Age of Elegance and the Age of Steam had met to adorn London.*

(26) *The train sheds beyond, however, were rudimentary and mean.*

(27) *A photograph taken about 1933 of No. 7 platform, the original departure platform shown in the middle picture.*

Greenford on the Northolt line to West Ealing on the main line. In 1903 it was used by the roundabout service for the Royal Show (p. 114), but regular services did not begin until 1 May 1904, since when it has been a useful link for through freight and an occasional passenger special. The exiguous local traffic was maintained by an auto train service between Ealing Broadway, Greenford and beyond. On electrification at Greenford the trains, diesel railcars since 1958, were terminated there. Lying as it does behind the marshy Brent valley, the district was late in developing. But after 1925 housing estates and factories grew up in Perivale, and traffic at the three intermediate halts has grown enormously, in contrast with its rural operating methods.

The BRENTFORD branch, 4 miles long, was built from Southall to Brentford Dock to provide a water outlet on the Thames for the broad gauge. The Great Western & Brentford Company was incorporated on 14 August 1855, leased to the GWR in 1859 and vested in it on 1 January 1872. The branch was opened for goods on 18 July 1859, and passenger traffic began on 1 May 1860 but was never important. It was more convenient to reach London by LSWR, while trams and buses captured the local traffic. The infrequent auto trains were withdrawn on 4 May 1942.

But the line has always been important for goods transferred to and from water and in later years in connection with local factories. In 1860, 58,000 tons of goods and minerals were carried. In 1956, 180,054 tons of merchandise and 20,572 tons of minerals were dealt with at Brentford Dock (closed 31 December 1964). From here vehicles and spares, steel tubes, copper wire, tinplate, china clay and food-stuffs were shipped, and steel, timber, wood pulp and feeding-stuffs landed. Brentford Town, serving the factories along the Great West Road, handled in 1956 38,355 tons of goods and 193,510 tons of minerals.

Originally the branch was single, but in October 1861 a narrow-gauge track was laid down. The broad-gauge line was narrowed in 1876 and the line worked as an orthodox double track. Today it is single between Southall and Firestone Box (Brentford Town), beyond which it has been lifted.

The UXBRIDGE branch was authorized on 16 July 1846 when the Great Western & Uxbridge was incorporated.

Opened from West Drayton on 8 September 1856 as a single line 2·625 miles long, it was narrowed in 1871 and doubled in 1880 (*see* p. 141 for its subsequent history).

Also from West Drayton is the branch to STAINES WEST, a single line opened to Colnbrook on 9 August 1884 and to Staines, where a farmhouse was used for the station offices, on 2 November 1885. A temporary connection with the Southern was put in at Staines in 1942. The branch was rural rather than suburban and was worked by a diesel car until closure to passengers on 29 March 1965. Colnbrook is an important goods depot serving the new Poyle Industrial Estate. In 1958, 30,000 tons of merchandise were dealt with, but only 15,000 passengers.

THE LONDON & NORTH WESTERN RAILWAY

The first section of the London & Birmingham Railway was opened from Euston Square to Boxmoor on 20 July 1837, the full service to Birmingham beginning on 17 September 1838. On 16 July 1846 the London & North Western was formed by an amalgamation of several companies, including the L & B.

Paradoxically the Premier Line, so important to Britain's economy as a whole, had probably the least direct influence upon the growth of nineteenth-century London of all the railways entering it. The Company was interested only in its vast long-distance traffic and did even less than the GWR to foster suburban traffic. Its chief interest in such associates as the NLR, West London and NSWJ was in the opportunities they provided for developing through traffic.

EUSTON

Euston Square had been laid out about 1815 on land belonging to the Fitzroy family, a branch of the ducal house of Grafton with a seat at Euston Hall in Suffolk. On Drummond Street the L & B erected the famous *propylaeum*, the Age of Elegance applied to the transport revolution. But the portico gave access to mean train sheds. Sir John Summerson, the architectural critic, comments: 'As an approach to the modest little station building . . . [the portico] was manifestly absurd.'

But it was an attempt, rare in England, to make a great station a worthy ornament of the city it served.

The range of buildings behind the portico was begun in 1846. Within was the magnificent waiting-room, the Great Hall, designed by twenty-four-year-old P. C. Hardwick (son of Philip Hardwick, designer of the portico) and famous for the breadth of the unsupported ceiling and the stairway up to the noble Shareholders' Room. But behind lay a dark warren of offices.

The arrival (the 1962 No. 3) and departure (No. 6) platforms and intervening sidings were covered by a low roof, raised in 1872, being considered 'too squat and shed like'. Platforms 9 and 10 date from 1840, the former being 'The York' from its original function of dispatching trains for the Hudson Empire via Rugby.

Thenceforward Euston grew hideously and chaotically. In 1861 there was still only one arrival platform, though five (Nos. 6–10) were available for departures. The original turnplates for marshalling the tiny fourwheeled coaches were still in place and G. P. Neele, one of the LNWR's greatest officers, says 'the clatter incidental on a train coming in or going out over these tables was amazing'.

In 1871–3 platforms 1 and 2 were built for arrivals and in 1892 four long departure platforms were provided. These had separate entrances and were styled the West Station. But only certain trains were scheduled to leave from here and chaos resulted from cabs arriving at the wrong entrance and trying to get round to the right one. A director complained 'you have turned Euston into a Waterloo'. Eventually the separate entrance was closed except to parcels vans. In 1891 the 'wooden platform' (Nos. 4 and 5) came into use.

The Euston of 1962 had fifteen platforms, some rarely used. Nos. 1–3 were for main-line arrivals, 4 and 5 were electrified and 6 used for both arrivals and departures. No. 7, still 'the Kensington' as it was used for one of the few suburban services of the early LNWR, and 8 were too short, save for an occasional Tring local or parcels loading. Nos. 9 and 10 were chiefly, and 11 solely, used by parcels trains and 12–15 were the main-line departure platforms.

Judged on statistics of train and passenger numbers Euston

has always been one of the quietest London termini, as it has
lacked a heavy suburban traffic. On a 1960 day commuters
leaving between 4.0 and 7.0 p.m. numbered only 4,384. But
it has been well known for the important expresses it deals
with and could usually give an impression of intense activity,
for travellers encumbered with children and baggage, and
mountains of parcels and mails all take up much more space
than do commuters.

In 1841 there were 13 departures daily, only the 3.0 p.m. for
Aylesbury terminating short of Rugby. By 1878 there were 38
departures and even by 1903 arrivals totalled only 78, of which
36 were considered suburban.

This was the station that passed with the steam age. Of it
Sir John Summerson said: 'The station itself . . . is the great
museum piece, commemorating as no other structure in the
world the moment of supreme optimism in the marriage of
steam and progress.' But passengers and railwaymen can only
welcome the convenience of the new station, the first complete
reconstruction of a London terminus since that of Waterloo.

Work started in earnest in 1963 and the station was formally
opened by the Queen on 14 October 1968. From 3 January
1966 all trains were electrically hauled. There are 15 passenger
platforms, 9 and 10 being equipped for D.C. trains. There are
also 4 long and 2 short parcels platforms. The main feature is
the great concourse. With its associated passenger facilities, it
has the functional utility and architectural impersonality that
render it indistinguishable from any modern airport or
railway station anywhere in the world. The 15-acre flat roof
and unimpressive frontage in overcrowded London are an
appalling indictment of contemporary planning. The L.C.C.
refused commercial development over the station, while
allowing free rein near by.

After electrification, passenger traffic expanded rapidly, over 40
per cent in the first year. In 1969 expresses left for Birmingham
every 30 minutes from 4.15 to 7.15 p.m. In 1965 Northampton
had no service between 8.45 and 11.45 a.m., but electrification
brought an hourly service. In 1969 a minimum of 69 expresses
left daily, together with 121 A.C. outer suburban trains and
D.C. locals to Watford.

MAIN LINE FROM EUSTON

Natural obstacles were heavier than on the GWR. From the platform ends at Euston the line rises for a mile on a deep cutting up the 1 in 77 Camden Bank. Considered impracticable for locomotives, cable haulage was used from 1837 to 1844. For many years after that trains were piloted. If the assisting engine was going no farther than the summit it would be slipped and would draw ahead, the driver waving to a trusted points-man, who would switch the pilot into a siding and reverse the points for the train. From 1 January 1869 less spectacular assistance in the rear was provided.

At Camden the L & B laid out its main yards and originally planned the passenger terminus for this remote spot. Railway yards are the principal element in the landscape of St Pancras Borough. Not only are they the main source of employment, but they are largely responsible for depressing land values and spoiling amenities.

The complex layout at the approach to Primrose Hill tunnel (1,220 yards), piercing the Hampstead Ridge, dates from 1922. G. F. A. Wilmot has pointed to the 'elbow bends' by which this and subsequent lines crossed the ridge in order to shorten tunnels and reduce gradients.

Beyond, the line traversed the width of the clay plain, making for the Hatch End gap in the South Herts Plateau before crossing the Chilterns by the Gade and Bulbourn valleys and the Tring Gap. Deep cuttings were needed through the gaps. Harrow (1831 population 3,861) was the only place of consequence short of the market town of Watford (5,293 in 1831) and was given the only intermediate station.

Until 1844 a suburban service was non-existent and was very sparse after that. G. P. Neele found out the hard way. 'On one occasion, travelling from Euston by a train I fully expected to call at Kilburn [his home] I found myself landed at Harrow about 5.0 p.m.; there was no train due back until 7.0 p.m.'

In the 1850's the LNWR offered free seasons up to fifteen years to commuters buying property near Harrow. But the train service was unattractive and not until the late 1860's, when there was a good NLR service to the City from Willesden Junction, was there significant growth in nearby Harlesden.

On 1 July 1858 a 'third line' (up goods) was completed between Watford and Primrose Hill. By 1875 there was also a 'fourth line', and all four tracks were being used by passenger trains. The extra tracks were gauntleted through Primrose Hill tunnel until a new bore came into use on 1 June 1879. On that date it was possible to put on an hourly local service to Watford and in 1885 workmen's tickets were introduced at the stations out to Willesden.

By 1900 suburban traffic was growing in spite of the LNWR, and next year tube extensions were authorized from Golders Green to Watford. Action was forced on the North Western, which started work on the 'New Lines' to develop suburban traffic beyond Willesden. They were opened between Kensal Green tunnel and Harrow (where a well-designed new station was built) on 15 June 1912 and on to Watford on 10 February 1913. The original intention was to extend them, from South Hampstead in a deep-level tube, to a new station below Euston. But in 1911 it was arranged for Bakerloo trains to be projected over them. On 31 January 1915 the Bakerloo was extended from Paddington to Kilburn Park and on 11 February to join the LNWR at Queen's Park. The tube trains ran to Willesden from 10 May and to Watford (weekdays only) from 16 April 1917.

Operation of the LNWR's electric trains had to await the completion of the third Primrose Hill bore. The full service from Euston and Broad Street was not inaugurated until 10 July 1922. In 1961 the basic service to Watford was 8 trains an hour. The off-peak Broad Street service ceased in 1962, and from 14 June 1965 the LT trains terminated at Queen's Park, leaving only the 4 trains an hour from Euston. A.C. electric haulage of main line trains was extended from Bletchley to Willesden (freight) in September 1965 and to Euston for some passenger trains in November.

WILLESDEN JUNCTION

In 1841 or 1842 a tiny roadside station was opened on Acton Lane and enjoyed a service of two up and two down trains. Neele says passengers believed it was provided for the sole benefit of Captain Huish, who lived near by. Certainly it was a long way from the small village of Willesden. On 1 September 1866 it was replaced by Willesden Junction, where the West London and NSWJ diverged and where the Hampstead Junction threw two connections across the main line to join them. Low-level platforms were provided as well as high-level ones on both connections.

The two groups of high-level platforms were quite separate, and from each was a 30-minute service to the City. Passengers were given no indication from which the next train would be leaving, so with this and the labyrinth of entrances and passages, the station was known variously as 'Bewildering Junction' or 'The Wilderness'. On 12 August 1894 a rebuilt station was opened with a single group of high-level platforms.

New Lines station is an island with a stairway up to the wide island platform on the Richmond line. The main line station was a depressing place with seven platforms and two bays, served in 1961 only by 28 outer suburban trains. These ceased to call after 3 December 1962 and the station was demolished for electrification. The extensive marshalling yards are the main terminal of electrically hauled freight trains from the North-West. On the site of the steam sheds is the freightliner terminal, operational from 29 August 1967 and greatly enlarged in 1969. Near by, the 'Proler' installation reduces cars to pellets of scrap for railing to steelworks, while bulk chemicals are handled at the former goods depot. All this is indicative of changing rail freight patterns.

SUBURBAN GROWTH

Thus LNWR policy and Middlesex clay inhibited London's north-western spread. Neele says of the mid sixties, '[south of the Thames] a residential element had very largely grown up at almost all stations, but along the North Western system there was hardly any growth'.

Kilburn and Kensal Green grew between 1860 and 1900 as depressing extensions of Paddington, and Queen's Park was laid out at the end of that period as an experiment in better quality working-class housing. There was some building at Harlesden and in 1875 Stonebridge Park was 'a cluster of sixty or eighty smart new villas for City Men'. But the expansion of Willesden and Wembley was initiated mainly by the Metropolitan and the trams.

Willesden grew from 3,879 in 1861 to 15,869 in 1871. But by 1901 it housed 114,582. But in 1892 the L.C.C. reported: 'The North Western and Great Western touch Willesden Junction and probably no part of London is so poorly provided with workmen's trains.'

Farther out there was little development until after electrification. But after 1920 it became spectacular. Factories sprang up in Willesden and Wembley (especially on the grounds of the 1924 Exhibition), and all along the New Lines villas multiplied and new stations opened. Carpenders Park, opened in 1914 as a wooden halt to serve a golf course, dealt with 200,000 passengers in 1937. In 1957, at the newly rebuilt station (1952) sandwiched between an L.C.C. and a speculative estate, 1·3 million ordinary and 32,011 season tickets were sold and 361 trains a day called.

BRANCHES

On 25 June 1886 the HARROW & STANMORE (absorbed in 1899) was incorporated to build a single-track branch, 2 miles long. Opened on 18 December 1890, 'its construction resulted in a very considerable growth of residential buildings around the terminus' (Neele). During the 1930's the area was built over, but Stanmore, more conveniently served by the Metropolitan branch (p. 145), was closed to passengers on 15 September 1952, the shuttle service terminating at Belmont (opened 1932) until closure on 5 October 1964.

On 3 July 1860 the WATFORD & RICKMANS-WORTH received powers for 4·5 miles of single line from Watford Junction to the small market town of Rickmansworth, with its silk mill and watercress beds. Opened on 1 October 1862, it was vested in the LNWR in 1881.

At Bushey station the New Lines were diverted away from the main line to make a triangular connection with the Rickmansworth branch at Croxley Green Junction, whence it was doubled to Watford Junction and the High Street rebuilt as an island platform. The Junction was enlarged and now has five electric platforms, four main-line ones, and two through ones and a bay on the St Albans branch.

The Act of 26 July 1907, authorizing the New Lines, also sanctioned a short single line from Croxley Green Junction to CROXLEY GREEN, which was opened for passengers on 15 June 1912.

Electric trains began running to Croxley Green on 30 October 1922 and to Rickmansworth on 26 September 1927. The passenger service to the latter was withdrawn on 3 March 1952, and freight facilities beyond Goodyear Tyre siding in May 1966. Consent to closure of Croxley Green was refused and an exiguous peak-period service plies from Watford Junction.

THE WEST LONDON AND THE WEST LONDON EXTENSION

The Birmingham, Bristol & Thames Junction was incorporated in 1836 to connect the London & Birmingham and the GWR with the navigable Thames. In 1840 it became the West London and, after much delay, on 27 May 1844 it opened a 2·5-mile single line of mixed gauge and of rudimentary stations from West London Junction on the LNWR at Willesden, across the GWR on the level at Wormwood Scrubs, and on to the basin of the short Kensington Canal. The district was then open country and the line was so much lampooned in *Punch* as leading from nowhere to nowhere that it became 'Mr Punch's Railway'.

A half-hourly passenger service was started – with no connections! It was impossibly lavish and its withdrawal on 30 November was no surprise. Not only was traffic sparse – it was alleged a winkle-seller was the only passenger on the first train – but also the GWR were obstructive. The West London's Minutes of 25 October 1844 tell a sorry story. The 5.55 p.m. from Kensington was delayed so long at the crossing that it did not reach West London Junction until 7.0 p.m. and the solitary passenger had missed the last train on to Harrow. He was brought back to Kensington 'very much disappointed and dissatisfied' and hired a post-chaise at the Company's expense. The affair was an illuminating commentary on contemporary communications in West London.

In 1860 the GWR crossing was replaced by a bridge, but the line remained little used until 1863 when the West London Extension was opened on 2 March, allowing Mr Punch's Railway to reach somewhere at last.

Jointly owned by the LNWR and GWR (one-third each) and

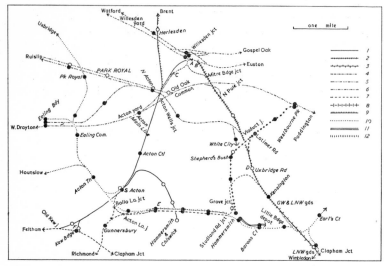

FIG. 13. The railways of west London: 1, North & South Western Junction Railway. 2, West London Railway. 3, West London Extension Railway. 4, LNWR. 5, GWR. 6, GWR—Ealing & Shepherd's Bush. 7 and 8, LSWR. 9, Midland. 10, District. 11, Piccadilly. 12, Central London. A, N & SW Junction. B, West London Junction. C, N & SW Old Oak Junction. D, GWR and LNWR goods depots. E, Turnham Green station. F, Midland goods depot.

the LSWR and LBSCR (one-sixth each), the West London Extension was authorized in 1859 as a double-track line of mixed gauge linking the WLR with Clapham Junction. The two northern lines leased and doubled the WLR.

At various times connections were laid in with the Ealing & Shepherd's Bush (p. 116), the Hammersmith & City (p. 115), the GWR main line from North Pole Junction and the Hampstead Junction at Willesden (p. 77). The LSWR branch from Richmond (p. 129) came in at the north end of Kensington

station, and at the southern end there were connections with the
LSWR, the Brighton and the Chatham.

This multiplicity of connections led to considerable development of transfer freight traffic between the northern and the
southern lines, while the former also opened depots south of
the river. In spite of the equivalent possibilities for through
passenger traffic, this did not begin until 1904 and never
attained large proportions. Most spectacular of all was the rise
and decay of suburban traffic.

KENSINGTON had but one platform until 1869, when
it was rebuilt in LNWR style with two long platforms, each with
a bay at each end, and served by loops off the through roads
with scissors connections in the middle. At the same time it was
named Addison Road, though in Russell Road.

From 1 April 1863 the GWR operated a service between
Southall and Victoria until 22 March 1915, broad-gauge trains
being replaced in 1866. On 1 July 1864, a broad-gauge service
from the Hammersmith & City was put on. On 1 August 1872
this became part of the 30-minute MIDDLE CIRCLE
between Moorgate and Mansion House. In September 1867
the LNWR inaugurated a 30-minute service between Broad
Street and Kensington (later Victoria LBSCR), extending it to
Mansion House on 1 February 1872 to become the OUTER
CIRCLE. This was augmented by trains from Euston or
Willesden to various destinations south of the river. A LSWR
service was established from Richmond to Waterloo and to
Clapham Junction on 1 January 1869 (p. 130).

Addison Road thus became the key point in West London
suburban services, and was soon surrounded by large houses
spreading over the fields from Kensington and Chelsea. Today
they are rather fallen from grace south of Cromwell Road, but
are almost as superior as ever to the north. From them emerged
frock-coated business men to board their trains of four-wheeled
coaches hauled by diminutive tank engines to the City by
routes inconceivable today.

Addison Road epitomized the age of steam, gaslight and
horse-cabs, and its glory died with them. Underground and
buses offered direct routes to West End and City and local
north–south passengers deserted rail for road.

Even so, 4·1 million passengers used the station in 1903 and it shared in the first period of electrification. On 5 November 1906 electric trains took over the Middle Circle (curtailed at Earl's Court on 1 July 1900 and at Addison Road on 1 February 1905). The Outer Circle, also turned back at Earl's Court because of congestion on the District from 1 January 1909, was replaced by a Willesden–Earl's Court service in 1912. Then, on 1 May 1914, District electric trains were introduced, replaced on 22 November by LNWR ones.

Between the wars a steam service was still provided by the Southern between Clapham Junction and Addison Road, supplemented by a few LMSR trains from Willesden to Clapham Junction. By 1938 passenger user at Addison Road had shrunk to 1·3 million, a figure which included exhibition traffic which reached 30,000 a day. War hastened the demise of the now uneconomic services. The advertised steam services ceased on 20 October 1940 and the electric ones, LMSR from Willesden and LT now from Edgware Road, on 3 and 20 October respectively.

On 19 December 1946 Addison Road became Kensington (Olympia) and reopened on exhibition days for an LT shuttle service from Earl's Court. In 1968 two passenger trips still came from Clapham Junction and about 30 freight trains passed each way daily, but the route never realized its potential for through passenger traffic. In 1904 services from the North to Kent and Sussex resorts were inaugurated, but daily services ceased in 1939. Advertised holiday trains continued to run and special workings are common. Increased importance came to Kensington after 24 May 1966 when the Motorail terminal was opened with four platforms. In 1968 there were up to 79 departures weekly. If the Channel Tunnel is built, still more traffic might be brought to the line.

THE NORTH & SOUTH WESTERN JUNCTION AND ITS ASSOCIATED LINES

In 1851 the North & South Western Junction was authorized to link the eponymous railways by 3·75 miles of double line from Willesden (N & SW Junction) to Old Kew Junction on the Hounslow Loop. Neele says it was promoted by Southampton interests and neglected by the main lines, T. C. Mills, goods manager at Camden, preferring to cart goods across London. Eventually Archibald Scott of the LSWR realized its potential value and arranged for his company to work the freight traffic.

This began on 15 February 1853 and local passenger services, always the NLR's concern, on 1 August. The district was completely rural and traffic was light at first. In 1858 trains were extended on to Twickenham and in 1863 to Kingston. To avoid reversals curves were opened on 1 February 1862, one to New Kew Junction and the other by-passing Barnes station.

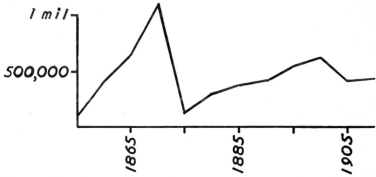

FIG. 14. Passenger traffic on the N & SW Junction. The peak in 1870 is probably due to the opening of the line to Richmond and the subsequent decline to competition from other routes thereto.

On the former a station (Kew Bridge from 1868) was built, which later became an important bus and tram centre.

The route on from Kew Bridge was so indirect that the LSWR obtained powers in 1864 for a 3-mile line from South Acton Junction (the site of the present station) to Richmond (New), a terminus adjoining the LSWR's Old Station. It was opened on 1 January 1869, after which NLR trains ran alternately to Richmond over the new line and to Kew Bridge only. The Barnes curve was abandoned.

On the same day the LSWR opened a 3·25-mile branch from the Acton–Richmond line at Gunnersbury through Hammersmith (Grove Road) to Addison Road. At Hammersmith two connections were provided, with the Hammersmith & City at Grove Junction, opened on 1 June 1870, and with the District at Studland Road Junction opened seven years later.

At the northern end of the NSWJ were three links, the main one, with the Hampstead Junction (p. 77), being opened in 1860. Then, on 1 October 1868, the DUDDING HILL LOOP was opened to goods trains between Acton Wells Junction (0·75 mile south of Willesden) and the Midland at Welsh Harp (where there was a station from 1870 to 1903). A triangle here was completed by a spur to Cricklewood (opened in 1870 as Child's Hill). This 3·75 mile link was promoted by the Midland and South Western Junction, a concern not to be confused with the better known Wiltshire company, incorporated in 1864 and absorbed by the Midland in 1874. It has always been an important freight link, the trains being worked by both the Midland and the LSWR and their successors, and is much used by passenger specials. At Acton Wells the GWR opened a spur from their main line. This is traversed by numerous through freight trains, and was used for a Southall–Willesden passenger service between 1888 and 1912.

The value of the NSWJ and the closely associated Acton–Richmond line was greatly enhanced by these connections. Over the years suburban trains of six companies worked into Richmond. Since the town was apparently adequately served by the Windsor line to Waterloo, some explanation of its attraction is necessary.

In the 1860's Richmond was the first place of consequence beyond Kensington and Chelsea, so was one of the few possible termini. It was one of the chief riverside towns and was already becoming a high-class dormitory suburb, from which the prosperous commuters were finding the journey on to the City from Waterloo tedious. Finally, Richmond and Kew were great centres for Londoners' day outings.

The NLR provided a 30-minute service from Broad Street, alternate trains being for Richmond and for Kew Bridge. In 1912 the erstwhile Outer Circle was diverted down the NSWJ, doubling the frequency of service. On its part, the LSWR inaugurated an hourly service from Richmond to Addison Road, trains continuing alternately to Ludgate Hill and Waterloo via the West London Extension. Later the frequency declined and the service ceased after 3 June 1916. GWR and Metropolitan trains arrived at Richmond via Grove

Junction, but as this connection was never electrified, the Metropolitan service ceased at the end of December 1906, when the Hammersmith & City was converted, and the GWR steam service ceased at the end of December 1910.

The Midland operated unsuccessfully and intermittently over the NSWJ between 1875 and 1902, after which the two intermediate stations on the Dudding Hill Loop were permanently closed to passengers. A SUPER OUTER CIRCLE (1878–1880) ran from St Pancras to Earl's Court via Dudding Hill and the LSWR's Acton Curve, which had completed the triangle North of Gunnersbury in 1878.

On 1 August 1905 the District service to Richmond was converted to electric traction, and on 1 October 1916 the LNWR followed suit with the Broad Street–Kew Bridge and Richmond service. On 12 September 1940 all the Kew Bridge trains were withdrawn. Richmond now has a basic service of three LMR and four LT trains an hour. Gunnersbury, now the basement of an office block, achieved notoriety on 8 December 1954 when the roof of its island platform was blown off by a freak tornado.

Riverside location and Georgian architecture give Richmond and Kew much charm and inflated property values. North of the river houses and gardens are smaller and Acton is heavily industrialized, the whole area served becoming built up between 1890 and 1914. The NSWJ, though leased to the LNWR and the South Western until 1871, when the operating partners became the LNWR, NLR and Midland, kept its identity until 1923, so traffic figures can be summarized (Fig. 14).

Unlike the West London, the NSWJ still retains its suburban traffic and unlike the former it has never been important for through passenger trains. But it is one of the vital links in London's freight routes. In 1956, 80 westbound goods trains were scheduled daily through Acton Wells Junction and 45 passed on to the Southern.

A single line to HAMMERSMITH and CHISWICK from Acton Gate House Junction (at Acton Lane) was the NSWJ's only branch. Used for goods since 1 May 1857, it had an erratic and primitive passenger service from 8 April 1858 to 1 January 1917 and was abandoned from 3 May 1965.

Clay, Houses and Electric Traction in Middlesex

> Gaily into Ruislip Gardens
> Runs the red electric train,
>
> .   .   .   .
>
> Where a few surviving hedges
> Keep alive our lost elysium—rural Middlesex again.
>
> JOHN BETJEMAN.

THE DISTRICT AND THE PICCADILLY IN WEST LONDON

In 1960 suburbia stretched continuously along the 8½ miles of line between North Ealing and Ickenham where forty years previously scarcely a house would have been visible from a train window. This social change was largely due to electric railways, projected by enterprising promoters into open country. For while it is true that Middlesex clay was formerly considered undesirable for building, it is also true that the GWR and LNWR had done little to encourage suburban traffic.

The District reached the area by slow stages. Its Act of Incorporation (p. 89) sanctioned an X layout at Earl's Court with arms to the Inner Circle at South Kensington (via Gloucester Road) and at High Street, to Addison Road, and to a station alongside West Brompton on the WLR. On 12 April 1869 a West Brompton–Gloucester Road service was inaugurated (extended to Blackfriars on 1 August 1870 and Mansion House on 3 July 1871). An engineer's report of 7 September 1869 states the other lines were ready, but neither was used until the Outer Circle was started in 1872.

Because the company lacked money and credit, but, to quote Sam Fay, 'cast their eyes enviously upon the fair and rich

(28) *The Inner Circle in steam days. A train on the 'Outer Rail' approaches Aldgate station about 1902.*

(29) *District locomotives built to haul 'Outer Circle' trains eastward from Earl's Court on a train of contemporary* LNWR *suburban coaches.*

(30) *An early District electric train at an unidentified spot, perhaps on the Ealing & South Harrow. Note the American influence upon the rolling stock under Yerkes's regime, and the invasion of building upon rural Middlesex after District incursions.*

FAR-FLUNG METROLAND

(31) *Quainton Road, a distant outpost of the urban Metropolitan Railway, in the 1920's presents a striking contrast with the Inner Circle. The Brill branch curves away to the right.*

(32) *Branches were built in anticipation of suburban development, as this view of the Stanmore branch under construction about 1931 shows. The neighbourhood is now fully built up.*

(33) *A Metropolitan freight train, in rural Bucks, illustrates the Company's desire to achieve main-line status.*

traffic district of the South Western suburban system' (and on GWR preserves), westward extensions were made through nominally independent companies.

The HAMMERSMITH EXTENSION built the mile of line from Earl's Court to Hammersmith Broadway, opened on 9 September 1874. Further extensions were abandoned when the LSWR granted running powers over its Richmond line, the HAMMERSMITH JUNCTION Company opening a connection to Studland Road Junction on 1 June 1877. A District branch was then opened on 1 July 1879 from Turnham Green on the LSWR to EALING BROADWAY. The GWR persuaded the District to drop its attempt on Uxbridge by consenting to a connection at Ealing and the inauguration of a Mansion House–Windsor service, which lasted only from 1 March 1883 to 30 September 1885. The West Brompton branch was extended to PUTNEY BRIDGE on 1 March 1880, trains eventually reaching Wimbledon on 3 June 1889.

By 1880 Hammersmith had become the edge of the built-up area, but good District services and, after 1900, tramway extensions advanced London's frontier to beyond the NSWJ by 1914. Electric traction began between Earl's Court and Ealing on 1 July 1905, Richmond on 1 August and Wimbledon on 27 August (Putney Bridge on 23 July). To deal with the increasing traffic the LSWR quadrupled its line between Studland Road Junction and Turnham Green, giving the District sole use of the southern pair of tracks. After the LSWR service ceased in 1916 its pair lay derelict.

The HOUNSLOW & METROPOLITAN Company, promoted by local landowners bent on increasing property values, was incorporated on 26 August 1880 to build a branch from the District's Ealing line at Mill Hill Park (Acton Town from 1910) to Hounslow Barracks (West from 1925). When opened on 1 May 1883 it deviated from the authorized route at Osterley to terminate at Hounslow Town. A single line from Lampton Junction (Osterley) to Hounslow West was opened on 21 July 1884, the section to Heston Hounslow (Central from 1925) was doubled in 1910. But the remaining 62 chains remained single until 1926; 300 trains a day were using this single line in 1913. The spur to the Town station was closed on 1 April

1886, but was reopened, together with a spur to complete the triangle, upon electrification. The Town station was finally closed on 2 May 1909 with the opening of Hounslow East. There are proposals to extend to London Airport.

The EALING & SOUTH HARROW Railway was incorporated on 25 August 1894 to build a 5-mile line from Hanger Lane Junction, just east of Ealing Broadway. It was part of the District's second drive on Uxbridge and there were hopes it might be used by the still-born London and South Wales as its approach to London. Ready in 1901, Yerkes used it as a test track for electric trains, a service being provided between Acton Town and Park Royal for the Royal Show of 23–27 June 1903. The next day a full service was put on through to South Harrow.

On 13 June 1905 an electric service was inaugurated between Hounslow Barracks and South Acton via Acton Town. It used a double-line spur between the two last named, hitherto unused for public traffic. The junction with the NSWJ was removed in 1915 and the spur singled in 1932. On 1 July 1905 electric trains began running eastward from Acton Town to Earl's Court. The South Acton service degenerated into a shuttle over the spur, maintained by a one-car train until 28 February 1959 inclusive.

In 1932 four tracks came into use all the way from the point at which the Piccadilly emerged at the surface to Northfields on the Hounslow line, incorporating the parallel District and Piccadilly (p. 103) tracks to Hammersmith, and the existing four tracks between Studland Road Junction and Turnham Green, which were leased from the Southern. The remainder of the ex-LSWR branch east of Studland Road was abandoned.

Thus on 4 July 1932 Piccadilly trains were projected on from Hammersmith to South Harrow, to Northfields 9 January 1933, to Hounslow 13 March 1933, and to Uxbridge 23 October 1933, and now provide all the services except a few (8 each way in 1961) peak-hour District trains to Hounslow. Piccadilly trains use the inside pair of tracks, running non-stop from Hammersmith to Acton Town, and District trains the outer, calling at all stations.

In 1914 continuous building extended to Chiswick Park, but while Hounslow and Ealing were expanding rapidly the lines thither and to South Harrow ran through open and nearly deserted country. The whole area became closely built over between 1925 and 1939 and pockets of industry sprang up. Local job ratios are higher than average, but all the lines are extremely busy with both London-bound and local commuters. Because of this virtually all the stations have been rebuilt. The 'little halt' at Northfields now has two long island platforms. Among the smaller stations, Sudbury Town, its traffic swollen from 60,000 to 1·25 million a year, was rebuilt in 1931 in the adventurous style of Charles Holden which became a model for later LT stations.

THE METROPOLITAN 'EXTENSION'

The stages by which the Metropolitan all but acquired trunk line status were piecemeal. On 13 April 1868 a single line, mostly in tunnel, was opened from Baker Street to Swiss Cottage by the METROPOLITAN & ST JOHN'S WOOD (incorporated on 29 July 1864, worked like all the other subsidiaries by the Metropolitan and absorbed in 1882). Through running from the City ceased in 1869 and did not begin again until 1907. Anything like a full service had been impossible since 1892, when alterations left only a single road from the 'Extension' to the Circle (Outer Rail), but this began on 4 November 1912, when the present layout came into use.

By 1903 Baker Street had 929 steam trains arriving daily from east and west along the Circle and from the 'Extension', while 13·2 million passengers passed the barriers. Thirty years later the number of trains had risen to 1,438, all electric of course. In 1959 a census showed 14,550 people *entering* the station between 4.30 and 7.0 p.m. to catch Metropolitan and Bakerloo trains. Nine thousand passed the barriers between 5.0 and 6.0 alone. The large exchange traffic is additional.

A double-track extension, emerging finally into the open at Finchley Road, was sanctioned on 5 August 1873 from Swiss Cottage to the River Brent. At the same time the line to Swiss Cottage was to be doubled though uncompleted until 10 July 1882. The new line was opened on 30 June 1879 to West Hampstead and on to Walm Lane (now Willesden Green) on

24 November. Then suburban development was little more than the large villas of St John's Wood. West End Lane, on which West Hampstead station stands, had for years been a favourite country drive for Queen Victoria.

The KINGSBURY & HARROW, jointly owned by the Metropolitan and the St John's Wood companies, was authorized on 16 July 1874 to build on further. The 5·5 miles were opened on 2 August 1880 with but one intermediate station. There are now five. Harrow-on-the-Hill station was in 'Queen Anne' style and established the tradition of good architecture maintained by the Metropolitan and London Transport. Thirty-six trains arrived daily. In 1961 there were 185 down trains from Baker Street.

The project included a connection back at Finchley Road with the adjacent Midland. From 1 October 1880 it was used to exchange freight traffic, for the Metropolitan had opened goods depots along the Extension served by its own trains. Used until 1948, the connection was severed in 1953.

Under Watkin's leadership the pace of extension accelerated, though the objective remained a close secret. The HARROW & RICKMANSWORTH Company, incorporated on 7 August 1874, opened its line to Pinner on 25 May 1885 and to Rickmansworth on 1 September 1887. 'What could be the object of carrying the line through a district consisting only of farms and fields?' asked a contributor to a local newspaper. But construction was hastened forward far into the Chilterns, the small town of Chesham being reached on 8 July 1889. From a junction at Chalfont Road (now Chalfont & Latimer) the line pushed on through Amersham and the Wendover Gap out on to the Midland Plain to reach Aylesbury on 1 September 1892.

Still the Metropolitan forged on. On 1 July 1891 it took over the AYLESBURY & BUCKINGHAM Railway, hitherto worked by the GWR. The line had been opened on 23 September 1868 from Aylesbury to a point on the LNWR's Bletchley and Oxford branch so isolated that it was called Verney Junction after the local landowner. In 1897 a through service began between Baker Street and Verney, 50·5 miles, a second track having been laid north of Aylesbury.

The motive behind this northward thrust only became public in 1893 when the Manchester, Sheffield & Lincolnshire, also under Watkin's chairmanship, obtained sanction for its long-coveted London Extension and became the Great Central. It was to build southward to Quainton Road on the Verney line and to enjoy running powers thence to Harrow South Junction. From there to Canfield Place, alongside Finchley Road station, the Metropolitan would build an extra pair of tracks to be rented to the GCR for its exclusive use.

Watkin had envisaged fusion of the two companies, but was no longer in control and union with an impoverished GCR did not attract the now flourishing suburban railway. For Willesden had almost doubled its population in ten years, while Wembley and Harrow, ill served for so long by the LNWR, were growing fast.

'METROLAND'

The Metropolitan now concentrated on developing the country-side of Middlesex and South Bucks. Suburban settlement was encouraged not only by electrification, frequent services and low fares, but also by lavish advertising and by land and building speculation. These last activities were handled by the Surplus Lands Committee, whose work was transferred in 1919 to a subsidiary company, Metropolitan Railway Country Estates. By 1939, 4,600 houses had been built on 'Met' estates.

From Wembley far into the Chilterns became 'Metroland'. The very word evokes a way of life, widely denigrated, but, judging from the competition to share in it, the ideal of the modern English, and one created by the electric railway.

Wembley, a hamlet in Harrow Parish until 1894, numbered 10,277 in 1881, 31,217 in 1911 and 124,843 in 1961. The old town of Harrow, spreading over the plain around the Hill, mushroomed from 49,020 in 1921 to 96,756 in 1931 and 219,494 in 1951. Job ratios are low, and in 1951, 25 per cent (23,000) of Harrow's working population and 29 per cent of Chorley Wood's travelled into Central London. Where there are pockets of industry figures are similar to those of Rickmansworth, with only 15 per cent employed in Central London.

Between 1925 and 1939 the flood-tide of red-brick houses swept across Middlesex. From these houses the Metropolitan carried breadwinners to the City daily, wives to the West End weekly and families to the occasional dinner and show. In the other direction hikers crowded week-end trains out to the Chilterns. Since 1950 the building flood has swept right through the Chilterns, where any land that can be wrung from the Green Belt carries an inflated price.

DEVELOPMENTS ON THE EXTENSION

On 1 March 1906 the Harrow–Canfield Place tracks were leased to the GCR, and on 2 April all Metropolitan property north of Harrow was leased to a Metropolitan and Great Central Joint Committee. Thereafter increasing traffic matched the constant improvements which by 1962 had converted an ordinary steam line into one of the foremost 'rapid transit' systems in the world.

On 1 January 1905 electric working began between Baker Street, Harrow and Uxbridge with multiple units. Electric locomotives were built to haul the through trains, steam taking over at Willesden Green until 1 November 1906, Wembley Park until 19 July 1908 and Harrow thereafter. On 5 January 1925 electric working was extended to Rickmansworth, but further advance was delayed until 12 September 1960, when multiple-unit trains began running out to Amersham and Chesham.

In 1932 the Metropolitan carried 4 million tons of merchandise and minerals. Pullman cars (introduced 1 June 1910) made four return trips a day from Aylesbury and branches reached far into the rural fastnesses of North Bucks. But from 1 November 1937 the LNER took over the goods workings and provided the steam locomotives for passenger trains north of Rickmansworth. The Pullmans were withdrawn on 7 October 1939. Finally, all LT trains ceased to run beyond Amersham after 9 September 1961 and thereafter all its services were provided by multiple-unit trains.

Meanwhile quadrupling between Finchley Road and Willesden Green was completed in stages between 30 November 1913

TABLE 9

TRAINS ON THE METROPOLITAN 'EXTENSION' LINE
(*Mondays to Fridays*)

	1901	*1913*	*1961*
Leaving Baker Street	123	295	449*
Terminating at:			
Willesden Green	31	62	—
Neasden	46	91	6
Wembley Park	—	—	43
Stanmore	—	—	155
Harrow	21	49	27
Uxbridge	—	42	107
Pinner	—	27	—
Rickmansworth	13	—	2
Watford	—	—	63
Chesham	3	14	2
Amersham	—	—	19
Aylesbury	3	10	25†
Verney Junction	6	—	—

* Includes 251 Metropolitan and 198 Bakerloo trains.
† The LT service was cut back to Amersham after 9 September 1961.

and 31 May 1915. The section on to Harrow went into service on 10 January 1932. But beyond, electric and steam trains, passenger and freight, LT and LNER, all continued to share one pair of lines. The 1935 Plan (p. 187) provided for further quadrupling, but work did not begin seriously until October 1959. It was completed to Watford South Junction (junction with the Watford Branch) in time for the revised service introduced on 18 June 1962.

South of Finchley Road there were only two tracks, and to eliminate this bottleneck the Metropolitan planned a tube from Kilburn to the Circle at Edgware Road, rebuilding the latter in 1926 as a start. Then, as part of the 1935 Plan, a tube was built from the Bakerloo at Baker Street to the Extension at a rebuilt Finchley Road. This was opened on 20 November 1939 and has two intermediate stations to replace the three on the Extension.

Beyond Finchley Road the tracks were rearranged to allow Bakerloo trains to use the centre pair and call at all stations to

Wembley Park. Here they diverge on a burrowing junction for Stanmore, their places being taken by Metropolitan stopping trains as far as Harrow. Beyond, the fast and stopping lines are in pairs. Stanmore trains may be diverted to the Fleet Line (p. 109).

In 1903, 15 trains left Baker Street between 6.0 and 7.0 p.m., 5 for destinations beyond Neasden and 3 for beyond Harrow. After 1962, 28 Metropolitan and 15 Bakerloo trains left Finchley Road (where all trains call for exchange purposes). Destinations were: Stanmore 15; Uxbridge 12; Watford 8; Amersham 7; Chesham 1. Over 20,000 passengers would have been carried in the 43 trains. In 1962 the rails between Harrow-on-the-Hill and North Harrow were estimated to carry 36,000 passengers daily.

UXBRIDGE

What was to become the Extension's busiest branch was originally promoted by a District subsidiary, the HARROW & UXBRIDGE, incorporated on 6 August 1897 to extend the District's South Harrow line (p. 134). The parent company's resources proved insufficient to raise the necessary capital. Accordingly local interests persuaded the Metropolitan to work the line. This move was authorized on 9 August 1899, together with a link from Rayners Lane to the Extension at Harrow North Junction. The District was consoled with running powers from South Harrow.

The branch was finally opened on 4 July 1904 and worked by a steam shuttle service until electric trains began running through from Baker Street on 1 January 1905. Disputes delayed through running of District trains until 1 March 1910.

It was an area of meadowland with oaks in the hedgerows and only the village of Ruislip (3,566 in 1901) and the hamlet of Ickenham (433 in 1921) were served by the branch *en route* to Uxbridge. Ruislip was the only intermediate station, and the service of 48 Metropolitan and 15 District trains each way operated in 1910 was a very lavish one. But speculative builders were slow to develop the clay lands, even after wooden halts were opened. That at Rayners Lane, dating from 26 May

1906, for years served 'two or three well separated houses, a sewage farm and a rifle range' (A. A. Jackson).

Ruislip Manor Halt, opened 5 August 1912, had only a field path for access and trains stopped only on request. The estate which it served was built between 1910 and 1920, but the main activity began after 1929. The number of residents served by the line grew from 48,000 in 1931 to 95,000 in 1938, while between 1931 and 1951 the population of Ruislip–Northwood Urban District rose by 326 per cent, the largest increase in Greater London.

The halts formed the nuclei of the new communities. Parades of shops were built at the entrances and the fields disappeared beneath red-brick and tile semi-detached villas and their tiny gardens. Industry is virtually non-existent, but the 23 per cent of Ruislip–Northwood's working population which commutes to Central London, though high, is not exceptional. There are nearer opportunities for employment at places such as Greenford and Wembley.

R. M. Robbins considers that these communities represent the better side of Middlesex development. Fortunately too London Transport rebuilt the halts as worthy centres of the new suburbs. Bookings at Ruislip Manor rose from 17,000 in 1931 to 1·3 million in 1939 and those at Rayners Lane from 22,000 in 1930 to 4 million in 1937.

Uxbridge itself has a different and longer history, being one of several towns which grew up where important roads, in this case the Oxford Road, crossed the broad and marshy valley of the Colne. With a large market, it also grew to prosperity on the coaching traffic, and in 1831, with 3,043 souls, was one of the more important Middlesex towns. The townsfolk therefore bitterly opposed the GWR Bill, but there is no evidence that, once it was passed, they refused the line passage through the town. In any case there was rejoicing when the branch from West Drayton put the town on the railway map (p. 117). The VINE STREET terminus is close to the town centre and some through trains ran to Paddington. But passengers were few, especially to Central London, and the service was withdrawn from 10 September 1962. Freight traffic ceased on 13 July 1964.

Powers were obtained on 28 June 1861 by the Uxbridge & Rickmansworth Company to extend the branch up the Colne to the LNWR at Rickmansworth, but they remained unused. Instead, on 2 August 1898 the GWR received sanction to link it with the GW & GC near Denham. In the event the new line was built only to a terminus in HIGH STREET, which robbed it of any utility. A sparse passenger service from Denham was operated between 1 May 1907 and 31 August 1939. High Street was closed to goods traffic on 25 September 1939, but handled coal until 2 April 1962.

Neither branch much affected the town, which stagnated picturesquely, its coaching trade dead and its flour-mills dying, and the 1901 population figure was almost the same as it was seventy years before. The significant year was 1904, which saw the coming of both the Metropolitan and the electric tram. Immediately the latter was of more effect, cars running through from Shepherd's Bush and finally ending Uxbridge's isolation. During the decade 1901–11 the population grew threefold to 10,374. By 1931 it reached 31,887 and by 1961, 63,762. Uxbridge is largely a residential centre, but there is much industry near by and in 1951 only 8 per cent of the employed population worked in Central London.

The Metropolitan's terminus was in BELMONT ROAD. It had a simple red-brick building on one platform, but the other was shelterless and here District and Piccadilly trains were exiled. It became hopelessly inadequate, and on 4 December 1938 the L.P.T.B. opened a spacious modern station in the High Street. Adjoining is the bus terminus, the whole a model traffic centre, its architecture worthy of its central site. The old station became a wholesale merchant's depot after closure for goods from 1 May 1939.

GREAT CENTRAL

On 25 July 1898 coal trains began running over the Great Central's London extension, but passenger traffic did not begin until 15 March 1899 and merchandise until 11 April, for Marylebone was not ready. It was approached from Canfield Place by two miles of double track built by the GCR and bitterly

opposed in St John's Wood by the artists' colony and by an
M.C.C. fearful of Lord's being desecrated.

The GCR's advent found favour with a public obsessed with
the apparent monopoly enjoyed by established companies, and
the *Railway Magazine* lyrically hailed the newcomer. But the
London extension, at least south of Woodford Halse, was probably a mistake. The first three trains out of Marylebone carried
52 passengers between them. 'Eminently satisfactory', trumpeted
the *Railway Magazine*, but other journals were more sceptical.
Nor did traffic ever develop satisfactorily. In November 1903
13 passenger, 1 parcels and 12 freight trains passed on to the
GCR at Quainton Road daily, and the number of down trains
from Marylebone never varied greatly over the next fifty
years.

In 1902 Sir Sam Fay was recruited by the GCR as general
manager. His characteristically vigorous policy included the
building up of suburban services, for the Company could ill
afford to neglect any source of revenue. Fay set an example by
living at Gerrards Cross.

As far as the Aylesbury line was concerned, the agreement
with the Metropolitan precluded any stops short of Harrow.
Outside peak hours the service was irregular until 1962 when
there were 23 daily suburban departures from Marylebone,
calling at Harrow, Chorley Wood and stations beyond, instead
of 11 as in the previous year.

Though the Neasden–Northolt line was built through open
country, lavish station accommodation was provided. But in
spite of housing developments traffic did not come to the four
stations, for it was abstracted by the parallel Ealing and South
Harrow. In 1968 the service was probably the sparsest in
London. Beyond West Ruislip traffic is heavy and there is a
basic hourly service to High Wycombe. There are plans to
divert this to Paddington and close the Northolt–Neasden link
which now carries no other traffic.

THE DECLINE OF MARYLEBONE

The red, Tudoresque façade of Marylebone, strangely provincial
in conception, and the pretentious hotel building, at present

headquarters of the Railways Board, conceal the four platforms of London's least-used terminus, now part of the London Midland Region. In 1903 there were only 14 daily arrivals and the passenger user was but 471,000. In 1958 arrivals had increased to 61, but 53 were suburban services non-existent in 1903. The 5 down Manchester trains were carrying an average of 79 passengers apiece. In 1959 all services, apart from a few overnight ones, were cut back at Nottingham, and on 5 September 1966 regular passenger services ceased north of Aylesbury.

A 1961 census day saw 6,069 passengers leaving on 49 trains, 2,836 (47 per cent) on the 10 leaving during the busiest hour. From 18 June 1962, with all suburban services operated by diesel multiple units, there were 23 departures for Aylesbury via Harrow, 32 for High Wycombe, Princes Risborough or Aylesbury, 12 for West Ruislip and 8 'Main Line', 75 in all.

Marylebone was much used to relieve other termini for excursions, holiday overnight trains and, during rebuilding, trains diverted from Euston via Bletchley and the war-time Calvert curve.

Freight traffic at Marylebone ceased in 1952, the goods shed becoming a parcels depot until 1967, when traffic was diverted to Euston. The coal depot closed in 1965, when the 28-acre goods yard was sold to the GLC for a housing site. Neasden yard and loco sheds are closed and how to accommodate the Aylesbury service elsewhere is the only problem preventing total closure of Marylebone. The Great Central, last trunk line into London, has ceased to exist as a through route.

METROPOLITAN & GREAT CENTRAL BRANCHES

With the opening of the GCR extension to Quainton Road the line to VERNEY JUNCTION sank to branch status. From 6 July 1936 Metropolitan trains ceased to run beyond Aylesbury and the LNER also withdrew their local service. Through parcels and freight trains ran until 6 September 1947, when they were all diverted over the Calvert Spur.

The line to BRILL was the oddest ever to come within the

LT fold. Built privately by the Duke of Buckingham and opened in part during 1871, it was taken over by the Oxford & Aylesbury Tramroad Company in 1894. As part of an abortive attack on the West Midlands, the Metropolitan took over on 1 December 1899. Thenceforward an aged but spotlessly clean 4-4-0T and a rigid eight-wheeled coach maintained a service until the L.P.T.B. closed this working museum from 1 December 1935. In its last year the line carried a daily average of 58 passengers and 34 tons of goods.

The electrified CHESHAM branch still remains single, winding sinuously down the side of the Chiltern Valley. A lavish shuttle service and through City trains at peak hours have always been provided. The old market town is now growing rapidly, the 1961 population of 16,236 being 42 per cent up on that of 1951.

On 2 November 1925 the Metropolitan and LNER opened a jointly owned 2·5-mile branch from a triangular junction south of Rickmansworth to WATFORD. Thirty-five electric trips were made daily and 35 by steam trains from Marylebone, until the folly of this dawned on the LNER and in May 1926 their trains were replaced by Metropolitan ones. A shuttle service to and from Rickmansworth lasted from 1925 to 1934. The Watford terminus is inconveniently sited, but suburban development keeps the line busy enough for a basic service of 3 trains an hour.

The newest branch is from Wembley Park to STANMORE, promoted by the Metropolitan and opened on 10 December 1932. Though running through open country 144 trains a day were provided. As a result the district became largely built over in five years. Since 20 November 1939 all trains have been Bakerloo. Four or five trains an hour run in slack hours and 15 per hour at peak periods.

In 1924 the LNER opened WEMBLEY STADIUM station for the Empire Exhibition. It had a platform on a single track which made a complete loop from the Northolt line just west of Neasden, which, until 1968 enabled a roundabout service to be run every few minutes from Marylebone on Cup Final and other occasions.

CHAPTER VIII

The Midland and the Great Northern

Rumbling under blackened girders,
Midland, bound for Cricklewood . . .

JOHN BETJEMAN.

THE COMING OF THE MIDLAND

THE Midland and the Great Northern were both major carriers of coal and freight and had an important express passenger business. But their policy towards suburban traffic diverged and consequently the pattern of suburban growth differed as between Hendon and Hornsey, Boreham Wood and Barnet.

Prior to 1857 all the Midland's London traffic had passed through Rugby, but in that year the Company reached Hitchin on the GNR. On 1 February 1858 it began to work passenger trains into King's Cross. The service was sparse, there being but 7 departures a day from King's Cross in 1864, but with the limitation on line capacity imposed by primitive signalling and braking, congestion on the GNR was severe. Naturally if anyone had to suffer it was the tenant company, and in 1862, 1,000 Midland passenger trains and 2,400 freight trains suffered severe delay. The LNWR were also prone to place embargoes on Midland traffic on the grounds of congestion.

Independent access to London was a necessity. As a first step, though enjoying full rights at King's Cross Goods, on 2 January 1865 the Midland opened St Pancras Goods on a branch from the GN – NLR curve, giving access from either the GNR or the LNWR (via the NLR). On 22 June 1863 a line was

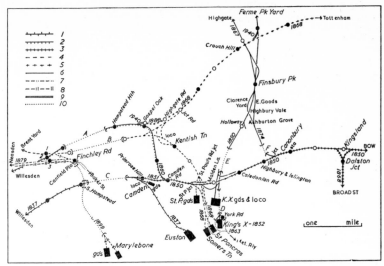

FIG. 15. The approaches to the northern termini: 1, LNWR. 2, Hampstead Junction Railway. 3, NLR. 4, Midland. 5, Tottenham & Hampstead Junction Railway. 6, GNR. 7, Metropolitan. 8, GCR. 9, War-time spurs. 10, Lines in tunnel. Tunnels: A, Hampstead. B, Haverstock Hill. C, Primrose Hill. D, Gas Works. E, Copenhagen. F, Canonbury.

sanctioned from Bedford to a passenger terminus on the Euston Road, also to be called St Pancras.

As with other lines entering London from the north, the principal natural obstacles were the Chilterns, the South Herts Plateau and the Hampstead Heights. These were crossed by the Luton Gap, in Elstree tunnel and through the long Haverstock Hill tunnel, approached by similar elbow bends to the parallel one at Primrose Hill. In addition the Brent valley was crossed on a nineteen-arch viaduct south of Hendon. On the south side of the valley land was purchased to lay out a marshalling yard. After passing through the small cathedral city of St Albans no other place of consequence was reached before Kentish Town.

There is much confusion as to the opening date of the St Pancras extension, but the ground has recently been cleared by Geoffrey Webb, who is of the opinion that through merchandise (not mineral) traffic began on 9 September 1867. On 13

July 1868 a local (it could hardly be called a suburban) service began between Bedford and Moorgate Street, using the 'St Pancras Branch' which diverges a mile north of the terminus at St Paul's Road Junction and which leads down to the Metropolitan. St Pancras itself was opened on 1 October.

ST PANCRAS

By 1865 London had expanded northward to Kentish Town and the last 1·5 miles were through a built-up area. There was the usual outcry about loss of amenity when it was found that 6 of the 400 trees in Camden Square would be destroyed. But the 3,000 houses razed in Agar Town and Somers Town were no loss, being one of the most horrifying slums in London and 'bounded by mountains of refuse from Metropolitan dustbins, strewn with decaying vegetables and foul smelling fragments of fish heads', an area inappropriately named La Belle Isle. Fortunately the Norman church of Old St Pancras was spared, though the present Churchyard Sidings commemorate a near miss.

Like the LNWR and the GNR, the Midland had to cross the Regent's Canal, but unlike them continued on the level, so the terminus was raised on arches 12 to 17 feet above the Euston Road. The street level was, and still is, given over to the storage of beer from Burton, always an important traffic to the Midland. To ensure economy of space the arches were built with spans of 24 feet 9 inches, a multiple of beer barrel diameters.

Over the Euston Road looms Gilbert Scott's immense Gothic façade, once an hotel but now let out as offices. Reflecting the solid but romantic opulence of the mid-Victorian period, contemporary opinion rated it 'one of the chief architectural ornaments of the metropolis'. Twentieth-century taste regards it with aesthetic horror, though the *avant garde* are rediscovering merit in it.

The station behind is equally bold in conception and deserves to be better known. The seven platforms and ten roads are covered by a 25,000-square foot glazed roof with a single elliptical span 240 feet wide and 100 feet high. F. S. Williams, writing in 1877, says 'in result we have an arch, not only of extraordinary lightness and beauty, but of equally extraordinary strength'. It was the work of W. H. Barlow.

In 1874, 18 Midland and 6 Great Eastern (p. 151) trains left St Pancras on weekdays and at St Paul's Road Junction these were joined by 59 trains from Farringdon Street and 14 more working through from the LCDR. In 1903 there were 38 suburban and 28 main-line arrivals at St Pancras, the latter being somewhat less than at Euston or King's Cross, with 42 and 41 respectively. But ordinary passenger user that year was 2·5 million compared with Euston's 2·6 million. So train loads were heavier, doubtless due to third-class comfort on the Midland. In addition there were a calculated 7·3 million season-ticket journeys compared with 1·9 million at Euston.

In recent years passenger traffic has grown with accelerated schedules to the Midlands and the eclipse of Marylebone. On the 1961 census day, 77 trains left with 16,636 passengers. Between 4.0 and 7.0 p.m. there were 14 departures with 5,561 passengers. This represents a peak hour concentration of only 35 per cent, vividly underlining the relative unimportance of suburban traffic.

It is on medium- and long-distance traffic that St Pancras concentrates. Prior to 1923 it was a station for Scotland and for Ireland too. But the Heysham boat trains now leave from Euston and few people travel the whole way to Glasgow and Edinburgh. But there is a steady flow of passengers to and from the industrial cities of the Midlands and North encouraged by fast and frequent services built up after 1950. St Pancras is also the gateway to the 'Grassy Shires' of beef cattle and hunting fame. Tweeds have been as familiar a sight on the concourse as briefcases.

THE MAIN LINE

Adjoining St Pancras is the Somers Town goods station, dating from 1887 and developed by the Midland as a potato market. In the 1960s it was worked as a single depot with St Pancras Goods, dealing with outward traffic, while the inward is concentrated at the latter. Together they formed a typical large London goods station. About 85,000 consignments a week were dealt with, collected and distributed by 330 lorries. In 1960, 12 'fitted' and 2 'non-fitted' trains arrived, mainly from midnight onwards from such centres as Glasgow, Leeds, Sheffield, Burton and Bedford.

The passenger locomotive shed was at Kentish Town, as were the original carriage sidings (Tartan Arrow's rail terminal has been on the site since 1967). The main carriage depot was provided later at Cricklewood, 5 miles out. With increasing train lengths and frequencies the demand for storage rose, but land values prevented provision nearer in. Just to the north, Brent marshalling yard is one of the largest in London. During the 1950s an average of 25,000 wagons a week passed through. Hendon was the terminus of the 'Condor' all-container service to Glasgow, precursor of the freightliners, which ran between 16 March 1959 and 20 October 1967. The main line was quadrupled to Elstree by 1895, and up it trundled an endless succession of coal trains, now much reduced. But even in 1956 there were 50 up freights scheduled daily through Elstree.

At one time the BRB planned to divert passenger traffic from beyond Leicester to Euston (probably via Nuneaton), to provide a service from Leicester to Moorgate and to close St Pancras. In 1969 the plans were officially shelved due to the cost of adapting the widened lines and to the growth of traffic at Euston and at St Pancras itself. Unlike that of the GC, the Midland's trunk line will continue as such for the foreseeable future.

THE TOTTENHAM & HAMPSTEAD JUNCTION

On 29 July 1862 the Tottenham & Hampstead Junction was incorporated to build 4·5 miles of double track from the GER Cambridge line at Tottenham North Junction to Gospel Oak station on the Hampstead Junction. Eventually the GER and the Midland each put up a third of the capital.

The 4·25 miles from Tottenham to Highgate Road opened on 21 July 1868 with a GER service from Fenchurch Street via Stratford. This lasted only until 31 January 1870, for even then it was impossibly circuitous and only at Holloway was there much building.

A short time later a triangular layout was completed at the Tottenham end and on 3 January 1870 the Midland had completed a spur from Kentish Town to Highgate Road, eventually providing a triangular junction. On 1 October a service was inaugurated between Moorgate Street and Crouch Hill, extended on 1 May 1871 to a new station at South Tottenham, built in open country. Later, in 1894, Midland trains were projected over the Tottenham & Forest Gate to Barking (p. 199).

An infrequent GER service started in 1885 between Chingford and Highgate Road and on 4 June 1888 was extended to Gospel Oak. Normal traffic was light, but on bank holidays the families of artisans and clerks, who largely inhabited the area, poured out to Epping Forest and Hampstead Heath. The regular service ceased in September 1926, but trains ran on bank holidays until 1939. There was no physical connection at Gospel Oak until 23 January 1916, and then for freight only. It lay unused after 1920 and was removed on 3 September 1922.

On 1 July 1902 the T & H J passed into the joint ownership of the GER and the Midland. Today the boundary between the Eastern and London Midland Regions is just west of Crouch Hill. The main passenger traffic flows over this important link have been: (a) The Midland suburban service described on page 152 and (b) the much sparser GER service; (c) Midland trains, regular and excursion to Southend, operated between 1895 and 1961; (d) the GER service of up to 6 trains a day each way between St Pancras and Cambridge (1870–1923) (considering St Pancras more convenient for the West End than Liverpool Street, the GER acquired running powers in return for allowing Midland goods trains to work into the docks. Race specials ran to Newmarket by this route and Royalty even patronized it); (e) The Tilbury boat trains, St Pancras being preferred to Fenchurch Street for its facilities for passengers encumbered with baggage until 1963, when electric trains began to be used.

The main function of the T & HJ nowadays is as a link in the freight 'belt line'. This was made possible by the permanent restoration of the Gospel Oak connection on 11 March 1940 and by the use between 8 January 1940 and 28 April 1968, of a spur to the GNR line at Ferme Park (partially built in 1870 and used during the first world war). In 1953, 36 westbound freights were booked through Upper Holloway daily. They originated from the LT & S (via the Tottenham & Forest Gate), from the docks and Temple Mills (via Tottenham South Junction) and from Ferme Park. Destinations were equally diverse, including Brent, Wellingborough, St Pancras, Acton, Feltham and Hither Green.

SUBURBAN SERVICES AND SUBURBAN GROWTH

The Midland's Half-yearly Report of 19 February 1869 says of the new London extension: 'It is proper to mention there is every possibility of a large passenger traffic in the suburbs of London.' At first it was encouraged and eventually there were six stations on the 4 miles from St Pancras to West Hampstead and nine on the T & HJ.

In January 1874 of 59 down trains leaving Farringdon Street, 24 were for the South Tottenham line and 35 for the main line, 10 terminating at Finchley Road, 5 at Haverstock Hill and 20 going to Hendon and beyond. Largely because of this very adequate service, the whole of the district served by the T & HJ became built up between 1870 and the opening of St Ann's Road station in 1882. By 1900 suburbia also reached out to Cricklewood and there had been some development around Hendon and Mill Hill stations.

Much traffic was lost to trams and tubes after 1905, but though the Midland suffered as severely as other lines, it had other than suburban fish to fry and made no attempt even to prevent further loss. The T & HJ service was greatly reduced, while five of the nine stations were closed over the years. On the main line the service was reduced to a pale shadow of its former self and Camden Road (1916), Haverstock Hill (1916) and Finchley Road (1927) were closed.

The Midland, and later the LMS, made no attempt to develop traffic with the Middle Zone and, uniquely, the service down the main line remained unimproved throughout the 1920–40 period. Between West Hampstead and Elstree, eight miles away, there were only three intermediate stations. The enormous development of Hendon was due to the tube extension, and the people of Mill Hill preferred to take a bus to Hendon Central tube station.

The trend was not reversed until an interval service of diesel multiple units was started on 11 January 1960 on both the main and Tottenham lines. Forty-five trains now called at Elstree daily instead of 30, while competitive fares were introduced. Thus encouraged, traffic soon increased by 20 per cent. Though outside Greater London, St Albans (now with 100 trains instead of 79) may be taken as an individual example. In March 1961, 88,723 passenger journeys were made from the station, a 27 per cent increase over the 69,220 in March 1959.

Even so the 1969 frequencies are low by London standards and the three stations which adjoin each other in West End Lane provide an illuminating contrast. At West Hampstead, rebuilt in 1939, Bakerloo trains call every few minutes and traffic is heavy. At West End Lane, Broad Street–Richmond trains maintain a 20-minute service and traffic, though moderate, is steady. At the gloomy ruin of West Hampstead (Midland) diesel trains pause hourly, often fruitlessly.

THE GREAT NORTHERN RAILWAY

The Great Northern was also a major carrier of coal, merchandise and long-distance passengers. But it also allowed suburban traffic to develop to such an extent that, like the legendary Sorcerer's Apprentice, the Company found it had created a rising tide that threatened to swamp the difficult approach to King's Cross. The 'suburban opportunity' became the 'suburban incubus' and the period 1875–1940 was spent by the GNR and LNER in attempts to remove it.

Under powers obtained on 26 June 1846 after a bitter struggle (to be described in the volume on Eastern England), the GNR built its main line from Doncaster to London. The Hitchin Gap was used to cross the Chiltern scarp, and southward from Hitchin to Wood Green the full width of the South Herts Plateau was traversed. From the summit at Potters Bar the line descended continuously for 8 miles at 1 in 200, involving the passage of five tunnels. The final obstacle was the spur of high ground outside King's Cross, pierced by two tunnels on a 1 in 107 grade. It was the tunnels that made widening costly and did most to turn the 'opportunity' into the 'incubus'.

A goods depot was provided on Maiden Lane (now York Way), and here a temporary passenger terminus was opened on 7 August 1850. Goods traffic began on 12 December and coal traffic early the next year, the delay being due to disputes with the South Yorkshire Railway and lack of interest by the coal-owners. The GNR was the first railway to bring coal to London in quantity. The struggle with sea-borne coal was intense and a rate war brought prices down from 30s. to 17s. a ton.

In 1851 the Great Exhibition brought a flood of excursionists, the first mass movement on pleasure bent by the working classes. Since there was no telegraph, Maiden Lane had no knowledge of any special trains until they arrived. The return was equally chaotic. On one occasion 3,000 would-be passengers arrived to find the trains would accommodate 1,000. A party of Yorkshire-men invaded a Lincoln train declaring it must take them home. Edmund Denison, the chairman, was restrained from attempting to dislodge them single-handed while cattle trucks were brought up, presumably for the Lincoln passengers.

KING'S CROSS

The short extension to King's Cross was ready in 1852, and the first train to leave was the 7.0 a.m. Parliamentary for York on 14 October. The station had an arrival platform (the present No. 1) and a departure one (No. 10) separated by fourteen tracks. The whole was (and is) covered by a great twin-arched roof, each with a 71-foot span. The offices were all placed along the departure platform.

A separate and severely plain hotel, still in use, was provided, and Lewis Cubitt's façade is even plainer. If the frontage of St Pancras next door might be anything but a railway station, that of King's Cross could hardly be anything else. Cubitt said it was 'to depend for its effect on the largeness of some of its features, its fitness for its purpose, and its characteristic expression of that purpose'. Modern taste applies the architect's yard-stick both inside and out and finds King's Cross measures up.

Denison commented on its low cost and the shareholders protested at 'the extravagance in erecting so splendid a station'. Their view would appear to have prevailed at most other GNR stations. Incidentally the elegance of Euston (1837), the simplicity of King's Cross (1852) and the excesses of St Pancras (1868) epitomize the social history of the period.

In 1855 there were 19 departures, 4 of them expresses. By 1862 there were 30, 10 expresses, 13 locals and 7 Midland. On 1 October 1863 the 'suburban and City' service was inaugurated to Farringdon Street (p. 83), and from 1 January 1866 through goods and passenger trains began to the LCDR. On the East Branch a platform corresponding to the present York Road station was in existence in 1866, but down trains had to set back into the main station.

During 1862 a platform with one 'stepped' face was provided on the arrival side and numbered 2, 3 and 4. On 30 September 1868 the Midland used King's Cross for the last time, but the relief was only temporary. Numbers of trains still grew, mainly with the opening of suburban branches. By August 1873 departures had swollen from 30 to 89; 20 were main line, but there were 60 suburban trains from the Metropolitan and 9 from King's Cross. Accordingly a suburban station was opened in 1875 with three platforms (Nos, 11, 12, 13) and two lines. It was used solely for departures.

Not until 1 February 1878 was there a platform (No. 16) on the 'Hotel Curve' up from the Metropolitan, saving down trains setting back into the terminal platforms. But it is on a 1 in 60 gradient. Until dieselization on 23 March 1959, at peak periods the steam trains would emerge from the smoke-choked 'rat hole' every few minutes, the engines at full throttle. Then, with a load increased by a couple of hundred commuters, the big tank engines would have the task of getting the packed 8-coach trains into motion on the heavy gradient.

By January 1893 there were 539 movements into and out of the station daily. There were 43 main-line and 31 local departures from the terminal platforms, while 98 passenger and 77 goods trains stormed up the 'Hotel Curve'. The main-line trains were all started from No. 10. This led Sir William Acworth, the railway economist, to quote 'a competent critic' as saying: 'The King's Cross porters despatch human beings and the Finsbury Park people collect tickets faster than on any line I know.'

However, on 18 December 1893 a new island platform (Nos. 5 and 6) came into use, one side for departures and the other for arrivals. On 4 April 1895 an extra line of rails was provided between platforms 11 and 12 and the suburban station assumed its present appearance, save for modernization of the offices in 1938–9. In 1903, 15·4 million passengers were dealt with, making it much the busiest northern terminus. This was due of course to the heavy suburban traffic, 54 per cent of the passenger journeys being made by season-ticket holders.

In 1922 the rigid division into arrival and departure sides was broken down by running up suburban trains into platforms 11–13. On 15 December 1924 this part of the station was enlarged by the addition of platforms 14 and 15. These replaced locomotive sidings, which were moved to their present site, formerly occupied by the gas-works which gave their name to the tunnel at the platform ends.

Few more changes were needed to give King's Cross its present form. In September 1926 two more departure platforms, 7 and 8, came into use. They were very narrow and in 1938 they were widened by abolishing No. 9 road. There is thus no platform 9 and similarly no No. 3, as the 'step' was removed converting No. 4 into one long face.

King's Cross now monopolizes the Edinburgh, Dundee and Aberdeen traffic and has always provided the services to the West Highland line. Traffic to the industrial West Riding and North East is heavy all the year round. Since 1950 the tendency has been to provide more frequent and faster services of lighter expresses. So, except perhaps at night, the mighty caravans of seventeen or eighteen coaches are no longer seen. A number of the new services are all-Pullman. Norwegian boat trains leave for Newcastle.

Suburban traffic has greatly declined since 1903. In 1952 less than half the number of trains arrived before 10.30 a.m. as they did fifty years earlier. Growing commuter traffic from the Outer Zone stations between Potters Bar and Letchworth has partially compensated for the large losses in Middle and Inner

Zone traffic diverted to tube extensions. But even in 1970 development is less south of the Thames. It is fully described in Volume V, Chapter 6.

In 1960 daily user averaged 30,000 in winter, 18,000 suburban and 12,000 main line. But in the summer the latter figure swelled to 25,000 a day and to 50,000 on Saturdays.

MAIN LINE DEVELOPMENTS, KING'S CROSS TO FINSBURY PARK

Even in 1864, twelve years after opening, congestion of the double track approaching King's Cross had become serious. James Allport, general manager of the Midland, complained: 'The Midland can never tell with anything like certainty at what time their trains will reach King's Cross.'

The terminus lay at the foot of 1·5 miles inclined at 1 in 107, the line passing through Copenhagen and Maiden Lane (or Gas Works) tunnels. Between the two the lines to goods station and engine sheds branched off.

In 1866 a second Copenhagen tunnel was sanctioned and in 1872 a spur from Finsbury Park to the North London at Canonbury. The latter was to allow freight trains, which hitherto passed over Maiden Lane spur on to the NLR *en route* for the docks and the Royal Mint Street depot (outside Fenchurch Street), to avoid Copenhagen tunnel altogether. Unfortunately Royal Mint Street was somewhat remote, though less so than King's Cross, a serious matter as cartage costs were high due to the rise in horse prices in the 1870's. So the GNR leased a site at Farringdon Street in 1871 and opened a depot on 2 November 1874. Trains thither would have to use the tunnels, and the situation was as before.

So in 1874 powers were sought for a second Gas Works tunnel. The situation was by now quite out of hand. In that year commuters were 2½ times as numerous as seven years previously. Suburban trains were taking half an hour on the 1½ miles from Holloway to the Metropolitan. Indignation meetings were held and a deputation sent to wait on the GNR. Thoroughly alarmed, the latter sought relief by running powers for suburban trains into Broad Street via the Canonbury Spur.

The LNWR prevented the North London from granting these
and in desperation the Great Northern invited the NLR to run
trains from Broad Street out to its suburban stations.

GNR goods trains began running over the Canonbury Spur
on 14 December 1874 and on 18 January 1875 the NLR
suburban trains. These still operate though on a much reduced
scale. Instead of the 73 up trains in 1906 the 12 daily trains in
1960 brought in just over 2,500 commuters. LNER and Eastern
Region stock and crews have been used since July 1945. The
usual GNR termini were Potters Bar, High Barnet, Gordon Hill
and Alexandra Palace.

Goods trains began using the new Copenhagen tunnel in
August 1877 and a flying junction was soon after provided at
Holloway for the goods branch. The duplicate Gas Works
tunnel went into service on 4 March 1878. The two tracks in
this were both up, those in the original tunnel becoming down.
Segregation of Metropolitan traffic on the outer roads was now
possible south of Belle Isle.

General traffic increases soon nullified all these improvements
and the bottleneck was as bad as ever. The chairman, Lord
Colville, reported in January 1882, 'towns were springing up
within two or three miles of King's Cross as fast as people could
build them'. In two years season-ticket holders increased by
25 per cent, from 11,250 in 1879 to 14,420 in 1881, and they
were complaining as bitterly as ever. Goods traffic over the
Widened Lines had reached massive proportions. Finally, two
serious accidents had given rise to justifiable public alarm over
the signalling system. On 10 December 1881 four trains had
run into the back of each other in the darkness of Canonbury
tunnel and a collision occurred in dense fog at Hornsey on
25 January 1882.

There was no alternative to seeking powers for third double-
line tunnels at Copenhagen and Gas Works. On 10 February
1882 Lord Colville said: 'The matter can be delayed no longer.
We are now carrying traffic which produces £3,400,000 on the
same rails near London as twenty years ago when there was a
traffic producing £1,300,000 only; besides we are influenced
by the enormous suburban traffic. . . .' The new tunnels were
brought into service in June 1886 and June 1892 respectively.

Since then signalling improvements and diversion of suburban traffic to the tubes have kept the situation well under control.

In 1960 there were some 24 daily departures from King's Cross Goods, giving next-day deliveries over much of the North. Niddrie Yard (Edinburgh) was reached in about twelve hours. Freightliners were first dispatched in 1966.

Holloway station, just north of Copenhagen tunnel, was opened as a 'ticket station' in 1854 and closed on 1 October 1915. Near by were the cattle docks serving the Metropolitan Cattle Market, used to dispatch Motorail trains to Edinburgh and Perth from 1962 until their diversion to Kensington in 1969.

MAIN LINE DEVELOPMENTS, FINSBURY PARK TO POTTERS BAR

The original stations were Hornsey, Colney Hatch (New Southgate), Barnet (New Barnet) and Potters Bar. On 1 July 1861 a wayside station was opened on the Seven Sisters Road, 2·75 miles from King's Cross. Hornsey Wood with its tea gardens was near by, but little other traffic was expected at the two wooden platforms. But by 1867 it had become the junction for the Edgware branch and there were four lines. Traffic was increasing so fast that the directors recommended a footbridge and 'waiting shed'. But the next year the proprietors were protesting at expenditure on platform canopies.

In 1869 Hornsey Wood became a public park, called Finsbury Park, and this became the name of the station. On 14 December 1874 rebuilding with four platforms was completed. By 1912, 550 trains a day were calling at the four island platforms served by six lines, for Finsbury Park had become the key point in the suburban system. Here passengers from the northern suburbs interchanged between King's Cross, Moorgate and Broad Street trains, or took the tubes to City or West End. Here too suburban trains were terminated to relieve pressure on the lines down to King's Cross. To speed this exchange traffic each local line was served by two platforms and the knowledgeable used trains as bridges between platforms. Platforms 9 and 10 and an extra road were added in 1911.

Today there are no trains to the 'Northern Heights', passengers have deserted the Main and Hertford lines for the tube, and the services to Moorgate and Broad Street are skeletal. In 1961, 218 trains called, less than half the 1912 figure.

South of Finsbury Park land had been bought in 1866 for sidings and eventually some 40 acres were laid out. Clarence Yard dealt with down traffic and East Goods with up. Off the Canonbury line are Highbury Vale and Ashburton Grove, mainly engaged in sorting wagons for local services.

Six tracks have extended to Wood Green since 1892. Up and down traffic is rigidly segregated. There are both up and down yards at Ferme Park, opened in 1888 and partially closed in 1968. Carriage sidings are at Waterworks, beyond Hornsey, and the main ones at Bounds Green, just north of Wood Green.

Beyond Wood Green the five tunnels made widening difficult. Quadrupling to New Barnet was sanctioned by the GNR Act of 1882, but subsequent financial stringency prevented completion until June 1892. But three of the tunnels were in the 2·5 miles from Greenwood Box to Potters Bar summit, and this section remained double for sixty-six years, yet another of the bottlenecks from which the GNR has always suffered. It was not until 3 May 1959 that the widening was completed.

As a measure of later activity on the GNR main line, there were 56 northbound goods trains daily through Wood Green in 1957. Among the up services were the express fish and meat trains from Aberdeen, Hull and Grimsby, vegetable trains from Peterborough and coal trains from there and Doncaster.

SUBURBAN GROWTH ALONG THE MAIN LINE

In 1852 King's Cross was on the extreme edge of London, and Maiden Lane led out to Copenhagen Fields, a resort of holiday-makers. The *Illustrated London News*, describing the journey of the official train at the GNR's opening, said that on emerging from Copenhagen tunnel the train 'went skimming along a region of cornfields. This sudden transition from the busy haunts of life to quiet rural scenery, undisturbed even by the presence of a villa, is what chiefly strikes one. . . .'

But the reporter sent by the same journal to cover the opening of the Alexandra Palace in 1873 found that it was not until Finsbury Park had been passed that 'bricks and mortar began to give way to fields and hedges'. Throughout the 1860's there had been much building in Holloway and along the Seven Sisters Road. This was respectable enough, but noisome slums had deflowered Copenhagen Fields.

In the early days North Middlesex and South Herts was a land 'of indifferent farming and a thinly peopled countryside'. The *Railway Times*, reporting evidence to the Committee considering the London & York's Bill in 1845, says: 'Passing over the first ten miles only, along which there was absolutely no population except a few farmers, country gentlemen and rusticating merchant princes . . . they commenced their case with witnesses from Chipping Barnet.' Lest its readers might think the latter a metropolis, the journal added: 'Barnet with its grocers came on the scene and looked as big as could be wished.'

In 1866 passengers awaiting the 8.45 a.m. at Hornsey watched a hare being chased across neighbouring fields. But in the 1870's rows of small terrace houses spread across Hornsey and Wood Green, a process completed in the next decade. These were Lord Colville's 'towns' (p. 158). Of yellow stock bricks and slate roofs they are as characteristic of the age as the houses of Metroland are of a later one. Every front downstairs window has a bay and in most an aspidistra could be seen through the lace curtains. In 1931 the L.C.C. survey found 248 in every 1,000 of the occupied population to be clerks.

Hornsey grew from 19,387 in 1871 to 61,097 in 1891. But the main period of growth in districts north of Wood Green was slightly later. At first the demand so far out was for larger houses, and Thorne says of Friern Barnet in 1875 that it was a scattered suburban area, many of the houses being residences of wealthy citizens. At that date East Barnet had but 992 souls, though nearby Southgate was growing rapidly.

The high ground was chiefly sought after for these large villas. So, when the rate of building accelerated after 1890, rows of small houses were built along the line. The GNR policy of frequent services and reasonable season-ticket rates created a salient of continuous building which reached out to New Barnet by 1914. This is an equivalent distance out to Harrow and Sidcup, both of which were then far beyond the edge of Greater London. In this the GNR showed a lack of a consistent policy towards suburban development. Regarded by 1870 as an 'incubus', it was nevertheless constantly encouraged from the fringes of the built-up area, leading to continuous expansion. Even today New Barnet remains the edge, and open country intervenes between it and Potters Bar.

THE NORTHERN HEIGHTS

To the north of London the scenery is hilly and diversified. The uplands of the South Herts Plateau are about 350 feet high, but there are deep valleys, including that up which the main line climbs to Potters Bar. From the plateau two prongs of high ground reach out south-westward, the Hampstead ridge, and, behind it and much more cut into by valleys, that on which Barnet and Edgware stand. These are popularly the 'Northern Heights'.

Because for the most part they are crowned with gravel, making water supply and drainage easy, the Northern Heights had more and larger villages than had the clay plain to the west. Highgate and Hampstead had become favourite suburbs for the wealthy and artistic during the eighteenth century, and by 1860 such people were beginning to 'discover' the villages and the small town of Barnet which lay to the north.

But the LNWR passed miles to the south and west of the area and the GNR skirted it to the east. A number of schemes were mooted to provide much-needed communications with this isolated district, and on 3 June 1862 the Edgeware [sic], Highgate & London was incorporated to build a single line from Seven Sisters to Edgware, 8·75 miles away. The company was sponsored by the GNR and absorbed by it on 15 July 1867.

The line was opened on 22 August 1867. Nothing but fields existed between Finsbury Park and Highgate and beyond only Finchley (4,937 in 1861) and Edgware (705 in 1861) were of any importance at all. Mill Hill was tiny and remote from its station (now Mill Hill East).

On 13 May 1864 a short branch was authorized from Park Junction, 0·5 mile beyond Highgate, to Muswell Hill. The ridge here is capped with glacial clay and gravel and there were no villages, the objective being the proposed Alexandra Palace. The 0·75-mile extension to the walls of the Palace was the concern of the Muswell Hill Railway.

The branch was ready for the opening of the Palace on 24 May 1873. The day was fine and the ensuing rush was, according to Grinling, the GNR's historian, still talked of in the King's Cross booking office twenty-five years later. On the first sixteen days 99,000 people travelled out to the Palace along the new line. Then on 9 June the Palace was burnt out and the branch was closed until 1 May 1875 when the Palace reopened. The Muswell Hill Railway, one of the shortest in England, was not absorbed into the GNR until 1911. Its vicissitudes were manifold, the Palace and with it the line being closed seven times between 1875 and 1898.

The 4-mile branch from the optimistically named Finchley and Hendon (later Finchley Church End and now Finchley Central) to High Barnet, authorized on 16 July 1866, was opened on 1 April 1872. What such a line meant to individuals may be judged from the evidence given to the Parliamentary Committee by the vestry clerk of Finchley, W. Hammond. He was a lawyer living in Whetstone who had business interests in the City. He travelled in by bus and coach, taking 90 to 105 minutes to the Bank, at a cost of £30 a year. First-class seasons on rail were to be £10 or £12 and the journey time 50 minutes.

Both branches were built as double track and the original line was doubled to Finchley Central by January 1870. The section beyond Finchley remained single and was treated as a branch after the opening of the High Barnet line.

Until 1914 the service was extraordinarily good by contemporary standards. In 1872 there were 23 weekday departures from High Barnet, 15 from Edgware and 6 more from Finchley. By 1904, 51 up trains were leaving High Barnet, but of the 23 from Edgware all but three terminated at Finchley. There were

46 departures from Muswell Hill, including 29 trains from Alexandra Palace and several additional trains from East Finchley and Highgate. Over 100 trains called at stations on the London side of Park Junction.

The climb up to the Northern Heights was extremely severe. From King's Cross Metropolitan to Finsbury Park was bad enough, but thence to Park Junction the 2·5 miles are continuously inclined at 1 in 75 and 60, up which the diminutive tank engines would blast their slow way at rush hours dragging long trains of crowded four-wheelers.

They were crowded because a good service, cheap fares and healthy pleasant heights encouraged suburban development. Stroud Green station was opened in 1881 to serve the new streets covering the slopes of the Highgate ridge. Muswell Hill grew up between 1890 and 1910, and after 1904 Hampstead Garden Suburb came into being between East Finchley and Golders Green stations. Beyond, right out to Barnet, houses were springing up around the stations. The Edgware branch, however, still penetrated a rural backwater. Barnet had grown from 3,375 in 1871 to 11,335 in 1911, but in that year Edgware's population was still under a thousand.

After 1920 building extended out along the Great North Road to join Barnet with London and Finchley with Hendon. But a salient of country still separates Finchley–Whetstone from New Mill Hill–Edgware. Old Mill Hill, Totteridge and Arkley remained in 1960 curiously rural to remind us how much suburban growth, as it was a century earlier, was still tied to railway stations.

After 1914 train services fossilized and from 1915 the midday and evening trains to Moorgate and Broad Street ceased. The articulated stock provided after 1925 was sufficiently austere, but even in 1935 the LMSR were running sets of four-wheelers out from Broad Street, perhaps to make Moorgate passengers thankful for the LNER's small mercies. Competition from trams and later trolley-buses along the Great North Road to Barnet was also acute.

The truth was that the steam service, notoriously unreliable in winter, had been saturated with new traffic and the LNER lacked capital for the radical improvements needed. The 1935

COMMUTER FASHIONS AT LIVERPOOL STREET I

(34) *In the 1880's segregation of classes by train as well as by carriage was still rigid. The 12.55 p.m. for Enfield (on Saturday, 25 October 1884) carried workmen exclusively.*

(35) *But the homeward-bound workman who happened to be later would have felt ill at ease among the bowler- and top-hatted clerks waiting for the 1.55 p.m. (Saturday, 25 May 1889).*

COMMUTER FASHIONS AT LIVERPOOL STREET II

(36) *Bowlers had given way to boaters on the new 'Jazz' Service of 1920, while the war had broken down the male exclusiveness of the City.*

(37) *Passengers travelled on the new electric trains from Chingford and Enfield in 1961 in undiminished numbers. But on this one at least women appear in the majority among the hatless commuters.*

Plan (p. 187) therefore provided for the whole Northern Heights service to be transferred to London Transport.

The Northern tube was to be extended from Archway to the surface at East Finchley. Tube trains would then run out to Barnet and, over a doubled track, to Edgware. The Northern City Tube (ex-GN & C) was to be extended from Drayton Park to a new island platform at Finsbury Park LNER and the tube trains were to run to Alexandra Palace. Highgate would be rebuilt as a two-level exchange point between the two services, and Park Junction–East Finchley would go out of use for passenger trains.

Tube trains began running to East Finchley on 3 July 1939 and to High Barnet on 14 April 1940. Steam trains continued to run out to East Finchley until 2 March 1941. The Finchley–Edgware service was suspended from 11 September 1939 to facilitate doubling, but on 18 May 1941 tube trains were extended over the single line to Mill Hill East, principally to serve the barracks. All further work was suspended because of the war.

After 1945 London Transport had second thoughts. Costs had risen more than fares were likely to, the Green Belt was more rigidly protected, and war damage to the City had caused a marked fall in commuters thither. Work was not resumed, and in February 1954 London Transport announced the scheme would be permanently abandoned.

Meanwhile steam trains still chugged up to Alexandra Palace, but in the periodic post-war crises of staff and coal shortages it was the Palace services which were first reduced or suspended. Patrons were thus driven to the 212 bus service to Finsbury Park to take the tube there. By 1954 two-coach trains, making some dozen trips a day from Finsbury Park, had an average load of 45 passengers; they ceased to run from 5 July 1954 and the branch was abandoned.

The 57 steam trains from High Barnet were replaced by 212 electric ones, and originating journeys from the eight stations (including Highgate), now served by tube trains, increased from 3·5 million in 1934 to 12 million in 1947. In 1959, 11·6 million originating journeys were made.

These figures not only reveal a slight declining trend. G. F. A.

Wilmot, in his excellent recent monograph, *The Railway in Finchley*, shows them to obscure a rapid increase in peak-hour loadings. In 1950 trains leaving Finchley Central for High Barnet between 5.30 and 6.0 p.m. carried an average of 1,690 passengers between them. Ten years later the figure had swollen to 2,303, a 36 per cent increase. The corollary, of course, is the considerable decline in off-peak loading, and increased operating costs are the result.

A large proportion of the working poulation travels to Central London daily, in 1951, 31 per cent from Finchley and 22 per cent from Barnet. For them the electric service is more reliable than in steam days. Whether crowded tube trains represent an advance in human dignity is a different matter. But the line does show some of the difficulties and limitations in converting an urban 'rapid transit' route into an outer suburban one.

Since all trains stop at all stations into Central London schedules are little quicker than the steam ones. Provided that parking is possible it is quicker and more convenient to drive from Finchley to the West End. This is not the case from places an equivalent distance out on Southern or Great Eastern systems.

ENFIELD AND HERTFORD

Wood Green station, on the main line, was opened in 1859, and in April 1871 a 4-mile branch was opened to Enfield, an old-established and flourishing town, but already served by the Great Eastern (p. 172). The intervening country was almost deserted, its cold clay soils unpopular for agriculture and building.

In 1875 Thorne described Palmer's Green as 'a little gallery of houses along the Enfield Road', and, because of landowners' reluctance to sell, not a single house went up in the area between 1876 and 1888. Bowes Park and the Bycullah Estate (Enfield) grew up after 1880, but the main building period did not come until trams were introduced along the parallel Green Lanes in 1907–9.

The GNR's desire to bypass the Greenwood–Potters Bar bottleneck led to the branch acquiring strategic importance when incorporated into the HERTFORD LOOP, a move eventually preferred to the original scheme of extending the High Barnet branch. The Loop was opened to Cuffley on 4 April 1910 and a single track on through Hertford to rejoin the main line at Langley Junction was ready on 4 March 1918, a second track being brought into use in 1920 (Vol. V, pp. 123-4).

The newer line starts beyond Grange Park station. On it a station was provided at Enfield Chase, the old terminus being retained as a goods depot. In 1962 this became one of the earlier coal concentration depots in Greater London. Establishment of these has enabled most smaller yards to be closed. Because of limited accommodation at Enfield Chase, peak-hour suburban trains are reversed at Gordon Hill. There is a basic service at half-hour intervals out to Hertford North. In addition the Loop justified itself as an alternate route. In 1957, 11 down and 13 up through freight trains were booked over it, though passenger trains have been diverted only in emergencies.

THE PICCADILLY EXTENSION

From the suburbs, new and old, along the main GNR line and the Enfield branch the percentage of the employed population travelling into Central London is among the highest in Greater London. In 1951 the figures were 37 per cent from Hornsey, 35 per cent from Southgate and 30 per cent from Wood Green. The area was thus a special concern of the North and North East London Traffic Enquiry of 1925. The report stated:

> As far as concerns the suburban services of the L.N.E.R., it was generally admitted that if regard be had to their statutory obligations and to the limitations of a steam railway, there was little fault to be had in the manner in which the Company operated their local lines. But in not electrifying their suburban system they have exhibited a want of consideration for the needs of suburban traffic which the travelling public . . . feel they are entitled to expect from an important company possessing a monopoly of railway facilities north of Finsbury Park.

An extension of the Piccadilly from Finsbury Park was recommended and financed through the Development (Loan,

Guarantees & Grants) Act of 1929, which guaranteed interest on capital raised to give employment. The 4·5-mile line, almost wholly in tunnel, was opened to Arnos Grove on 19 September 1932, while trains reached Enfield West (now Oakwood) on 13 March 1933 and Cockfosters on 31 July. In all 7·5 miles were built, the last three on the surface.

To Bounds Green the line served a built-up area, relieving road traffic (30,000 a day were then coming in to Finsbury Park by tram and bus) and cutting deeply into LNER traffic. Northward was the open farmland of Enfield Chase. This part of the new line was speculative, but the builder was quick to follow. Arnos Grove, 'Old' Southgate, Oakwood and Cockfosters, some not even villages, all became large suburbs in less than five years. Southgate became a borough only in 1933, but by 1961 had a population of 72,051.

TUBE TO EDGWARE

Though powers to extend the Hampstead Tube from Golders Green to Edgware had existed for twenty years, work was not started until 1922. On 19 November 1923 the 1·75 miles to Hendon Central were opened, and the 3 miles on to Edgware on 18 August 1924.

The extension released a tremendous housing boom in Hendon during the 1920's and at Edgware during the next decade, for the neighbourhood had hitherto been retarded by the poor services offered by the Midland and the GNR. The 'London Electric Doric' stations became the foci of shopping streets interspersed with drinking palaces in 'Brewers' Tudor'. Hendon Central and Edgware also became the centres of numerous feeder bus routes radiating out through the avenues of semi-detached villas.

At Edgware the old GNR terminus survived unaltered to deal with goods and parcels. The LT terminus near by was built as a through station, and under the 1935 Plan it was proposed to extend the line through virgin country to Bushey Heath. There was also to have been a connection to allow the tube trains from Finchley to enter the LT station. Work on the extension was begun but was interrupted by the war. As explained on page 165, it was afterwards decided not to proceed. The abandoned works can be traced north of Edgware, while the car sheds, erected near Elstree, became the Aldenham bus overhaul works when these were removed from Chiswick.

After the ending of steam suburban workings on the Northern Heights, the LNER, and later the ER, ran freight trains (mainly for coal) out to Edgware, High Barnet and Cranley Gardens to serve the nine depots and the Mill Hill gasworks. In 1956 nine trains were run daily, eight from Highbury Vale and one from King's Cross goods. These were gradually withdrawn as the depots were closed. The last scheduled goods train ran to Edgware on 4 April 1964, and the track beyond Mill Hill East was lifted later that year. The line from Finsbury Park up to Park Junction (Highgate) with the LT line was retained until 1970 for stock movements to and from the LT car sheds.

GREAT NORTHERN ELECTRIFICATION

In spite of the diversion of the Northern Heights services to the LT's Northern Line, suburban traffic from King's Cross along both the main line and the Hertford Loop remains heavy, though the main growth is from the outer suburban area beyond Greater London. The 1956 Modernization Plan envisaged suburban electrification as incidental to conversion of the whole GN main line, and in 1958 G. F. Fiennes, then line traffic manager, predicted completion of the former by 1964. The larger scheme was, however, shelved soon after. From time to time an imminent start to the suburban scheme was announced, but so far no definite date has emerged. Dieselization of suburban services was carried out between 1958 and 1962.

CHAPTER IX

Suburban Traffic Extraordinary:
the Great Eastern

It is not in the showy evolutions of buildings, but in the multiplicity of human habitations . . . that the wonderful immensity
of London consists.

DR JOHNSON (as quoted by BOSWELL).

IN 1840 the north-eastern suburbs of London were more
extensive and more industrialized than those of any other
sector. Sixty years later this was still true, and it was also true
they had become the most homogeneous, now being almost
exclusively peopled by workmen, artisans and clerks. All this
was largely the result of policies consistently pursued by the
Great Eastern Railway after its formation in 1862.

By 1920 the GER had built up a steam suburban system
unrivalled anywhere in intensity and capacity. But steam was
already outmoded for such a task. Thus the period until 1935
saw this system, incapable of radical improvement short of
electrification, fighting a losing battle with overwhelming
traffic increases from expanding suburbs.

After 1935 came a period of struggle to electrify, a task not
completed until 1960. Conversion took two distinct forms – the
Southern system of handling only suburban traffic by electricity,
and the Northern Heights pattern of converting branch lines to
'rapid transit' by projecting tube trains over them.

The story of the GER is told in Volume V. Its nucleus was
the Eastern Counties line, authorized on 4 July 1836 to build
a 5-foot-gauge railway from London to Norwich. The first

section was opened from Devonshire Street, 0·75 mile east of Bethnal Green, to Romford on 20 June 1839. Though Brentwood was reached on 1 July 1840, because of financial stringencies the line was not opened to Colchester until 1843 and Norwich until 1849. On 1 July 1840 a westward extension was opened to the permanent terminus at Shoreditch in the closely built-up eastern suburbs.

On 4 July 1836 the Northern & Eastern Company was incorporated to build a line from Islington to Cambridge, to be the first stage in a trunk line to York. But the N & E was even more impecunious than the ECR and was forced to seek authority to divert the London end to join the ECR at Stratford. From Stratford to Broxbourne was opened on 15 September 1840, Harlow the next year and Cambridge in 1845.

The ECR was, as always, meanly intransigent. Only declining fortunes forced them to allow in N & E trains at all, and tolls were so high that the N & E had to charge higher fares than those of competing coaches and buses. Thus suburban traffic was discouraged, apart from the miserable service. The situation was resolved by the leasing of the N & E to the ECR from 1 January 1844 and in September and October both lines were converted to standard gauge.

On 2 April 1849 the Blackwall Railway, anxious to increase traffic into Fenchurch Street, opened a link from Stepney to the ECR at Bow Junction (1 mile west of Stratford). Typically the ECR were reluctant to grasp this opportunity of reaching a terminus much more conveniently sited than Bishopsgate, and no physical connection was made until 1854.

On the ECR services were infrequent and fares high. Small wonder suburban traffic failed to develop. By 1864, however, there had been a change of policy by the newly constituted Great Eastern. There were now 29 departures for the Broxbourne line, 14 of them for Enfield (branching off at Angel Road). Down the Romford line there were 16 trains, 12 calling at all stations. But the inconveniently sited Bishopsgate (as Shoreditch had become under an 1846 Act) was also becoming inadequate, while the Fenchurch Street (used since 1854) tolls were a constant burden.

On 17 December 1862 the general manager and the engineer

recommended a Cityward extension on grounds which included the possibilities of further developing suburban traffic. 'The importance of this Company's suburban traffic', they said, 'will be felt when the fact is known that within 18 miles of London the passenger traffic considerably exceeds £100,000 per annum.'

The recommendations were accepted, and on 31 December 1863 the Board announced the formation of the Great Eastern Metropolitan Station & Railways Company to extend the line to Liverpool Street, the new terminus being opened for suburban traffic on 2 February 1874. 1,071 people, considerably fewer than in the case of the Broad Street extension, were displaced, but the Act obliged the GER to provide workmen's trains. The Company, however, developed these services far beyond the statutory minimum, with major consequences for the growth and social composition of the north-eastern suburbs.

Bishopsgate became a goods depot (rebuilt 1881; burnt out 5 December 1964 and abandoned) to supplement the original Brick Lane depot (later Spitalfields; closed 1967). Besides general traffic the two depots have played a large part in provisioning London from the farmlands of East Anglia. Twenty-seven thousand sacks of grain and flour were received at Brick Lane in a December week of 1847, and in 1906, 100,000 tons of potatoes were received at Bishopsgate, 1,000 tons of green peas being dealt with on 7 July alone.

THE LEA VALLEY AND HACKNEY DOWNS GROUP OF LINES

From Stratford the N & E ran up the Lea Valley, but the settlements were on high ground to the west. The stations were thus inconvenient, while Tottenham, serving a town which numbered 8,584 in 1841, was the only one of any importance. Until access to Maiden Lane became possible it was used to unload cattle destined for the London market.

To reach some more of these settlements a single line branch, authorized in 1846, was opened on 1 March 1849 from Angel Road through Lower Edmonton to Enfield. Both these were important places in 1841, with populations of 9,027 and 9,367.

Edmonton had become a residential suburb for wealthy Londoners and industry was unobtrusively represented by glass and soap works. Charles Lamb had said of Enfield: 'I had thought in a green old age to have retired to Ponders End – emblematic name, how beautiful.' But industrialization of the Lea Valley had already begun with the establishment of the Royal Ordnance Factory at Enfield Lock.

On 23 June 1864 the GER obtained powers for a line from Loughton Branch Junction, just north of Stratford, through Walthamstow (7,137 in 1861) to High Beech in Epping Forest, already a popular resort. Then on 29 July another line was authorized, from Bethnal Green northward to Hackney Downs. Here it would split, one branch continuing up the high ground west of the Lea to join the Angel Road–Enfield line, the other swinging eastward across the Lea to join the proposed High Beech line, with a north-facing spur from Clapton Junction to Copper Mill Junction on the Lea Valley line.

On 26 April 1870 a single line opened from Lea Bridge on the Lea Valley line to Shern Hall Street (Walthamstow), worked by a shuttle service. This line and an extension to Chingford were sanctioned by an Act of 20 June 1870, together with the abandonment of the original High Beech scheme. The Chingford extension was opened on 17 November 1873, when Shern Hall Street was replaced by Wood Street.

Walthamstow was growing rapidly, but in the early 1870's trains would wait in Hoe Street station for any intending passenger seen running across the surrounding fields. Chingford, a small village of 1,137 souls in 1871, was the gateway to Epping Forest and excursion traffic reached enormous proportions. On Whit Monday 1920 over 100,000 passengers arrived. But thereafter numbers declined as rising living standards made longer trips to seaside and country more common.

The branch was doubled by 2 September 1878 and opened to the present, larger terminus a mile to the north. The station has four platforms and is laid out for an extension never built. The old station served as the goods yard.

The Hackney Downs line was finished in 1872 and most of

the Lea Valley trains were diverted this way, a shorter but more difficult route.

The first part of the Hackney Downs route, from Bethnal Green to Stoke Newington, had been open since 27 May 1872 and on 22 July the local service was extended to Lower Edmonton, where a new high-level station was provided near the original one with its single platform. On 1 August the connection with the old line from Angel Road at Bury Street Junction was ready and the Hackney Downs trains began running over the newly doubled track to Enfield Town. The latter had been rebuilt, involving the demolition of the original station building, a seventeenth-century house and later a school attended by the poet Keats. A third platform was provided in 1920. Until 1939 a few trains ran from Lower Edmonton Low Level to Angel Road. The line remained open until the goods depot closed on 7 December 1964.

The new route to Enfield crossed the Tottenham & Hampstead Junction at Seven Sisters (not to be confused with the station which became Finsbury Park). Only one of the three spurs authorized here was built, that of 1 January 1880 connecting Seven Sisters and South Tottenham. From the former a 2-mile line branched off for Palace Gates, opened to Green Lanes (later Noel Park) on 1 January 1878 and throughout on 7 October. Palace Gates, which is hard by the GNR's Wood Green and which is rather optimistically named, was designed as a through station, for it was intended to continue over the GNR to an end-on junction at Alexandra Palace with the Muswell Hill Railway (p. 163). But the line merely petered out in a goods yard, since 1958 equipped for mechanized retail coal distribution. In 1929 the LNER laid in a siding connection with the Hertford Loop and in 1944 this was fully signalled. It was regularly used by freight trains and excursions to Southend.

The present layout was completed on 1 October 1891 with the opening of the Churchbury Loop from Bury Street Junction to the Lea Valley line at Cheshunt. The district was undeveloped and the inconvenient shuttle service could not compete with electric trams, which were running out to Waltham Cross from 1904. Regular trains ceased on 1 October 1909, though workmen's trains in connection with munitions factories operated between 1 March 1915 and 1 July 1919. Thereafter it was used only for local freight until reopened fully on 21 November 1960 (p. 189).

TRAIN SERVICES AND SUBURBAN DEVELOPMENT

From 1872 a lavish interval service of 6 trains an hour called at Hackney Downs (Table 11, p. 186). Fares were equally attractive and workmen's trains were run from Enfield at 2d. return for the double journey of 22 miles. Though the 1864 Act provided for one workmen's train from Edmonton and one from Wood Street, in 1891 the GER were operating 5 from Enfield and 6 from Walthamstow alone.

There were 6 '2d. trains' from Enfield in 1915, 2 non-stop from Edmonton Low Level via Angel Road and 7 from Wood Street, all leaving before 6.30 a.m. A little later the '3d. trains' left, 2 each from Enfield, Edmonton (non-stop from the Low Level) and Palace Gates and 3 from Wood Street. Later still '4d. and 5d. trains' were run to reach Liverpool Street before 8.0 a.m.

A 30-minute service was now provided to both Chingford and Enfield, augmented at peak periods. Eight trains left Liverpool Street for the Hackney Downs line in the 16 minutes between 5.18 and 5.34 p.m. Outside peak hours, when there were through trains, Palace Gates enjoyed a frequent shuttle service and there were peripheral routes such as those from Palace Gates to North Woolwich via South Tottenham.

Thus was stimulated a mass migration from the overcrowded Inner Arc and already decaying Inner Zone suburbs of Hackney and Stoke Newington. It was the earliest such in London and for the first time the working and lower middle classes were beginning to travel to work by rail on a really large scale.

Through the seventies and eighties rows of small, jerry-built brick boxes, 'chopped off at the ends where another street crossed at distances prescribed by by-law' (Robbins), spread across Tottenham, Edmonton and the east of Wood Green. The proportion of artisans living in Enfield and Walthamstow was lower. Consequently the housing was somewhat better. But in the main the whole area was inhabited by lower-income groups.

The population of Tottenham doubled between 1871 and 1881 and doubled again by 1891, when it reached 97,174. In the same period Edmonton expanded almost three times from 13,860 to 36,351. Enfield, farther out, developed later, increasing by only 3,000 between 1871 and 1881 to 19,104. But by 1901 it had 43,042 inhabitants. Walthamstow numbered 11,092 souls in 1871, doubling at each succeeding census until 1901, when there were 96,720.

By 1914 a salient of suburban development reached Enfield, Ponders End and Walthamstow, relatively farther out than any other sector of Greater London. But after 1930 expansion north of Enfield was halted by the highly capitalized glasshouse industry which had raised land values. East of the Lea, Epping Forest interposed another barrier. However, there was some building around Ponders End and Enfield Lock and particularly in Chingford, which grew from 9,482 in 1921 to 48,355 in 1951. Here housing densities were much lower and incomes higher. In the last few years land values have so risen that horticulture is retreating up the Lea Valley before the rapid advance of the builder. Inter-censal increases (1951–61) of 39·2 per cent were recorded in Waltham Holy Cross, 53·3 in Cheshunt and 30·3 in Hoddesdon.

Rail traffic remained heavy from the outer stations, but began to decline from the inner ones after 1926. Highams Park, on the Chingford line, is one of the less important outer stations, but in 1956, 50,000 ordinary tickets and 1,500 seasons were sold monthly; 170 passenger trains a day called. The Palace Gates branch experienced the most spectacular decline; in 1938 there were 73 up trains, in 1961, 6, while the line was closed to passengers on 7 January 1963 and completely on 28 December 1964.

INDUSTRIAL DEVELOPMENT

The foundations of industry had been laid in the Lea Valley by 1840, development being aided by the Lea Navigation, which still carried two million tons in 1960. The railway began to play a big part after the opening of the Doncaster–March line in 1882, which turned the Lea Valley approach to London into a trunk freight line. A large-scale movement of Yorkshire coal to

East London began and a northern outlet for industry was provided. (The full story is told in Volume V.)

Development accelerated after 1920, when many firms moved out from the East End and many more were newly established. The whole Lea Valley is highly industrialized as far as Broxbourne, factories lining the railway from Lea Bridge. From Enfield Lock to Hoddesdon extend the glasshouses and over all tower the chimneys of the power-stations at Brimsdown and Hoddesdon and the gas-works at Tottenham.

Some idea of the range of industry and of it as a source of rail transport may be gained from details given by C. J. Allen of the make-up of the *Lea Valley Enterprise* on a typical 1960 day. This express freight train was introduced on 2 November 1959 between Tottenham and March. The train left with a single wagon, but after four stops left Broxbourne with 53. Nineteen contained flowers, tomatoes and watercress, and the rest, among other items, ventilating machinery, deck-chairs, confectionery, cables, electrodes, bacon slicers, paper, roofing felt, plastics and paint. In 1957 Waltham Cross, one of the seven goods depots between Temple Mills and Broxbourne, dealt with 19,300 tons of sundries, mainly fruit, vegetables, fertilizers, peat and machinery, 22,244 tons of minerals and 28,610 tons of coal.

Large numbers are employed locally. In 1951 only 12 per cent of Enfield's working population travelled to the Central Area and only 2 per cent from Waltham Holy Cross. From Walthamstow and Tottenham the figures were 18 and 19 per cent. Thus most journeys are short and unless services are highly competitive passengers will easily be lost to road transport.

THE LOUGHTON GROUP OF LINES

It was the Blackwall Company who first had designs on the country between the Lea Valley and Romford lines. But the powers were given to the Eastern Counties, and it was not until 22 August 1856 that the 7 miles were opened from Loughton Branch Junction to the small town of Loughton.

The district served was the rural flanks of the Roding Valley rising to the Epping Forest ridge. Already the villages housed some wealthy business men and there were prospects of suburban traffic. Wanstead and Chigwell numbered 5,000 and 3,000 respectively and were the largest places.

On 24 April 1865 the line was extended 11·5 miles to Ongar from a junction just short of Loughton terminus, which became the goods yard. It ran through a remote area of low, boulder-clay-covered hills north of the Roding. At first single, it was later doubled to Epping. On 1 May 1903 a 6·25-mile FAIRLOP LOOP was opened from a triangular junction with the Romford line at Ilford to a south-facing junction north of Woodford.

Services were sparse compared with those over the Hackney Downs lines. In 1874 Loughton had 22 down trains, Epping 9 and Ongar 6. But by 1894 there had been much suburban development at the southern end and 62 trains were now booked to pass on to the branch, 11 to terminate at Snaresbrook and 1 at Woodford; 28 went on to Loughton, 8 to Epping and 14 to Ongar. By 1920 the total had risen only to 68 – 51 originated from Liverpool Street, 14 from Fenchurch Street and 3 from Stratford. In the same year the Fairlop Loop had 22 services between Woodford and Ilford. A shuttle service ran during slack hours, but at peak periods roundabout trains were run from the London termini.

The comparatively infrequent services and more particularly the absence of workmen's facilities inhibited suburban growth and confined any there was to better-class housing. Leyton and Leytonstone grew up between 1870 and 1900, the same period as Walthamstow. Wanstead's main period of growth dates from 1900 to 1920 and the terrace and semi-detached houses are larger. Woodford is almost unique in the Middle Zone of north-east London, consisting largely of the detached houses of middle and upper income groups.

Between the wars Woodford grew rapidly and there was considerable expansion around the stations at Buckhurst Hill, Loughton and Theydon Bois. Since the post-war electrification, growth has continued on a large scale all the way to Epping, though there is still some open country between stations. Epping's 1951–61 increase was 44·1 per cent. Beyond Epping the aluminium tube trains bounce incongruously through woods and fields.

Save where Ilford had spread out to Newbury Park, there had been little development along the Fairlop Loop prior to 1914. Between the wars the L.C.C. built a large estate at Barkingside, served chiefly by trams, and there was considerable expansion around the substantial branch stations to the north, expansion which is continuing rapidly since 1950.

THE ROMFORD LINE

An agreement between the ECR and a Stratford farmer stipulated before construction began he could remove 'as many of the mangel-wurzel plants as may be growing on the said lands' as he thought fit. Market gardens, interspersed by mansions in their parks, extended over the fertile plain to Romford, after which the line climbed into the low, wooded hills around Brentwood. Stratford, Ilford, Romford and Brentwood were the only places of any consequence along the High Road to Colchester. Romford, numbering 5,317 in 1841, was by far the largest.

For many years the local service was sparse in the extreme beyond Stratford. Forest Gate, 1·5 miles to the east, had but two trains a day and its receipts, the most meagre on the line, were so small it was closed from 1844 to 1846. But 350,000 passengers a month were using it in 1912. In 1864 there were 12 down locals beyond Stratford compared with the 40 on the North Woolwich line.

By 1874 the Lea had become the frontier of Greater London, and Stratford (23,286 in 1871) formed a sizable bridgehead beyond. The old centre along the Broadway retained its rural charm, but Hudson Town (the appropriately named railway settlement) spread northwards, grimly industrial. Besides the railway workshops, new plants included engineering, printing, match and soap making and tar distilling. Ilford and Romford were still market towns and grew very slowly. The infrequent local service was now augmented by an hourly suburban service to Forest Gate. It was not until 1900 that the rows of terrace houses engulfed Ilford and Seven Kings. Romford was still almost unaffected, but beyond it a model estate was taking shape at Gidea Park in 1910 when that station was opened.

In 1894 there were 36 suburban trains for Ilford, 14 of them going on to Romford and 8 more for places beyond. But by 1906 there were 83 suburban services from Liverpool Street and 44 from Fenchurch Street to Ilford. Fifty-seven went on to Romford and a further 22 terminated beyond, mostly at Brentwood and Shenfield.

In the inter-war period building spread out to meet the expanding Romford, which grew fourfold from 19,442 in 1921 to 88,002 in 1951. North of Ilford, along the new Eastern Avenue, a vast suburb grew up entirely devoid of any rail facilities. There was even further post-1945 development in North Ilford and in Romford, which grew by almost a third between 1951 and 1961. On the outskirts of Romford the L.C.C. built the Harold Hill Estate. Its 1961 population, estimated at 32,735, was entirely dependent on a rather inadequate bus service.

Shenfield now became the terminus of the intensive suburban service instead of Romford. The line had been quadrupled to Ilford in 1895, to just west of Romford in 1902 and to Gidea Park in 1931, being finally extended to Shenfield in 1934.

On 16 July 1883 the GER were accorded powers for a 21·25-mile line from Shenfield to Southend. This was opened to Wickford for goods on 19 November 1888 and for passengers on 1 January 1889 and on to Southend for all traffic on 1 October. Doubling between Wickford and Prittlewell was completed in 1901.

The line ran across low hills, separated from the gravel plateau on which Southend is built by a stretch of London Clay. The main objective was of course Southend. Apart from excursion traffic a business service was provided in 1911 with 5 fast up trains in the morning and back at night. The rather poor soils kept low the value of land *en route*, and after 1920 the good business service created a curious form of suburban development. While elsewhere the normal form was of continuous building of houses in small gardens, outward from the stations of Billericay, Wickford, Rayleigh and Hockley spread asbestos bungalows, huts, bus bodies and railway carriages in unplanned anarchy. For the most part they ranged at irregular intervals along a maze of unmade and unadopted roads.

RURAL OUTPOSTS

(38) *The small country station-house of the London & Croydon's Anerley station survives unchanged in a suburban shopping street.*

(39) *Walthamstow's Hoe Street station, now in the heart of the town, was still in open country in the 1870's.*

(40) *Modernization of a rural branch. A London Transport train from Ongar enters Blake Hall station in 1961, unaltered from* GER *days.*

AN EAST LONDON MISCELLANY

(41) *Early days on the Eastern Counties Railway: an animated scene at Shoreditch terminus about 1850.*

(42) *An East London key point: Stratford in GER days. The Lea Valley line diverges to the left and the Romford line to the right. The platform from which the photograph was taken has been superseded by the new Romford line/London Transport exchange platforms farther west.*

(43) *The Thames Tunnel. A train leaves the under-river section of the East London line and enters Wapping station at the northern end.*

Without the normal suburban amenities, most of these dwellings were on small holdings of an acre or so. Too small to provide a living, they were cultivated as a spare-time occupation by pensioners and commuters. Planning authorities can happily prevent the spread of huts and bus bodies, but since the area can no longer be designated agricultural, orthodox houses are springing up on vacant sites.

STRATFORD

Ever since the N & E made their junction with the ECR in 1840 Stratford has been the key point in the railway geography of East London. On 29 April 1846 the first section of the Woolwich branch was opened from Eastern Junction, a triangular layout being completed on 14 June next year. On 15 August 1854 the line from the North London at Victoria Park was opened through a new low-level station to Sheet Factory Junction on the Woolwich branch. From the north side of the low level a connection was laid to the Lea Valley line at Chobham Farm Junction and beyond that another spur from Channelsea Junction up to the main line on the Bow Junction side of the high-level station. In later years the Chobham Farm spur ran through the works, and to avoid them a new loop was provided from Lea Junction to Loughton Branch Junction.

In 1840 the ECR had set up their repair shops at Romford, but between 1845 and 1848 they were transferred to a site at Stratford adjoining the locomotive roundhouse on the up side of the Lea Valley line. Later they expanded over the land on the down side. The present locomotive depot, beyond the Chobham Farm spur, dates from 1888 and in 1897 the wagon works were moved out to Temple Mills. Stratford works are now due for closure.

The handsome buildings of the passenger station were erected in 1846–7 between the Lea Valley and the Romford lines. At present there are three platforms on both lines, but the Lea Valley platforms have not been used since 1969 and trains call at the Romford ones only at peak hours. The main activity is at the new station immediately to the west, where cross-platform exchange takes place between GER electric suburban services and Central Line Tube trains, which briefly emerge at the surface. Beneath are the two low-level platforms.

Just north of Loughton Branch Junction was a siding adjoining a water-mill formerly owned by the Knights Templars. We first hear of Temple Mills siding in a minute of 13 November

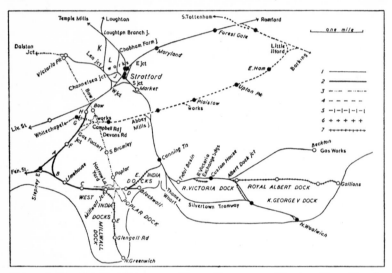

FIG. 16. Dockland railways: 1, Great Eastern. 2, Blackwall. 3, North London. 4, London, Tilbury & Southend. 5, Whitechapel & Bow. 6, Tottenham & Forest Gate. 7, Port of London Authority. A, Salmons Lane Junction. B, Limehouse Junction. C, West India Docks station. D, Poplar station. E, South Dock station. F, Burdett Road station. G, Bow Road (W & B) station. H, Bow Road (Blackwall) station. J, Fork Junction. K, Freightliner Terminal, L, LIFT.

1877 in which the Way and Works Committee authorized an extension. Every year between 1880 and 1893 further extensions were authorized, and in October 1930 the Cambridge 'hump' yard was opened. The eight groups of sidings were unified and modernized in 1954–9 with 48 sorting sidings and a daily capacity of 4,500 wagons. In 1958 there were 74 daily arrivals at the south end of Temple Mills and 51 departures from the north. On 4 July 1967 the London International Freight Terminal (LIFT) became operational on the site of part of the works, and the Freightliner terminal opened on the site of High Meads sidings on the opposite side of the Loughton Branch—Lea Junction spur.

LIVERPOOL STREET

Liverpool Street was opened to suburban trains on 2 February 1874 and to all traffic on 1 November 1875, when Bishopsgate was closed to passengers. It was reached by a four-road extension (increased to six in 1891), diverging just west of Bethnal Green and descending at 1 in 70, for the most part through a gloomy cutting in which were the smoke-wreathed platforms of Bishopsgate Low Level (open from 4 November 1872 to 22 May 1916). Originally the terminus comprised platforms 1 to 10, now known as the West Side. The eight platforms of the East Side went into service on 2 April 1894.

Convenient situation, lavish services and low fares made Liverpool Street into the busiest London station. In 1855, 2·14 million had used Bishopsgate, and in 1902 65·3 million were passing through Liverpool Street. In 1897 the '2d. trains' carried 2 million passengers into Liverpool Street and the '3d. and 4d.', or 'half-fare trains', 6 million. The workmen in caps and corduroy trousers and the junior clerks in bowlers and dark suits crowded the hutch-like four-wheeled coaches. The *Illustrated London News* observed: 'The passengers by the 2d. trains are not to be commended in either language or attire' but the 'half-fare trains' were patronized by 'the better class of workmen, warehousemen, shopmen and not a few poorly paid clerks.'

Between 8.0 and 9.30 the ordinary trains poured in the season-ticket holders, top-hatted and morning-coated senior clerks and executives. As yet women were conspicuously absent from business trains.

The L.C.C.'s enquiry into workmen's services accorded the GER their accolade. 'The Great Eastern is especially the workman's London railway – the one above all which appears to welcome him as a desirable customer.'

In 1902, 90·7 per cent (59·2 million) of the passengers were travelling to and from stations less than 12 miles out; 3·8 per cent (2·5 million) were to and from those between 12 and 30 miles out; and 5·5 per cent (3·6 million) to and from those over 30 miles. These figures underline the overwhelming predominance of suburban traffic. But the growth of long-distance traffic must not be overlooked. It now exceeded that of Euston or King's Cross.

By 1903, 75,000 passengers were arriving daily before 10.30 a.m. alone. The comparable Paddington figure was 1,800. 399 suburban and 36 main-line trains were booked to arrive daily, and this total was exceeded only at London Bridge. On the nine trains from Walthamstow between 7.30 and 8.0 a.m. there were 7,400 seats and about 7,100 passengers, but the last two were uncomfortably crowded. Then as now the problem of the peak loomed large.

Over 200,000 passengers and 1,250 trains movements were being dealt with daily by 1912, though trams were taking many short-distance travellers. By 1919 recovery from the war was under way. Boaters were now being worn by the peak-hour crowds and the war had turned the woman City worker into a commonplace. Traffic increases, and more particularly shortened hours, were causing an operating crisis. But electrification of the Enfield and Chingford lines, by far the most densely occupied, would have cost £5 million. With the low fares dictated by statute and by road competition this was not considered economic. Instead, after an intensive period of 'work study', Sir Henry Thornton, whom the GER had recruited from the U.S.A. as general manager, and the superintendent of operation, F. V. Russell, devised an increased service involving only minor alterations to the tune of £80,000.

On 12 July 1920 the 'Jazz' Service began, so called from the yellow and blue stripes painted under the coach roofs to distinguish first and second class. By the use of engine spurs at the platform ends and turnover locomotives, platform occupation could be cut to 4 minutes if the train could be loaded that quickly, and in practice a train entered each platform every 10 minutes. Seating was increased by 50 to 75 per cent and on the down suburban track 24 trains an hour could be run, representing 20,350 passenger seats. This has been claimed by many writers to have been more than any contemporary electric

TABLE 10

SAMPLE FROM A PASSENGER CENSUS TAKEN BY THE GER
WHILE PLANNING THE 1920 'JAZZ' SERVICE

	Boarding Alighting 6.5 p.m. Down		Boarding Alighting 7.40 a.m. Up	
Liverpool Street	1,241	—	—	1,022
Bethnal Green	81	2	6	35
Cambridge Heath	57	3	non-stop	
London Fields	22	2	non-stop	
Hackney Downs	62	14	33	65
Clapton	46	68	56	55
St James Street	9	551	286	0
Hoe Street	15	594	570	0
Wood Street	3	196	118	3
Highams Park	6	63	71	11
Chingford	—	49	48	—
	6.17 p.m. Down		7.3 a.m. Up	
Liverpool Street	979	—	—	1,167
Bethnal Green	65	14	10	82
Cambridge Heath	29	10	2	30
London Fields	9	18	0	25
Hackney Downs	20	41	10	44
Rectory Road	6	46	11	4
Stoke Newington	28	36	9	26
Stamford Hill	3	55	12	3
Seven Sisters	2	166	198	13
Bruce Grove	6	196	200	3
White Hart Lane	0	46	77	3
Silver Street	1	140	386	16
Lower Edmonton	13	227	236	5
Bush Hill Park	3	109	224	0
Enfield Town	—	60	31	—

system could have dealt with. Strictly in terms of *seats* this is probably true, but in 1936 passengers were being carried at the rate of 27,000 an hour west-bound through Charing Cross (District) and 26,000 an hour on one track of the Northern Line. But the GER *tour de force* enabled 51 trains to leave between 5.0 and 6.0 p.m., most in the charge of a diminutive but vociferously pugnacious tank engine, 27 for the Hackney Downs line, 8 for the Loughton line and 16 for Ilford and beyond.

TABLE 11

THE HACKNEY DOWNS GROUP OF LINES
DEPARTURES FROM LIVERPOOL STREET BETWEEN
5.0 AND 5.59 p.m.

	1874	1884	1920*	1958	1962	1970
White Hart Lane	2	—	—	—	—	—
Palace Gates	—	2	3	—	—	—
Enfield	2	3	10	4	6	6
Wood Street	2	1	6	—	—	—
Chingford	1	2	6	8	9	6
Broxbourne and beyond†	—	1	4	7	12	15
	7	9	29	19	27	27

* 'Jazz' Service.   † Including trains via Lea Bridge.

In 1924, 280,00 passengers a day were passing through, 40,000 in the busiest hour, which was more than many of the other London termini had in the twenty-four. But it was the apotheosis of steam suburban traction and no further improvements were possible, save in passenger comfort. For the service was still being operated by set trains of 16 four-wheeled coaches. Not until 1925 did Sir Nigel Gresley start introducing his quintuplet articulated sets, two per train, which lasted until electrification in 1960. Yet in 1925 the Metropolitan had been carrying its passengers for twenty years in electric trains of bogie coaches and the Southern was rapidly converting its suburban system to electricity.

Service cuts were made in the 1926 General Strike and further ones during the last war, never to be fully restored. For there was also a continuous decline in traffic from the Inner Zone stations. The Loughton traffic, too, was diverted to the Central Line. The average weekday user therefore declined to about 160,000 after the second world war. But by 1958 it had recovered to some 174,000 and a census taken in 1960 shows a 4 per cent increase in two years.

ELECTRIFICATION

The 'Jazz' Service represented 'the last word in steam operated suburban services' (C. J. Allen), and was rightly praised as such in the technical press. But the GER was a victim of its own success, for such was the suburban growth its services had created that as far back as 1890 it was felt north-east London required better facilities.

In 1894 the London, Walthamstow & Epping Forest Railway was authorized as an electric line from Finsbury Circus. The scheme lapsed, but in the 'Tube Mania' of 1901 there were two Bills, the North East London (Mansion House–Tottenham) and the City and North East Suburban (Cornhill–Waltham Abbey). Next year James Holden produced from Stratford Works a ten-coupled tank engine which at its test in 1903 could accelerate from rest a 15-coach train (of four-wheelers) more quickly than could electricity. It was a bluff, for excessive track damage would have been caused by the monster in regular service. But, though the City & North East Suburban's Bill was passed in 1905, no more was heard of it.

The 1905 Royal Commission recommended electrification of the GER and tube extension, and the 1925 London Traffic Enquiry (p. 167) echoed its recommendations. Town councils were continuously vociferous, and as counter-propaganda the LNER announced interest in a tube to Stratford and Ilford, which the GER had proposed in 1901. But the LNER took no practical steps, consistently maintaining that the type of traffic prevented a sufficient level of earnings to amortize the capital involved in electrification.

The opportunity did not come until 1935, by which time passenger user at Liverpool Street had fallen to 230,000 a day. In that year radical improvements were decided on as part of the agreement with the Treasury which guaranteed interest on loans for capital works to relieve unemployment (*see also* Vol. II, p. 190). The war badly delayed the programme, which was not finally completed until 1960.

The scheme fell into three clearly marked sections: the projection of Central Line tube trains over the Loughton line;

electrification of the Romford line; and electrification of the Hackney Downs lines.

The Central tube was to be extended eastwards from its Liverpool Street terminus, with cross-platform exchange with the District at a rebuilt Mile End station and similar facilities with the GER at Stratford. The line would finally surface to connect with the Loughton line just beyond Loughton Branch Junction. Tube trains would run over this all the way to Ongar, and round the Fairlop Loop from Woodford to Newbury Park. But instead of running on to Ilford there would be a new tube along the line of Eastern Avenue back to Leytonstone on the Loughton line. Thus, at last, North Ilford would have direct rail communication.

TABLE 12

SERVICE FREQUENCIES ON THE CENTRAL LINE – 1960

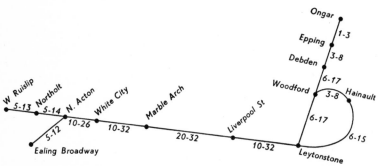

The figures show the number of trains per hour each way: the first is that of the basic service, the second that of peak periods.

Central Line trains began running to Stratford on 4 December 1946 and to Leytonstone on 5 May 1947, when steam trains ceased to run west thereof. The latter were also withdrawn from the Fairlop Loop from 30 November, and on 14 December the tube service was extended from Leytonstone to Woodford and through the North Ilford tunnels to Newbury Park. The curve from the latter round to Ilford was immediately disconnected, but goods trains used that to Seven Kings until March 1956. The rest of the Loop was reopened on

31 May 1948 as far as Hainault and on to Woodford on 21 November. On that day too the tube service was extended to Loughton. Epping was reached on 25 September 1949, but the steam shuttle service, retreating before the electrical advance, continued to serve Ongar until 18 November 1957.

Trains run out from Central London to Epping (or short thereof) and to Hainault via Newbury Park, shuttle services connecting Epping with Ongar and Woodford with Hainault. Since 5 April 1964 the latter has been operated with driverless trains. North Ilford is fully built up and traffic on this section is probably at its maximum. But increases from north of Woodford are already posing a problem. The line, too, is operated on the 'rapid transit' basis, all trains stopping at all stations, while they are formed of stock with low seating capacity and low maximum speeds. The Bank, 17·5 miles from Epping, cannot be reached in less than the standard time of 40 minutes, while in business hours trains reach Walton-on-Thames, 17 miles from Waterloo, in 21 minutes, and are far more comfortable.

The LNER electrified the Romford line with overhead wires carrying 1,500 volts D.C. Electric trains began running to Shenfield on 26 September 1949, and were extended on to Chelmsford on 11 June 1956 and to Southend on 31 December. In 1962 slack periods 3 trains an hour left for Gidea Park, 3 for Southend and 1 for Chelmsford.

In the last year of steam working 2·6 million ordinary passengers were carried between Shenfield and Southend and Chelmsford. In the first year of electrification these more than doubled to 5·4 million and in the second rose further to 5·9 million. Because of even greater increases in season-ticket holders, receipts rose by 117 per cent in the first year of the new working, while operating costs fell. The whole system was converted to A.C. at 50 cycles over the first weekend (4–6) of November 1960. (Chelmsford converted 20 March 1961.)

The Hackney Downs lines were electrified on the same system, the new services being inaugurated on 21 November 1960. Included in the scheme was the Churchbury (now Southbury) Loop. The basic service was of 6 trains an hour to Enfield and Chingford (later cut to 3) and 2 to Broxbourne, where at the new station they were divided into Bishop's

Stortford and Hertford East portions (the latter later became a Broxbourne–Hertford shuttle). The Lea Valley line south of Cheshunt remained diesel operated until electrified as far as Copper Mill Junction and the spur to the Hackney Downs line. On 5 May 1969 a service was inaugurated of 2 trains an hour to Bishop's Stortford via Southbury and 2 to Hertford via Copper Mill, with connections at Broxbourne. Some diesel trains from North Woolwich continued via Lea Bridge to Tottenham. The latter was now an important interchange with the Victoria Line.

The electrification scheme as a whole improved communications with the Inner Zone between Bethnal Green and Stoke Newington and Clapton, which had the worst rail service of any equivalent area, and with the rapidly growing Outer Zone beyond Cheshunt (Volume V, pp. 111–17) as well as to the Middle Zone. By 1967 traffic had exceeded expectations.

LIVERPOOL STREET TODAY

Liverpool Street has acquired a rather unjustified reputation for dirt and gloom, but even in steam days it was considerably cleaner and more cheerful than Broad Street, Euston or King's Cross. A clean, smartly painted and spacious station lies behind the Gothic hotel and office block, a milder and less aggressive façade than that of St Pancras. The revolution completed between 1949 and 1962 has eliminated steam. Not only does the ear miss the bark of hard-worked tank engines, but the even more characteristic beat of the Westinghouse brake pumps.

All services, main line and suburban, are now on an interval basis, save at peak periods. Traffic and therefore atmosphere at Liverpool Street accords far more with that of termini south of the Thames. The census of 4 October 1960 showed 181,152 passengers passing the barriers. Though busy at all times, in the evening peak the spacious concourse under its high arched roof is a seething lake of humanity fed by rivers converging on the station from various parts of the City and drained by others flowing through the platform barriers.

Here again is the problem of the peak. On the census day

43,675, or 46 per cent, of the 91,013 departing passengers left between 5.0 and 6.0 p.m., and there was a similar concentration of up traffic into the morning peak. The 5.46 p.m. for Chingford carried 1,289 passengers, the 2.8 p.m., 43.

Between 5.3 and 6.0 p.m. 29 electric trains down the Romford line carried 30,530 passengers on the census day, over 1,000 apiece. Incidentally a further 6,767 passengers joined at Stratford. The actual peak was from 5.33 to 5.43 when 6 trains took out 9,743 passengers (*nearly 1,000 per minute*), a further 1,503 people joining the 4 which stopped at Stratford.

The 1969–70 timetable shows 65 departures between 5.0 and 6.0 p.m. On the Hackney Downs line there were 24 electric trains, 6 apiece for Chingford and Enfield, 9 via the Lea Valley and 3 via Southbury, and 3 main line diesel trains for Cambridge. On the Romford line there were 38 electric departures, 20 for Ilford, Gidea Park or Shenfield, 11 for Southend and 7 for Chelmsford or beyond. The following year several more trains were put on the Romford line.

As at the Southern termini long-distance commuting is increasing fast and Southend and Clacton are the counterparts of the Kent Coast or Brighton. There is the same high proportion of holiday and day excursion traffic to seaside resorts. The 1,000 passengers a day to Clacton in winter multiply to over 8,500 in summer. Among these resorts are Southend and other popular ones like Felixstowe and Yarmouth, or the more exclusive such as Frinton. Here too is the continental traffic. There are 3 daily services to Harwich, running in duplicate and triplicate for much of the year, and occasional liner specials to the Royal Docks and Tilbury.

Long-distance trains are well filled. The 1960 census showed 11,200 passengers on the 52 main-line departures on Tuesday, 4 October, 215 per train on the average, though varying from 613 on the 5.16 p.m. for Cambridge and 508 on the 5.45 for Harwich to 2 on the 3.20 a.m. for Clacton.

Parcel and mail traffic is large, about 10 million parcels a year being dealt with. At Liverpool Street are the similar quiet efficiency, ordered haste and type of passenger as are to be found at Waterloo, though the frenzied *crescendo* of peak hours is more like that of Charing Cross.

CHAPTER X

Dockland and Suburbia on North Thames-side

Southend is only in its infancy, the district traversed by your Bow and Barking branch has yet to be built over; your Gravesend traffic is now at its minimum; there is a probability of docks being constructed at Tilbury. . . .

REPORT OF COMMITTEE OF INVESTIGATION,
LONDON, TILBURY & SOUTHEND RAILWAY, 1864.

THE shores of the Thames Estuary are generally low and marshy, but there is firm ground suitable for early town growth at a number of places on the Kentish bank. On the Essex side, however, this occurs only at Grays and Southend. Thus in 1830 only Barking and Southend were of potential importance below Poplar, then on the very edge of Greater London. Barking was a market town and small port on Barking Creek (the Roding Estuary), its fishing fleet numbering 120 smacks in 1833. Southend was a small and exclusive resort. Paradoxically, therefore, the first railways on the north bank were built to serve towns in Kent. But they soon effected such a revolution on the rural seclusion they had violated that the fate of the Kentish traffic became of very secondary import.

Apart from Howland Dock, the nucleus of the Surrey Commercial Docks, London's dock system developed in the early years of the nineteenth century on the low north bank between the high ground of the City and the Lea Estuary. Hard by the City, the London Docks date from 1805 and the adjacent St Katharine Dock from 1828, while, farther downstream, the West India Docks date from 1802 and the East India from 1806. The two last were connected with the City by the East India

Dock Road of 1810, along which a ribbon of industry and housing soon spread. But southward stretched the undeveloped Isle of Dogs and to the north fields and common land separated Poplar from Bow.

Steam vessels had increased the already heavy traffic on the river. The resorts of Margate, Ramsgate and Southend received their visitors by water; the normal way from Maidstone, Chatham and Canterbury to London was by road to Gravesend and thence by water; while Woolwich and Greenwich had a frequent ferry service Londonward.

THE BLACKWALL RAILWAY

In the 1830's the steamers on the 'Long Ferry' to Gravesend were carrying a million passengers a year. Most of these, and other river and cross-Channel steamers as well, called at Brunswick Wharf, Blackwall, for this was 6·5 miles from London Bridge by water, but only 4 miles from Aldgate Pump along East India Dock Road.

It was to speed communication between Brunswick Wharf and the City that the Commercial Railway was incorporated on 28 July 1836 to build a line from Minories to Blackwall. Its name was changed to the London & Blackwall in 1839 when the short extension to Fenchurch Street was authorized. The 3·3 miles of 5-foot-gauge line were opened to passenger traffic on 6 July 1840. Mostly on a viaduct, it was cable operated. A second track went into use on 3 August, when a 15-minute service was inaugurated.

The 415 yards into Fenchurch Street were opened on 2 August 1841, and the 1846 Commission (p. 22) was told this had increased traffic by 50 per cent. Intermediate stations were provided, but steamer passengers were the chief source of revenue. In 1846 the Blackwall railway carried 1·8 million passengers. In the month of June 1844, of the 331,644 passengers landed and embarked at Gravesend, over 200,000 were to and from Blackwall.

In 1848–9 the line was converted to standard gauge and to locomotive haulage in preparation for the link with the ECR, opened to Bow Junction on 2 April 1849 (p. 171). The

Blackwall Company were turning to sources of revenue other than steamer traffic, for, with the development of direct rail communication with places on the Lower Thames, steamer traffic had already begun to decline.

Other companies were encouraged to use Fenchurch Street as their City terminus. From 1850 an NLR service had operated (p. 75), the ECR began through working in 1854 (p. 171) and in the same year London, Tilbury & Southend trains arrived via Stratford and in 1858 via Gas Factory Junction (p. 199). 'Foreign' companies also used the line as access to goods stations serving the City and London Docks.

Another source of revenue was the growth of docks, industry and housing in the Isle of Dogs. The West India Docks were enlarged in the 1840's and Millwall Dock was opened in 1868. Housing for dock workers went up, mainly in Millwall and Cubitt Town (1843), and factories lined the river bank.

A railway system was laid out to serve the docks, the 'trunk' being 1·5 miles of single line from Millwall Junction, on the Blackwall line, to the River at North Greenwich. Built under the Blackwall's Act of 19 June 1865, ownership of the MILL-WALL EXTENSION was complex. The Blackwall had 5 chains at the north end and 31 at the south and, between, the London and India Docks had 41 chains and the Millwall Dock 52 chains.

The line to West India Dock was completed in 1867 and was opened on to Glengall Road on 18 December 1871 and to North Greenwich on 29 July 1872. It was operated by a joint committee of all the owners. In addition to goods traffic there was a passenger service from 1871, operated north of Glengall Road by horse cars until 1880. The trains, operated by three diminutive engines and primitive coaches, ran for the last time on 3 May 1926. The GER and the Blackwall bought the ferry to Greenwich. As late as 1900, 1·3 million passengers were carried over it, but it was closed in 1902 when the L.C.C. opened the foot tunnel.

By the 1950's the line had been taken up beyond Glengall Road; the rest was still the 'main line' of the Docks system operated by the Port of London Authority. In the 1950's this carried about 15,000 tons of goods monthly, 6,000 export,

7,000 import and 2,000 internal. On 1 May 1970 the P.L.A. ceased rail operations and rail traffic was lorried to the berths from goods depots.

On 1 January 1866 the Blackwall was leased to the GER, but the small company remained independent until 1923. The service was always intensive and in 1920 there were 57 down trains, but by then traffic had almost vanished. The service was withdrawn permanently from 4 May 1926 on the occasion of the General Strike.

Since the war the junction at Stepney has been severed, while the spur, opened in 1880 to allow through running from the Bow direction, carried but 3 trains a day in 1953. The principal entrance to the dock lines is the Harrow Lane yard at Millwall Junction approached from the NLR (p. 76).

THE NORTH WOOLWICH LINE AND ITS BRANCHES

In 1844 the Eastern Counties & Thames Junction was incorporated to build 1·75 miles of line from Stratford to what is now Thames Wharf on Barking Creek. Promoted by G. P. Bidder, a prominent railway contractor (p. 55), it was commonly known as 'Bidder's Folly', passing as it did through a completely undeveloped area. The next year an Act was obtained for the 2·75-mile North Woolwich Railway to extend the line through uninhabited and roadless marshes to the ferry at North Woolwich.

The line was opened from Stratford to Canning Town on 29 April 1846 and on to the spacious classical terminus on 14 June 1847. R. Ruegg, in *Rambles around Woolwich* (1847), said the only buildings at North Woolwich were 'a public house . . . a small house occupied by the family of a shepherd, and the terminus of the North Woolwich Railway. It is singular to hear the whistle of a locomotive . . . where twelve months since the heron, the plover and the bittern roamed'.

In 1847 the Thames Junction bought the North Woolwich, and Bidder ran an hourly service until 1854, when the Eastern Counties were at last persuaded to have dealings with the new line, starting a service from Fenchurch Street via Stratford. On 31 March 1858 the ABBEY MILLS SPUR was opened from the LTSR line east of Bromley to the North Woolwich line north of Canning Town, and thereafter many trains used this route. In 1854 trains began running over the Victoria Park–Stratford link (p. 181), worked by the NLR until 1866, by it and the GER alternate years until 1874 and by the GER thereafter, surviving in an attenuated form until 1942.

Meanwhile Bidder had bought up the unwanted marshes and in 1850 floated the Victoria Dock Company to utilize them. 'The principal feature which distinguished the Dock from its predecessors was that it was brought into direct communication with the railways of the United Kingdom' (J. G. Broodbank).

The North Woolwich line was diverted through Custom House station on the north side of the new dock, the old line on the south side becoming the Silvertown Tramway (legally the 'Woolwich Abandoned Line') serving factories along the river bank. Squalid houses, crushed between factories and docks, were erected, passenger traffic grew and Tidal Basin and Silvertown stations were opened.

In 1880 the Royal Albert Dock was opened and again the line was diverted, this time into a tunnel under the waterway ('The Substituted Line'). The original line ('The Transferred Portion') remained part of the dock railway, carried over the waterway on a swing bridge.

In 1870 a large gas-works was built on the marshes at BECKTON in order to use sea-borne coal. It was connected with the North Woolwich line at Albert Dock Junction by 1·75 miles of single track owned by the Gas Light and Coke Co. Opened for goods on 14 October 1872, it was leased and worked by the GER, which ran a passenger service for the workmen from 17 March 1873. In 1920 there were 5 services a day from Stratford but these dwindled to one, withdrawn on 28 December 1940.

To serve the Royal Albert Dock the dock company built 1·75 miles of double line from Albert Dock Junction parallel with the quayside lines to GALLIONS. Opened to Central station on 3 August 1880 and throughout by July 1881, it was used only for passengers and parcels, a shuttle service from Custom House being provided by the owners and through trains by the GER. At Gallions an hotel and a pier were built and liner passengers were landed. 'Is it Tilbury and a tender or Gallions and the Dock?' asked the hero of Kipling's *The Light that Failed.*

On 30 June 1896 the GER took over all the passenger workings, of which there were 54 down trains in 1900 and 40 in 1920. A much more attenuated service was in operation on 7 September 1940 when a stick of bombs on the line brought it

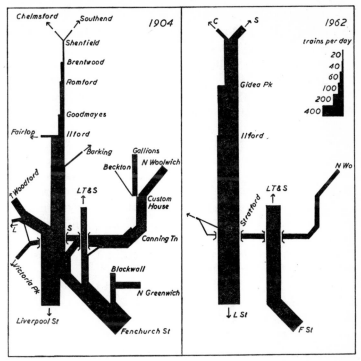

FIG. 17. The decline of inner and rise of outer suburban services in east London 1904–62. The thickness of the lines is proportional to the number of stopping trains on an ordinary weekday.

to a permanent end. The line was abandoned by the P.L.A., which had always staffed it, in October 1950.

The North Woolwich line has four tracks between Stratford South Junction and Tidal Basin. In 1958, 60 regular and 6 conditional freight trains were booked southbound through Stratford Market Station (closed 6 May 1957). Thames Wharf is the main goods depot, though North Woolwich is also important. From the former a goods line, opened in June 1848, leads across the Lea to the East India Dock, the sole rail access since the Blackwall connection was severed in 1947.

Goods traffic remains heavy, but road competition for passenger traffic intensified when trolley-buses were extended from Stratford to North Woolwich in 1938. But social changes led to the greatest loss of traffic. Before the second world war most dockers and factory workers lived near their work and went home for their midday break, making four short rail journeys daily. Slum clearance, accelerated by bombing, means the majority live as far afield as Becontree or Dagenham. Eating in canteens at midday, after work they take the bus all the way home or to East Ham station, where they continue on the District.

In 1920, 115 down passenger trains were booked through Canning Town daily and 17 terminated there. As late as 1939 there were 60 down services originating from Palace Gates, Stratford and Fenchurch Street. The latter ceased to run after October 1940 and in 1959 there were but 26 down trains and in peak hours only. In 1960, however, an hourly interval service was started, with extra trains at peak periods. It was to be the last intensive steam-worked service in Greater London, becoming gradually dieselized in 1962.

The Royal Docks, the Victoria, Albert and King George V (1921), are the largest group in London, with 233 acres of water and 11 miles of quay. They were served by the largest section of the P.L.A.'s railways, worked by their own blue diesel locomotives. Connection with British Railways was through the Royal Victoria Exchange Sidings, which had thirty-one roads and a capacity of 1,200 wagons. Boat trains to and from Liverpool Street were worked along the quayside by Eastern Region engines. Rail operations to the berths in the Royal Docks ceased on 1 May 1970 except to the heavy lift berth in Victoria Dock. Afterwards railborne traffic was brought by road from nearby goods depots.

THE GENESIS OF THE LONDON, TILBURY & SOUTHEND
RAILWAY

To meet the competition of the North Kent (p. 45) for the Gravesend traffic, the Blackwall joined with the Eastern

Counties, concerned with preserving for themselves the territory south of their Romford line. On 17 June 1852 they were
authorized to build a line from Forest Gate Junction on the
Romford line to Tilbury Fort, where two short branches to a
terminus made a triangle, and thence to Southend, 36 miles.
Separate 'Extension Shares' were raised. On 3 July 1854 the
two companies leased the line for twenty-one years to the
contractors, Peto, Brassey & Betts.

Opening to Tilbury was on 13 April 1854, to Leigh by 1 July
1855 and to Southend on 1 March 1856. East from Tilbury the
line was single and in the absence of a telegraph had to be
worked as a single section. As only three trains each way daily
could be operated, the line was soon doubled. Trains carried
Bishopsgate and Fenchurch Street portions joined and divided
at Stratford.

To eliminate delays at Stratford and to develop local traffic
west of Barking, on 7 July 1856 a cut-off was authorized
between Barking and Gas Factory.Junction (Bow) and running
powers thence into Fenchurch Street. It was ready on 31 March
1858 and all Tilbury line trains ran direct into Fenchurch
Street. The ECR inaugurated a Bishopsgate–Barking service,
GER trains running into Barking until 1918.

The proprietors of the Extension Shares now worked to rid
themselves of outside control and succeeded in incorporating
themselves as the London, Tilbury & Southend Railway. The
lessees were conspicuously failing to develop traffic, but the
lease did not expire until 1875, after which, failing to interest
the GER, the LTSR decided to work the line itself.

On 18 May 1869 the NLR, having obtained running powers
over the whole system, opened a spur from Bow to BROMLEY
JUNCTION. It operated a shuttle service between Bow and
Plaistow until 1916 and ran regular and excursion trains
through to Southend. The latter survived until 1955. Bromley
Junction was also used by goods trains until it was taken out on
14 September 1959, when about 20 trains a day were using it.

On 4 August 1890 the TOTTENHAM & FOREST
GATE Railway was incorporated to build a 6-mile line from
T & HJ at South Tottenham (p. 150) to the LTSR at its new
station of Woodgrange Park, just beyond Forest Gate Junction.

Traffic began on this costly line on 9 July 1894, and at the same time the LTSR opened a spur at Little Ilford to allow through running into East Ham as well as Barking. This is now built over.

The line was promoted by the Midland and Tilbury companies. The former was in an expansive phase and could thus reach Tilbury and its docks. The latter, without its own London terminus, gained entry to St Pancras, while the northern suburbs were put in contact with Southend without using GER or NLR metals. The Midland projected its T & HJ suburban service (p. 152) to Barking and East Ham and the LTSR operated through trains and excursions from St Pancras to Southend.

The Midland were thus brought into very close relations with the prosperous local company and became interested in acquiring it, taking over on 1 January 1912. Thus the LTSR eventually passed to the LMSR and retained much of its character until electrification in 1962, although control passed to the Eastern Region on 20 February 1949.

TRAFFIC GROWTH AND ECONOMIC DEVELOPMENT IN SOUTH ESSEX

When the lease expired on 3 July 1875 the LTSR was in parlous state. No attempt had been made to develop potential traffic and, said A. L. Stride in 1912, 'when we took over the line there was no rolling stock of any description, there was no telegraph system, there were no block signals. . . .'

That this ramshackle, poverty-stricken concern was converted over the next thirty years into a smart and prosperous line was largely the work of one man, A. L. Stride, who was engineer and general manager from 1875 to 1912. It was the continuity of his energetic management which raised the LTSR to the top flights of railway efficiency, with such profound effects on the district served. In the first six months of 1876 the line carried 0·86 million passengers and in those of 1912, 17 million. In the same period season-ticket holders increased from 499 to 10,892.

Because freight did not flow in any quantity from Tilbury Docks until after 1910 or from industry until 1930, the line was dependent on passenger traffic, residential and holiday. This it successfully stimulated by an excellent and reliable service, comfort, and above all very low fares. In the early 1920's bogie stock was commonplace when four-wheelers were standard on the Great Eastern.

SOUTHEND

Among the far-reaching consequences of LTSR policy was the phenomenal growth of Southend as a resort and suburb.

The low gravel hills of South Essex sweep eastward from Brentwood to reach the river between Benfleet and Shoebury-ness as low cliffs. Around a break in these grew up the hamlet of South End (of Prittlewell Parish), which in 1801 numbered fifty-one houses and was already something of a sea-bathing resort. By 1848 'quiet, dull Southend' extended over a mile of sea front and straggled up the High Street as far as the site of the Central station. In 1859, three years after the coming of the railway, Brassey laid out Cliff Town among cornfields and New Town was started. In 1863 three hotels were opened and day visitors were becoming more numerous. The Scratton Estate, south of the railway, was sold for building in 1869, but there was no development north of the line.

Soon after opening, 6 trains a day were provided to London, one a fast business service. But the early importance of Southend as a residential suburb must not be exaggerated. Prittlewell Parish grew only from 2,359 in 1851 to 8,009 in 1891. In 1889 there was still only a single business express.

On 24 July 1882 a cut-off was sanctioned from Barking through Upminster and over the Laindon Hills to Pitsea, thus avoiding the detour through Tilbury. This was opened through-out on 1 June 1888 and brought Southend to 35·25 miles from Fenchurch Street, 7·75 miles nearer. Fast trains now took only 50 minutes and the service was greatly increased.

As a result Southend grew fourfold in twenty years and doubled again in the next ten to reach 70,767 in 1911. In the eighties the town spread north of the LTSR line along the newly made-up Victoria Avenue, though even in 1898 the GER's station was on the northern edge of the town and Marine Park (now the Kursaal) the eastern. After 1900 expansion continued rapidly, Westcliff grew up and the old village of Leigh developed fast. The Chalkwell Hall Estate dates from 1900–5.

The 1882 Act also authorized the LTSR extension to Shoeburyness, where the school of gunnery had been established in 1859, and this was opened on 1 February 1884. Along it Thorpe Bay was started as a high-class residential resort after the station was opened in 1910.

The coming of the GER in 1889 brought still more trade to Southend, partly through the intense competition which resulted. The GER line allowed a northward expansion of Southend and today the built-up area extends out to Prittlewell, Rochford and Rayleigh stations. In the district as a whole there has been a continuous spread of building since 1920, interrupted only briefly by the second world war. The area between Leigh and Shoeburyness is now a single conurbation with a 1961 population of 184,000. The intercensal increase of Southend County Borough was 8·7 per cent and that of Rayleigh Urban District 103·9 per cent.

SUBURBAN GROWTH

Apart from Southend and Gravesend, the only source of traffic in 1876 was the district between Stepney and Barking. In Bromley and Plaistow factories were springing up alongside mean houses. Plaistow, where the LTSR had established its works, numbered 6,669 in 1871. The potato fields and the sheep grazing the Lea marshes were disappearing fast. 'The fields changed into streets which lead nowhere and which are left unfinished and fragmentary and lined with mean little tenements', said J. Thorne in his 1875 guide.

In contrast, contemporary East Ham merely 'straggled for a mile along the lane from Little Ilford to North Woolwich' (Thorne), and lay among market gardens noted for their pickling onions. Barking, numbering 5,766 in 1871, had a 'large corn mill on the site of the old Abbey mill', and immediately below were barges loading local onions and potatoes for London and 'fishermen lolling about'.

East Ham grew from 9,713 in 1871 to 69,758 in 1901, but the

main period of expansion was the next twenty years and in 1921 the borough numbered 143,246. A grid-iron of streets was laid over the market gardens and terraces of small houses were built, as superior to those of Plaistow as they were to be inferior to those of Becontree. A similar fate overtook Barking in the same period.

In 1870 the LTSR carried 1·8 million ordinary passengers and 440 season-ticket holders. In 1890, 6·8 million and 1,621 respectively were carried, most of the increase coming from the Stepney–Barking section. But ten years later the figures had soared to 15·7 million and 4,593 respectively.

It was not possible to enlarge Fenchurch Street to deal with traffic increases on this scale. Accordingly a relief route was provided by the WHITECHAPEL & BOW Railway, authorized in 1897 to extend the District line from Whitechapel to join the LTSR at Campbell Road Junction. Opened on 2 June 1902, it was owned jointly by the LTSR and District and was worked by the latter, its trains mostly terminating at East Ham.

The increased service forced the LTSR to quadruple the Campbell Road–Barking section, a work completed to East Ham in 1905 and the rest in 1908. In 1903 it was estimated 13·5 million of the LTSR passengers used Fenchurch Street, 2·4 million the Whitechapel & Bow, 230,000 St Pancras and 35,500 Liverpool Street.

District electric trains began running to East Ham from 20 August 1905 and to Barking from 1 April 1908, using the northern tracks of the widened section. The District also used its electric locomotives on through Ealing–Southend trains, with an engine change at Barking. Inaugurated on 1 June 1910, they lasted until 1 October 1939. In 1938 there were 4 trains a day each way.

East of Barking the great Becontree Estate, with a 1960 population of 90,800, was laid out by the L.C.C. between 1925 and 1935 to re-house East-Enders. In 1929 an L.C.C. survey, covering 37,000 wage earners on the estate, found 60 per cent still working in London and a further 8 per cent in places between.

The need for additional transport facilities was therefore urgent. Two additional tracks chiefly for the use of District trains were opened between Barking and Upminster on 12

September 1932 and five new stations provided on the 7·75 miles. One, Heathway, booked 2·25 million ordinary passengers in 1955 and sold 62,000 seasons.

In 1938 there were 301 eastbound District trains through Campbell Road Junction, 166 for East Ham or Barking, 38 for Dagenham and 97 for Upminster. In 1960 a higher proportion continued beyond Barking, there being a 10-minute off-peak service to Dagenham East, alternate trains continuing to Upminster.

The improved service encouraged speculative builders in Hornchurch and Upminster. Hornchurch Urban District grew from 17,489 in 1921 to 104,092 in 1951 and 128,127 in 1961. Beyond, the Laindon Hills became covered with a chaotic chicken-farm-cum-bungalow growth similar to that described on page 180 and centred on Laindon and Pitsea stations. Between these last the New Town of Basildon, epitome of planning, now numbers 88,459 people. In spite of the line passing through the civic centre of this large town, the general manager of the Eastern Region made the astonishing statement in 1961 that it was not worth while to build a station. Benfleet is the railhead for Canvey Island, now disfigured with the dire contagion affecting our coasts since the motor-car has enabled holiday-maker and rate-dodger alike to live in caravans and shacks remote from town or station. Beyond this again the Southend complex begins.

To fend the Great Eastern off Tilbury two short single-line branches were sanctioned on 20 August 1883, from Upminster to GRAYS and ROMFORD. The former was opened on 1 July 1892 and the latter on 7 June the following year. The shareholders feared they would be unremunerative, but in December 1959 the heavy local traffic had been boosted five-fold by the frequent new Diesel service. The Grays branch has been electrified.

Present-day passenger traffic on the LTS is enormous. In 1958, 60 million passengers were carried. West of Upminster LTS trains call only at Barking and Stepney, District trains taking all the local traffic. But even eastward congestion is rife at peak periods. In 1912 the Midland had undertaken to electrify as soon as possible, but the LMSR failed even to avail itself of the 1935 Treasury Agreement. In 1950 the B.T.C. announced that the LTS was next on the conversion list. But the hopes of the long-suffering commuters, riding in their aging rolling stock, were constantly deferred until 18 June 1962, when electrification was completed half a century after it was first thought vital. Traffic was expected to increase by 50 per cent with the introduction of the new services.

The Southend electrification is on the same system as the GE and the Gas Factory–Bow Junction and Forest Gate–Barking links between the two lines have been converted for special and emergency working. The LTS and District services have also been completely segregated on to the southern and northern pairs of tracks. Barking has been rebuilt as the main interchange station. In 1900 the station had two platforms at a level crossing, but was rebuilt with the quadrupling and again modernized in 1932. In 1958, 2·5 million tickets and 75,000 seasons were sold and 15,000 passengers a day were changing trains. Between 1959 and 1962 it was again entirely rebuilt with six platforms and two bays, and to enable better exchange facilities to be provided, the up District line was brought by flying and burrowing junctions outside the Southend lines. A further flyover connects the Forest Gate and Tilbury lines to allow freight trains to cross over clear of other traffic.

THE DOCK TRAFFIC

A 3·75-mile single line was opened on 7 June 1855 from Mucking on the Tilbury–Pitsea section to THAMES HAVEN. Steamers for Margate called and trains ran in connection, while the LTSR tried unsuccessfully to encourage the import of cattle from the Continent. Some general cargo was handled, but this ceased when the Tilbury Docks were opened in 1886 and no passenger trains have run since the end of the 1880 summer service except for workmen. Since 1945 two oil refineries with capacities of 10 million and 3·3 million tons a year have been built. During the 1960's traffic proliferated. Numerous block trains of petroleum products, chemicals, and gas-works feedstocks run daily and keep the branch a busy one.

The sprawling settlement (it cannot be called a town) which

is Tilbury dates only from 1886, when the first houses for dock workers were built. Previously the only traffic at Riverside station was to and from the Gravesend ferries. Until 1880 the LTSR could only carry rail passengers, but by purchase and lease it then gained the monopoly of the ferries, together with the use of West Street Pier at Gravesend. Over 3 million passengers a year are conveyed and there are through bookings from Gravesend to all LTS stations.

Tilbury Docks were the outcome of severe inter-company rivalry and were built by the East and West India Dock Co. to intercept traffic from other docks. They went into service in 1886, when the North End exchange sidings were opened. Tilbury Town station was opened on 15 June 1885 as Tilbury Docks. Because there were few storage sheds in the new docks, the owners leased the new LTSR Commercial Road goods depot (now used by the G.P.O. for overseas parcels post) and agreed special terms for the carriage of cargo to and from Tilbury.

Development was slow until the P.L.A. was created in 1909, when trade expanded rapidly. Until 1939 there was no road access and 87 per cent of traffic was railborne. By 1956 this had declined to 35 per cent. In 1961 250 of the loaded wagons were forwarded daily, but from 25 July 1969 all rail traffic was transferred by lorry between Riverside depot and the general cargo berths. The docks have been constantly enlarged and modernized, and now have specialized timber and rail-connected grain berths. In 1969 six container berths were ready or building, and that June the adjacent freightliner terminal went into service.

On 16 May 1930 the Landing Stage, used by liners to embark or land passengers, was opened. A new Customs Hall and the rebuilt Riverside station were designed as a single convenient unit by Sir Edwin Cooper. The station has four passenger platforms and two more for baggage. In 1955, 500 liners called and as many boat trains ran, carrying 147,298 passengers; 942,024 tickets were sold to local passengers. Trains also run to liners at their berths.

THE INDUSTRIAL TRAFFIC

At Purfleet an outcrop of chalk approaches the river and a lime and cement industry was established in the eighteenth century. The marshes were suitable for powder factories. But otherwise there was little industrial development until in 1930 the Ford Motor Company started on their vast plant. Since then the Essex shore from Barking to Thames Haven has become highly industrialized, and plants are still going up. Besides the cement, cars and petroleum already mentioned, paper and cardboard, soap, margarine, shoes, fertilizers and chemicals are produced. At Dagenham Dock and Purfleet and at numerous wharves petrol, coal and timber are landed, and power-stations are being erected to serve the new industries.

The LTS has become a major freight carrier, and since about 1955 the Eastern Region has successfully grasped the opportunity offered by industrialization. 'Railways are again a force to be reckoned with', said a local trader. In 1960, 1·75 million tons of freight originated on the LTS section.

In 1963 Ford opened their Merseyside plant and began to use rail to interchange components between Dagenham and Halewood, building up to 3 trains of pallet vans and open wagons each way daily. Several trainloads of cars and tractors are also dispatched daily from Dagenham (and Brentwood). Block trains of cement, petroleum and chemicals are also common, and general wagon-load traffic heavy.

Increasing freight traffic overwhelmed the LTSR yard at Little Ilford (now the electric stock depot) and in 1937 Ripple Lane Yard was started between Barking and Dagenham Dock. Rebuilt in the 1950's, it had fifty-one sorting sidings and a daily capacity of 2,000 wagons; its use declined with the growth of block trains. In 1953 there were 23 booked freight trains through Barking to Ripple Lane and 17 thence to Purfleet.

FENCHURCH STREET

The Blackwall Railway opened Fenchurch Street in 1841, probably with two platforms, and enlarged it in 1854 to deal with the ECR and NLR traffic. The Blackwall service, though frequent, soon became but a minor part of the station's activi-

ties. The NLR operated a 15-minute service from 26 September
1850, but ceased to be interested when they opened Broad
Street, though a shuttle service from Bow lasted to 31 December
1868. For the ECR it was the only City terminus from 1854 to
1874, when Liverpool Street was opened. But the GER still ran
a frequent service to Ilford and to North Woolwich, supplemented by business trains to Romford, Loughton and even
Southend. For the LTSR it was the only London terminus until
1894, and always the principal one.

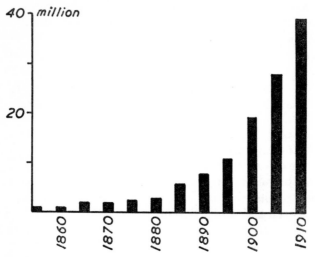

FIG. 18. Passengers on the London, Tilbury & Southend Railway.

Thus, until 1900, Fenchurch Street, with its very large
traffic with the Inner Arc and Inner Suburban Zone, was one
of the busiest London stations. As early as 1861 it was used by
7 million ordinary passengers and 1,286 season-ticket holders.
In 1903 passenger user was 23·9 million, 13·4 million by
LTSR trains and 10·5 million by those of the GER; 233 trains
arrived daily, 79 before 10.30 a.m.

But after 1900 traffic declined. The Whitechapel & Bow
diverted many LTSR passengers, traffic increasing over it from
2·4 million in 1903 to 9·4 million in 1905. Electric trams ate into
short-distance traffic. Fenchurch Street, too, was inconvenient

for the growing West End traffic. On a census day in October 1913, 48,386 passengers used the station, an annual rate of about 17 million. On the other hand the LTSR service frequencies had increased, so that while GER passenger user declined, train numbers rose. In 1913 there were 560 train movements, involving some 280 arrivals.

The service to Blackwall ceased in 1926 (p. 194) and all other LNER trains were withdrawn by November 1949, leaving the LTS trains in sole possession. Yet, such has been the growth of the Middle and Outer Zone, the 175 trains using the station daily in 1955 carried an average of 45,000 passengers. This represents a much greater passenger complement per train than in 1913. Since then delay in electrification in favour of the GER route to Southend led to a falling off. On the 1960 census day 37,700 were counted. But the 1962 census, after electrification, recorded 51,700 passengers. In 1962 there were 265 trains a day arriving and leaving, an increase of 90 over the steam service.

Fenchurch Street is convenient for the City, but suffers from being a short walk to either bus or underground. It suffers too the familiar problem of increasing numbers travelling in ever contracting periods. In the 1960 census 19,059 departing passengers were counted; 10,569, or *56 per cent*, left on the 13 trains between 5.4 and 6.3 p.m. There were 15,060 seats on the 13 trains. Only 5 trains left Stepney with more passengers than seats and only the 5.23 was badly overcrowded. The 4 Tilbury line services carried only 2,308 passengers, as traffic to Central London is small below Barking. Outside 4.0 to 7.0 p.m. the passenger complement exceeded 200 on only two trains.

Fenchurch Street has a severely plain but pleasant façade, spoiled by the neurotic zigzag of the GER canopy. Behind lie two island platforms at a high level. These were rebuilt in 1935 from five platforms, two of them very short and only No. 4 of any great length. In 1913 this was the only one available to LTSR trains and there were 12 departures from it between 4.57 and 6.7 p.m. In 1962 all four platforms were used to dispatch 18 electric trains between 5.2 and 6.0 p.m. Fenchurch Street is a clean, cheerful, intimate station, nowadays purely suburban in function, if it ever were anything else. With nationalization the LTS line at last got its own London terminus.

This chapter has largely been the story of the LTS, a compact, self-contained and intimate system with a tradition of good and imaginative management. In 1958 its 90 route miles and its 62 stations and depots earned £4·25 million from passenger traffic and £2·75 million from freight, over £75,000 per mile. Furthermore, there was an operating surplus of £300,000.

The whole system has the most up-to-date signalling, freight traffic is diesel-hauled and electrification of the passenger services has swept the shabby and outmoded stream trains into a merciful oblivion. South Essex has now a service of unprecedented frequency and speed. In off-peak periods 6 trains an hour leave Fenchurch Street for Shoeburyness, 2 fast and 2 stopping services via Upminster and 2 via Tilbury, while 39 trains a day include scheduled times of over 60 m.p.h. start to stop, enabling commuters from Southend to save up to three hours a week in their travelling time. The 'Tilbury and Southend' is once again a model of what a railway should be.

CHAPTER XI

Railways and Megapolis: a Conclusion

When a man is tired of London he is tired of life.

DR JOHNSON.

LONDON's development since 1840 has far exceeded that of previous centuries. It is no coincidence that the period has also been that of the Railway Age, for this development has been the result of the growth of trade, industry and commerce, in turn fostered by transport and communications developments, among which must be numbered the railway. But the spectacular growth of population and above all the even more spectacular growth in area since 1900 is almost wholly the consequence of rail transport.

Without the suburban railway the almost complete separation of work and residence could not have taken place. The railway, as yet, is the only possible mass mover on the scale necessary to allow this, while its special technical and economic characteristics alone make such journeys possible at a cost in time and money that hitherto is socially tolerable. The continuing necessity of suburban railways to London was acknowledged by the 1963 Beeching Report, which left Greater London virtually unaffected by its long list of recommended closures.

R. J. Smeed, of the Department of Scientific and Industrial Research, has demonstrated the complete dependence of London in its present form on its railways. One man travelling at peak hours occupies 1 square foot if travelling by rail, 3 if he walks, 4–10 if he goes by bus and 50–80 if by car. While the City has 0·14 square miles of roadway, if the 335,000 commuters walked to their work from peripheral termini or from underground stations they would need 0·02 square miles, 0·07 if they came by bus, and 0·65 square miles (parking would be extra) if by car, $\frac{1}{7}$, $\frac{1}{2}$ and 5 *times* the available space respectively. Without railways twentieth-century London might or might not be a better place to live in; it certainly would be a different one.

This separation of work and residence has permitted a constant rise in living standards generally and housing standards in particular. It also has important social consequences in that communities are no longer close-knit and all too many people no longer identify themselves with either their place of residence or their place of work.

The suburban way of life has been widely criticized from almost all points of view and scarcely a voice is raised in defence. Yet there is no denying the social attraction of Greater London. The Great Wen is swelling as fast as ever. The intercensal increase between 1951 and 1961 for the United Kingdom was 4·8 per cent, but that of the Home Counties was far above the national average. That for Hertfordshire was 36·5 per cent, for Buckinghamshire 25·9, Essex 11·8, Kent 8·7 and Surrey 8·1. It is true that Middlesex declined by 1·7 per cent and London County by 4·6. But there is no question of a decaying heart; the decline is due partly to slum clearances, partly to rising land values consequent on building for commerce and industry. But even now house and flat building is continuing fast in the Inner Zone.

Many take the view that the disadvantages of such growth outweigh any advantages and stand in the long line of those seeking to curb the growth of the Wen. This they would do mainly by limiting opportunities for employment. But others argue with equal force that so little is really known of the causes of city growth that indiscriminate pruning of the branches may well stunt the whole plant.

The indisputable fact remains that the railway is the instrument of growth, whether that has been for good or evil. The problems of Greater London are thus those of its railways. Since the one of major moment concerns the journey to work, so that of the railways is involved with commuting. 'The Problem of the Peak', a phrase once used by P. A. White of the Southern Region, is an apt description of the basic problem of

London's railways, which have to move more and more people in an ever shorter period of the day.

By the inevitable overcrowding not only is discomfort caused and probably efficiency lowered by fatigue, but costs are inflated to such an extent that to maintain its public transport in good order the community must choose between subsidy and facing its commuters with swingeing fares. For, though operating costs of rail transport are low, equipment costs are high. To keep fares in bounds this equipment must be given maximum use. As it is, some nine-car electric trains, representing a capital investment of £100,000 and annual recurrent costs of £10,000 before they are taken out of the sidings, may make only one effective revenue-earning journey each peak period, no more than 40 miles a day with a full load.

The later 1960's, covering the seven years between original publication and revision, saw not only a continuation of the trends described, but the emergence of new ones which may ultimately be of great significance. The population of Greater London continued the slight decline discernible since 1951, while the increase in employment in Central London levelled off markedly. The question now was whether automation of office work will greatly reduce numbers. Long-distance commuting, however, continued to grow in volume. Meanwhile, seven years after the Buchanan Report showed the goal to be a mirage, the G.L.C. pursues road plans aimed to cope with peak traffic. Planned investment in public transport is on a lesser scale in spite of its greater technical efficiency in handling traffic peaks. There is still a need to plan land use, roads and public transport as a coherent whole.

Transport is a social as well as an economic service. A great city and its transport are inseparably linked, and to neglect or ignore the social and economic implications of railways for 'Megapolis' is dangerous in the extreme. Their importance to Greater London is more now than at any time in the past.

The central aspect in this study, in which limitations of space have meant so many aspects have perforce been neglected or summarily dealt with, is the fact that some one and a half million people are moved into the small area which is Central London and then out of it again each day.

Bibliography and Acknowledgments

ONLY a small selection of the vast bibliography covering Greater London and its railways can be given here to serve as a starting point for further reading in a very scattered literature.

ORIGINAL SOURCES

These fall into a number of groups:

(1) The reports of various enquiries into London's transport, including the *1846 Royal Commission on London Traffic, 1865 Select Committee on Metropolitan Communications, 1901 Select Committee on London Underground Railways, 1903–4–5 Select Committees on Workmen's Trains, 1905 Royal Commission on The Means of Locomotion in London, 1925 Report of the Home Counties Traffic Advisory Committee, 1960 Royal Commission on Local Government in London, 1892–3–6–8 L.C.C. Reports on Workmen's Trains, 1959 Nugent Committee on the Future of Public Transport.*

(2) Local Acts of Parliament and the papers of the Committees preparing them.

(3) Reports and Minute Books of Railway Companies.

(4) Working and Public Timetables.

(5) Files of periodical and daily press: (*a*) the railway press of the nineteenth century, written mainly for investors, including *Herapath's Journal* and *The Railway News;* (*b*) the technical press of the twentieth century, including the *Railway Gazette, Modern Transport,* the *Railway Magazine* and *Modern Railways*; (*c*) House Journals, especially the *Great Eastern Magazine, Southern Railway Magazine* and *British Railways Magazine*; (*d*) the *Illustrated London News, The Times* and local newspapers.

(6) Statistical returns of the Board of Trade and Ministry of Transport.

(7) The maps of G. F. Crutchley published between 1825 and 1843, the various editions of the one-inch and six-inch Ordnance Survey maps, and the Railway Clearing House maps and Junction Diagrams.

In all writing on transport there is no substitute for field work, and hundreds of miles were covered by train, bus and on foot in the preparation of this book.

SECONDARY SOURCES

The best geographical description of London is still *London on the Thames*, H. Ormsby, 1930. *London and the Thames Valley*, R. L. Sherlock, 1947, covers geology and physiography. Social history is dealt with by R. J. Mitchell and M. D. R. Leys in *A History of London Life*, 1958, and industry in D. H. Smith's *The Industries of Greater London* and P. G. Hall's *The Industries of London since 1861*, 1962. But the serious student must be acquainted with H. Mayhew's *London Labour and the London Poor*, 1860; C. Booth's *Life and Labour of the People in London*, 1895–1903, and Sir H. L. Smith's (editor) *New Survey of London Life and Labour*. The journey to work is analysed in the London Transport Executive's *Travel Survey*, 1949, and in J. Westergaard's 'The Journey to Work', in *Town Planning Studies*, 1956. The architecture and urban structure are dealt with by S. E. Rasmussen in *London, the Unique City*, 1934.

R. M. Robbins's *Middlesex*, 1955, was of particular value. W. Pollitt's *The Rise of Southend*, 1957, is the best source for that town, while J. G. Broodbank's *History of the Port of London Authority*, 1920, and J. Bird's *Geography of the Port of London*, 1957, cover the port aspects. Of early guide-books the most useful were J. Thorne's *Handbook of the Environs of London*, 1875, and D. Lysons's *The Environs of London*, 1896, together with the early railway guides of G. Measom.

Of general works on the history of London's transport mention must be made of G. A. Sekon's *Locomotion in Victorian London*, 1938. O. J. Morris's *Fares Please* covers the development of road services. F. A. A. Menzler's 'London and its Passenger Transport System' (*Journal of the Royal Statistical Society*, 1950) is an unrivalled source of statistical information. The supplement to the *Railway Gazette* of 15 May 1946, *Improving London's Transport*, deals with the 1935 Agreement and consequent works. H. J. Dyos's 'Railways and Housing in Victorian London' (*Journal of Transport History*, 1955) is the best source for destruction of houses and development of workmen's services. Other sources were Sir William Acworth's *Railways of England*, 1900; H. G. Lewin's *Early British Railways*, 1935, and *The Railway Mania*, 1936. Published just in time for inclusion is *London Railways* by E. A. Course, 1962.

Files of the *Railway Magazine* and of the former *Railway and Travel Monthly* contain numerous local studies, many of a high order of scholarship, on which the author was very greatly dependent. Mention must be made of a series of articles by H. V. Borley on the railways of the Inner Zone in North and East London published in the *Journal of the Railway and Canal Historical Society* between 1957 and 1960, and of articles by C. E. Lee and R. K. Kirkland on underground lines, lines in South London and on various termini published in the *Railway Magazine* between 1938 and 1966.

Sources for individual lines were: for the Southern lines C. F. Dendy Marshall's *A History of the Southern Railway*, 1936; G. T. Moody's *Southern Electric*, 1958; R. W. Kidner's *The South Eastern Railway*, 1952; *The London Chatham and Dover*, 1953; E. A. Course's *The Bexleyheath Railway*, 1958. For the Great Western, E. T. MacDermot's *History of the Great Western Railway*, 1935, and T. B. Peacock's *Great Western Suburban Services*, 1949. For the London & North-Western, G. P. Neele's *Railway Reminiscences*, 1904; for the Midland, F. S. Williams's *The Midland Railway*, 1877; for the Great Northern, C. H. Grinling's *History of the Great Northern Railway*, 1898 (still a classic); and for the Great Eastern, C. J. Allen's *The Great Eastern Railway*, 1955. For the smaller lines, H. D. Welch's *The London, Tilbury and Southend Railway*, 1951, and R. M. Robbins's *The North London Railway*, 1953. The London Transport lines are covered by C. Baker in *The Metropolitan Railway*, 1951; C. E. Lee in *The Metropolitan District Railway*, 1956; and by T. S. Lascelles in *The City and South London Railway*, 1955. Model local studies are G. H. Lake's *The Railways of Tottenham*, 1945; A. A. Jackson's 'North West from Ealing' (*Railway Magazine*, 1959), and G. F. A. Wilmot's *The Railway in Finchley*, 1962. Finally, mention must be made of T. B. Peacock's *The Port of London Authority Railways*, 1952, and Sir John Summerson's article on Euston in *The Times* of 11 June 1960.

A number of unpublished theses contain much of value on the growth of London and on railway development. They are listed in the *Journal of Transport History*, 1960. The author gratefully acknowledges that by B. A. Bates, M.Sc.(Econ.) on *Some Aspects of the Recent Industrial Development of West London* (University of London, 1954) as the source of some statistics on traffic at West London goods stations.

Since the bibliography for the first edition was compiled, a number of works on Greater London have been published. Those of a general nature include *Greater London* edited by J. T. Coppock and H. Prince, 1964; *Atlas of London and the London Region* by E. Jones and D. J. Sinclair, 1968; *Greater London and Industrial Geography* by J. E. Martin, 1966; and *The Geography of Greater London* edited by R. Clayton, 1964. Looking to the future is P. G. Hall's *London 2000*, 1963. Of specialized transport literature, mention must be made of J. R. Kellet's *The Impact of Railways on Victorian Cities*, 1969; T. C. Barker and M. R. Robbins's *A History of London Transport—Vol. 1: The Nineteenth Century*, 1963 (Vol. 2 has not been published at the time of writing); E. A. Course's *London Railways*, 1962; and A. A. Jackson's *London's Termini*, 1969.

The chapters on North-East London should be read in conjunction with Volume 5 in the Regional History series— *Eastern Counties* by D. I. Gordon, and those on South London with Volume 3—*Southern England* by H. P. White. The author has developed the theme of suburban traffic at main line termini in 'London's rail terminals and their suburban traffic', *Geographical Review*, Vol. 44, 1964, pp. 347–65. Invaluable contemporary source material is provided by the *London Traffic Survey* by Freeman, Fox and Partners *et al.* for the G.L.C., successive volumes appearing from 1964 onwards.

The author wishes to place on record his gratitude to the Archivist of the British Railways Board and his staff for their assistance in gaining access to material and for his permission to publish it; to the Curator of Historical Relics, British

Railways Board, for his permission to reproduce photographs; and to the Council and Librarian of the Institute of Transport for the use of their library. He is also very deeply indebted to the public relations and publicity officers and their staffs who freely made available so much valuable statistical data, Messrs M. B. Thomas, Eastern Region; R. W. Crawshaw, London Midland Region; F. D. Y. Faulkener, Southern Region, and C. J. Rider, Western Region. To Mr R. M. Robbins the author owes a very special debt both in his capacity of commercial and public relations officer, London Transport Board, when he so generously furnished statistical information and facilities for research, and as transport historian, for encouragement in the early stages of planning this book. The Director of Housing, L.C.C., kindly furnished information on the council's estates. Especial thanks are due to Mr S. Miles Davey, formerly proprietor of Locomotive and General Railway Photographs, for his generosity in freely making available his unique collection of illustrations.

So many have helped with information and discussion that they cannot be listed here, only gratefully thanked. But the author must make individual mention of Professor M. J. Wise, Dr J. Martin (for suggesting 'The Inner Arc') and Mr J. Westergaard (for the concept of the 'job ratio' and information on the journey to work), all of the London School of Economics; to Mr B. N. Nunns for unwearied assistance in field work and in obtaining illustrations; to Mr G. F. A. Wilmot for criticizing the manuscript and for placing at the author's disposal his unique knowledge of the Finchley area; to Dr E. A. Course and Mr J. G. Spence for reading and commenting on the South London chapters; to Mr H. V. Borley for chronological information; and to Mr J. A. Patmore for assistance in preparing the second edition. Last but by no means least, thanks are due to Mr D. St J. Thomas, who has provided constant help and encouragement.

Index

Heavy type is used to indicate pages giving opening dates of sections (not individual stations except in the case of main-line termini). Branch openings are indexed at stations at the farthest end (from Central London). Popular names of lines are listed as well as those of the promoting companies. Towns known by compass-points are listed under these, but stations are listed under the town name: thus, West Drayton — but Croydon, West.
Abbreviations: elec. = electrification, tfc = traffic, xtn = extension.